Challenges

in a colonial county

duncanldubois@gmail.com

www.duncandubois.co.za

Sakura Book Publishing, Durban, South Africa

www.sakurabookpublishing.com

alta@sakurabookpublishing.com

Grateful thanks to Jan Pauw and Global Girmitya Centre - SA for their financial contribution.

Acknowledgment to UnSplash Sabesh-Photography for permitting free use of the cover photograph.

Thanks to Byron Du Bois for his technical and artistic contribution in arranging the cover.

ISBN: 978-1-0370-1063-7(print)

978-1-0370-1064-4(e-book)

Author's note

Challenges in a Colonial County is the sequel to the historical novel *Liaisons – Life in a Colonial County.* As such, *Challenges* begins in 1876 where *Liaisons* ended and contextualises authentic and fictitious developments, up until 1889 in Alexandra County on the Natal South Coast.

Like *Liaisons, Challenges* is a critical fabulation in that it inserts credible experiences in the gaps and silences of the historical record. Those gaps and silences involve tragedy, drama, love, predatory capitalism, controversy involving indentured Indian labour, reformist attempts to moderate social conventions, racial prejudice, obduracy of the colonial government towards infrastructure development and politics.

To avoid any misunderstanding, the interaction of the authentic characters with those around which the plot revolves is contrived. The following characters in the plot are fictitious: the Prescotts, Harrisons, Harringtons, Pryces, Gordon and Lily Snell, Geoffrey and Stella Southam, Sarika Singh, Hugh Lawson, Michael, Cynthia, Ruth and Margaret Moodie, Peter Richardson, Emma Johnson, the Smiths; Lucy, Luke, Ginger; Stella Hassall, Janki, Mr Tatham, Dulcie Lister, Yvonne Clark, Mr Butler, Isabel and Alice Greenacre.

The following places are fictitious: Michaelhouse, Sarika's stores, Dewsbury, Preston, Crofton, Glenmore, Taunton Manor, the Cutty Sark, and the Wiltshire.

Population statistics, tonnages of sugar, references to railway costs, infrastructure development, laws, newspapers, hotels, Goodricke's law firm, Greenacre's store, Acutt's, Natal Bank, Glasgow Insurance, are all authentic along with the associated names of officials and settlers.

The historical details are derived from my research published in *Sugar and Settlers: A History of the Natal South Coast 1850-1910* and *Labourer or Settler? Colonial Natal's Indian Dilemma*; "Hazardous to health? Sugar mills and river pollution in Natal 1869-1901," *Historia* – Journal of the Historical Association of South Africa, Vol. 63, May 2018.

Additional information was derived from *Valiant Harvest: The Founding of the South African Sugar Industry* by Robert F Osborn; *Inside Indian Indenture* by Ashwin Desai and Goolam Vahed and Prinisha Badassy's 2005 MA dissertation titled 'Crimes of passion, crimes of reason: Analysis of crimes against masters, mistresses by their Indian domestic servants 1880-1920.' The term 'sugarocracy' is derived from David Lincoln's article in vol. xi of the *Journal of Natal and Zulu History.*

Challenges in a colonial county

PART ONE

CHAPTER 1

The Cutty Sark pub in Umzinto one Friday afternoon in February 1876 was the occasion of farewell drinks for the departing Resident Magistrate, James Dunbar Moodie. A letter signed by 62 residents had been published in the *Natal Mercury* in which they regretted his transfer to Ladysmith in Klip River County and were profuse in their appreciation of how he had conducted his office since 1860. Raising his glass, the "Father of the District," as Reverend Joseph Barker referred to Field Cornet Alexander Brander, spoke in praise of Moodie's lone role as the top government official in the County. "You've become one of us, James. Your role and office have served to guide Alexandra County through the tenures of four Governors. You have asserted yourself beyond the requirements of your office by championing our causes."

Acknowledging his remarks, Moodie reflected on the experience he had gained during his sixteen-year tenure. "Alex County has provided me with legal challenges which few of my colleagues in other counties would face. The two rape cases involving Anne Prescott and the deportation of her abductor stand out in my memory. It was also a pleasure to have served in initiating the Umzinto Rifle Club which became the Alexandra Mounted Rifles in 1866. The tragic death of William Prescott in 1868 while on that camp when he was bitten by a black mamba, still weighs heavily on my soul and was the reason I resigned as the commanding officer of the AMR."

"My abiding memory of Alex County, however, is how you have persisted in the face of repeated government indifference to your transport and travel plight. There is not another county in the colony that suffers the neglect to which Alex County is subjected. But I can assure you that my successor as Resident Magistrate, Gould Arthur Lucas, is well aware of your plight. Before my appointment in 1860, he served in a temporary capacity following the retirement of Henry Francis Fynn."

****

Dewsbury was a 598-acre sugar estate south of the sprawling settlement of Umzinto. Simon Prescott inherited it from his deceased parents. A handsome 32-year-old, Simon was of average height, stout, athletic, clean-shaven and wore his sun-bleached hair fairly long. Quick-witted and intolerant of fools, his marriage to Cynthia Moodie, daughter of the recently departed resident magistrate, aroused the envy of not a few of the fairer sex in the district.

Having been impressed by the success of coffee cultivation on Woodhouse Lea, the estate of Eric and Frances Harrison in the Park Rynie area, in 1872 Simon had decided to devote 30 acres to coffee tree planting. Although it took four years before a harvest could be reaped, by 1876, coffee added to what Dewsbury's sugar crop and distillery earned for the Prescotts.

Thus, the state of Dewsbury's finances in 1876 made it possible for Simon to afford employing an assistant manager. His name was Peter Richardson. He had previously worked on sugar estates in Victoria County and was widely experienced particularly in rum production. Cynthia, was especially relieved that her husband had a competent assistant as in May 1876 she had given birth to their second son, named after her father, James Moodie. She needed Simon to be more domestically hands-on so she could cope with household chores, baby James and George, who was then five years of age.

Aged 29 in 1876, Cynthia had been married to Simon for nine years. They had met as young adults attending St Patrick's Anglican Church in Umzinto. Their mutual interest in outdoor life and her competence in horse riding made them a compatible match. Before her two pregnancies, she had been a teacher at the Umzinto government school. Physically well-endowed and vivacious, Cynthia usually wore her chestnut-coloured hair in a chignon. Like Simon, she was outspoken and readily identified with the frontier lifestyle on estates in Alexandra County.

****

At the age of 26, Sarika became a widow in July 1875 when her common-law husband, Michael Moodie, at the age of 23, was killed in a boiler explosion at Reunion sugar mill in Isipingo. Pregnant at the time, she gave birth in April 1876 to a son she named Michael. Although her husband was the son of the recently departed Resident Magistrate, James Moodie, the couple were regarded as social outcasts by Alexandra County residents because of her Indian ethnicity.

Charitably, the Harrisons, Eric and Frances had accommodated her on their Woodhouse Lea estate after Michael's death when she had discovered she was pregnant. Michael had previously been Eric's assistant before relocating with Sarika to the culturally diverse community of Isipingo to commence a life together less encumbered by the racial discrimination and the social ostracism they encountered in Alex County. Their relocation was made on the advice of Simon Prescott's sister, Victoria, aged 30, who was an outspoken opponent of what she called the "suffocating constraints" of Victorian social conventions. Married to Gordon Snell, a wealthy wine and spirit merchant in Durban, Victoria was an ardent proponent of social reform.

"Sarika, how do you see your future now that you have baby Michael to care for?" Frances asked one morning when they were having tea after Michael had been breastfed and was sleeping.

"With your indulgence, Frances, I would like to extend my stay with you while I investigate my options in Umzinto where I am contemplating establishing my own store and residence. The £200 I was paid in compensation for Michael's death will be more than sufficient for me to go into business and to have my own home. Having been a *dukahwallah* (an itinerant hawker) I know the ins and outs of trading. I could seek employment as a teacher at the Indian school in Umzinto or the one in Craigieburn near Umkomaas, but the salary is so meagre. Besides, I want to be independent. The Indian population in the County is growing faster than that of the white settlers, so the prospects of success for a general store are promising."

"That's so enterprising of you, Sarika. Eric and I are happy to have you stay with us as long as you like. We enjoy your company and our two boys, Edward and Nicholas, are very fond of you. When you feel that baby Michael can be left alone with me for a few hours, Eric or his assistant can take you to Umzinto so you can make some enquiries."

****

In 1874 the Harrington family settled on a rented sugar estate in the Park Rynie area. Since 1858 John and Emily Harrington had lived in Victoria County where John had worked as a manager on various sugar estates. The couple had immigrated to Natal from Preston in Lancashire in the wake of violent strikes and lockouts in the textile industry during 1853-54 which had inspired Charles Dickens' novel *Hard Times*.

Their relocation to Alexandra County was motivated by the desire to acquire their own estate. Whereas sugar planting in Victoria County was becoming increasingly dominated by a few powerful individuals and companies, prospects in Alexandra County were still favourable for small-scale entrepreneurs. In 1876 John Harrington took advantage of the economic slump aggravated by drought and purchased their rented estate renaming it 'Preston' after their hometown in England. For the Harrington children, Stewart aged 16, Priscilla 14 and David 12 years of age, it was their first proper home. Stewart and David relished the proximity of Preston to the coast where they intended to exploit and sample sea life. Priscilla was delighted to learn that their neighbour, Frances Harrison of Woodhouse Lea, offered piano lessons.

Remarks made by the new Governor of Natal, Sir Henry Bulwer, when he opened the 1876 session of the colony's Legislative Council, provided fresh impetus to the favourite topic of discussion at the Cutty Sark. In justifying the erection of bridges over the Klip and Tugela Rivers in the northern sector of Natal, Bulwer cited the need to improve communication with the Overberg trade. Since the development of the Diamond Fields in the Northern Cape, commercial activity to and from Durban had grown significantly. It was also the reason that railway construction from Durban northwards had commenced and was a priority.

"This is really frustrating," said Charles Knox, proprietor of one of the two European-owned stores in Umzinto. "One would have thought that after the near drowning of Simon Prescott's younger sister, Anne, in the Mkomanzi last year and the visit by the then Administrator, Sir Garnet Wolseley, a bridge over the Mkomanzi would have been a guaranteed priority of the government. If you recall, Wolseley was especially scathing in his comments about our so-called roads and the neglected state of the pont in use on the Mkomanzi."

"Our dilemma is that the powers in Pietermaritzburg don't see any economic incentive in developing our infrastructure. It took them ten years before they built a courthouse in this county. Yet four new sugar mills have been established here in the past year. The one in Sezela district is the largest in Natal," responded Field Cornet Alex Brander.

"What they don't seem to appreciate is that without proper roads and bridges, particularly over the Illovo, Mkomanzi and Umpambinyoni Rivers, our economic potential is being hamstrung. When it takes up to five days for an ox-drawn wagon to reach Durban, that's hardly a signal for commercial and property development here," opined David Aiken, joint owner of Maryville estate with his brother, James.

"I think we ought to be focused on getting shipping established on the Mzimkulu. I remember the Surveyor-General, Dr Sutherland, stating in 1866 that he saw potential in riverport shipping on the Mzimkulu. Of course, such a development would still be some 25 miles from Umzinto, but it would give us independence as a county and spur the development of Alfred County as well. Just think of the trade links shipping on the Mzimkulu could generate. It would attract commerce from Pondoland and East Griqualand. For us in Alex County, it would stimulate new markets for our sugar, coffee, tobacco and dairy produce," declared Charles Sinclair, owner of a transport business and a notary and conveyancer.

"Well, it is pleasing to note that our elected representative, James Aiken, told the Commission on European Immigration in Maritzburg that he regards the establishment of a harbour at the mouth of the Mzimkulu River as essential to bringing some relief to the transport woes of the lower South Coast. Apparently, he said if the Mzimkulu were in any other country but Natal, there would be steamers and sailing vessels running in and out of it already!" said Charles Paglar, keeper of the Umzinto prison, to the delight of the bar room regulars.

****

By 1876 new advances featured in Umzinto's social life. A cricket club had been formed with a founding membership of nineteen which included three of the late James Arbuthnot's sons as well as Charles Reynolds, nephew of Lewis Reynolds, the late owner of the 8,500-acre Umzinto Sugar estate. Highlights of the cricket season included limited overs fixtures against the Isipingo, Scottburgh and Ifafa clubs.

Although as the seat of the Alexandra County magistracy and the hub of its commerce, since 1862, when insolvency closed John Pearse's premises, Umzinto had been bereft of hotel accommodation. But in 1875, thanks to the initiative of William Thornton, the newly erected Royal Hotel opened for business. Whereas the previous year the first public ball in the County was held at the Umzinto school, in 1875 the Royal Hotel was the venue for the occasion.

As published in the *Natal Mercury* 13 July 1875

****

Sarika's eagerness to leave baby Michael with Frances for a day while she attempted to gauge her prospects for acquiring premises in Umzinto for the general store she wished to establish, was frustrated when Michael became ill. However in his sixth month, his growth pattern had stalled as a result of his body's inability to absorb Sarika's breast milk. Frances, as an experienced mother, feared that the little infant was suffering from dysentery.

Sarika resorted to traditional Indian treatments which included ginger and lemon. But the little boy's condition continued to deteriorate, his cries and discomfort proved greatly distressing for the household. For Sarika, his imminent demise brought home the still-recent memory of the loss of her baby's father. Mercifully, baby Michael's misery ended after nearly three weeks of suffering. After consulting Reverend Joseph Barker at St Patrick's Church, it was agreed that he could be buried alongside his father, Michael, in the church cemetery.

On an overcast, windy October morning, accompanied by the Harrisons and their two boys, Edward and Nicholas, Sarika committed her baby to eternal rest alongside his father in the graveyard at St Patrick's. Apart from Reverend Barker, no one else was in attendance. Sarika was *persona non grata* with the white community of the district because she had breached the social convention which scorned interracial relationships. Although Eric had informed Simon Prescott who was married to Michael's sister, Cynthia, of the death of their nephew, no response was forthcoming from Dewsbury.

Returning to Woodhouse Lea where they gathered sombrely at the lunch table, Eric asked if Sarika intended to inform the Moodies that their grandchild had passed on. "Yes, I intend writing to James and Margaret. Closure is important for me and for them, even though they disowned their grandchild. I did not shrink from confronting them at Michael's funeral and I won't avoid informing them of what we presided over today."

Tearfully, she recalled the last occasion which she and Michael had enjoyed at Woodhouse Lea. "Although at the time I felt a sense of finality that weekend back in June 1875, there was no indication that a dark destiny was looming. I remember preparing the biryani we ate that evening and the warmth of our mutual conversational interests that lasted well into the night. I am sure it was that night that I became pregnant as I remember coaxing Michael with the words "Let's make a baby!"

"Oh, Sarika! You have endured such bitter-sweet memories. Eric and I are privileged to have been able to assist you and Michael and to have provided you with support in the face of the ostracism of our fellow colonists. Until you are able to sort out your intended relocation to Umzinto, we are delighted to accommodate you. As far as we are concerned, you are part of our family and are welcome here any time in the future," said Frances.

That same day, Sarika wrote a short note to James and Margaret Moodie in Ladysmith informing them of the tragic end of their six-month-old grandson. No response from them was forthcoming.

****

The bar at the recently opened Royal Hotel seemed to appeal to newer residents of the Umzinto district as well as those, like Eric Harrison, whose support for Sarika had somewhat soured the reception he received at the Cutty Sark.

One Friday afternoon, John Harrington announced to his wife, Emily, that he was going to ride up to the Royal to acquaint himself with the locals. Warmly welcomed by William Thornton, the proprietor, John immediately felt comfortable even though he was new in the district. Arriving soon after him was Eric Harrison. Although they had not previously met as estate neighbours, John had heard that Eric's wife, Frances, would be giving piano lessons to his daughter, Priscilla.

After exchanging mutual family interests, the conversation turned to their respective estates. They both agreed that their sugar harvests looked promising despite the paucity of rainfall. On the issue of labour, John Harrington said he had experienced too many difficulties as an estate manager in Victoria County with indentured Indian labour. "I spent half my time trying to adjudicate personal disputes amongst them. Then the frequency with which they either absconded or feigned illness made life very frustrating."

In response, Eric recounted his experiences with indentured labour on Beneva, his Father-in-law, Edward Hawksworth's estate. "Unless one is out in the fields with them, they shirk. Absenteeism by feigning illness is another common practice along with requests to lodge a complaint with the magistrate. That convinced me to stick to native labour on Woodhouse Lea." They both agreed that having an estate assistant was necessary if one was to have any time to deal with the range of issues which competed for attention. "The difficulty, however, is to find a youngster who is willing and capable. My advice to you, John, is to cultivate that son of yours, Stewart. He might be only 16 now, but in the next three years he will be old enough to serve as your assistant on Preston," counselled Eric.

****

Another two new residents in the Umzinto district were Frank and Charles Reynolds. Following the death of their uncle, Lewis, in September 1875, their father, Thomas, had dispatched them from his Oaklands Estate in Umhlali to continue resuscitating the Umzinto Sugar Company estate which was in poor condition when Lewis bought it in 1873. Both under the age of 30, as regulars at the Royal Hotel bar, they provided fresh insights into life beyond Umzinto's relative isolation from the rest of the colony, regaling patrons with many lively tales about life in Victoria County. On a serious note, however, from what was developing on the North Coast, they made it clear that the days of small-scale sugar planting were rapidly coming to an end. In one of the discussions on the subject, Frank let it be known that their father intended to expand their Alexandra County enterprise in 1877 to be known as T Reynolds & Sons.

****

Within a week of burying her baby, Sarika travelled the short distance of some six miles from Woodhouse Lea to Umzinto to decide on the most appropriate site for her intended general store and residence.

Since Umzinto was never properly laid out as a village as Scottburgh was in 1861, clusters of businesses were haphazardly placed along its main thoroughfare to the south and north of St Patrick's Church. In between were overgrown expanses of vacant land. For Sarika, the first decision she had to make was at which end of the thoroughfare she should establish her store. She decided that the north end was closer to the route leading to Park Rynie and, therefore, promised to be more visible and commercially appealing.

Having made that decision, her next step in the process was to meet with the land commissioner, Alexander Brander, and enquire about purchasing a site or hiring one. As one of the earliest residents in the Umzinto district, Brander's disposition towards Indians was typical of prevailing white attitudes: they were not welcome as settlers and should keep to themselves. Making matters difficult was the fact that Brander did not have an office in the village but worked from his estate which was three miles south of the scattered Umzinto settlement. Sarika established that information by enquiring at the magistrate's office. She was also told that she would have to make an appointment to see Brander. To do so, she would need to mail him her request and await his response. Somewhat disappointed, but not really surprised, she wrote out her request at the post office which was placed in Brander's collection box.

A week later when Eric was in Umzinto to fetch the mail for Woodhouse Lea, it included a letter from Brander to Sarika. Typically, Brander's response to her request for an appointment was terse and discourteous: unless she had cash to buy a site outright, there would be no interview. Moreover, the only convenient time for him to see her was on a Monday morning at 7am.

Eric and Frances were outraged by Brander's response. "His arrogance makes my blood boil! According to the 1875 population statistics, there are more Indians in Alex County than the 500 or so white colonists. Brander and his ilk need to get their heads out of the sand and recognise the demographic and economic realities not just of Alex County but of the colony itself. Is he not aware that immigration to Natal by Indians far exceeds that of whites?

Anyway, Sarika, this coming Monday I will personally take you to Mr Brander's for your appointment. In fact, I am looking forward to it!" declared Eric.

****

On the last Thursday of October, the list of cricket players for the friendly limited overs match against Scottburgh was placed on the public notice board outside the Umzinto Post Office. It included several of the Cutty Sark regulars along with two of the Arbuthnots, St George and William, Simon Prescott and his Dewsbury assistant, Peter Richardson. At the Cutty Sark that evening, the discussion involved who should captain the side. The respect in which Simon Prescott was held for his shooting accuracy in the Alexandra Mounted Rifles made him the obvious choice. As regards the position of wicketkeeper, there were no volunteers. "I'm damned if I am going to crouch behind the stumps for 25 overs," declared Charles Paglar. "As it is, I struggle to bend down to pick things up off the floor. One of you more athletic types can be the wicky." After a brief discussion it was decided that Simon would appoint the wicket keeper.

At Dewsbury the same evening, Cynthia was displeased to learn that Simon would be away the whole of Saturday playing cricket in Scottburgh. "I look forward to having you around at the weekend. During the week I know you try to be a house help but even with Peter assisting you, there always seem to be issues that require you to be out in the fields or in the village," she complained. Taking her into his arms, Simon stroked her hair and nibbled her ear as he whispered, "I'll make it up to you on Saturday night and I'll also bring home one of those cakes you love from the Scottburgh bakery."

****

Cricket was not the topic of conversation at the Royal Hotel bar that same evening. Instead, it concerned Alex County's new magistrate, Gould Arthur

Lucas. "I see magistrates' salaries have improved from £300 per annum to £450. But does anyone recall Lucas from the period in 1860 when he had served briefly as magistrate here?" asked proprietor William Thornton. In response, Dr Lancelot Booth, the newly appointed District Surgeon, volunteered some thoughts.

"Lucas is actually a military man and holds the rank of Captain. Before he was appointed as magistrate in Klip River County he served with the 45th Regiment at Fort Napier. From what I gather, there was some controversy about appointing a military officer in a civil post. Apparently the General Officer Commanding British forces in Southern Africa was very reluctant to sanction Lucas's appointment but acceded to it only because of the shortage of competent men to fill such posts."

"So for how long was he magistrate in Klip River?" asked Robert Anderson.

"It must have been from about 1861 until the Langalibalele rebellion in Klip River County late in 1873. I do know from other doctors in the colonial service that Captain Lucas was involved in the suppression of the rebellion and apparently played a brutal role in breaking up communities and families of the Hlubi tribe," said Dr Booth authoritatively.

"Well, it seems his appointment here in Alex County has not excited any military concerns. But it does occur to me that when our departing magistrate James Moodie said that Lucas was well aware of our transport plight that he was being economical with the truth. Stuck out in Ladysmith and then busy soldiering, I don't think he has any idea of the infrastructure neglect of our County. I get the feeling that our loss of James Moodie is Klip River's gain," contemplated James Ross.

****

Amongst the Scottburgh cricket team were three sugar planters – Samuel Crookes of Ellingham and Thomas and Joshua Landers of Renishaw and

Maryland estates. Aged 37, Samuel Crookes was the captain. The night before the match there had been quite a downpour which had left the outfield very slow and the wicket spongy and damp.

The Umzinto XI had arrived in good spirits, partly due to some rum Simon had brought from Dewsbury. After meeting and greeting each other, the teams had tea and buns before taking to the field. Simon had won the toss and elected to field reasoning that the damp conditions made it a bowler's wicket. His decision proved correct – initially. His slow arm spinners were virtually unplayable and one by one, most of the Scottburgh team was skittled out cheaply. But just when the Umzinto lads thought they could dismiss Scottburgh for a low score and romp to an easy victory, Samuel Crookes came to the crease.

He had observed that the only way to score big runs was to loft the ball to the boundary because the slow outfield limited a batsman to stealing only occasional singles. With the fielders all in close, the risk of a run-out was also great. And so Samuel Crookes plundered Umzinto's bowling mercilessly, averaging at least eight runs an over. Simon's field adjustments made no difference to Samuel. He found the gaps and drove the ball repeatedly to the boundary.

For Umzinto, respite from Samuel Crookes' batting onslaught finally came when one of his lofted shots was caught in the last over of the innings. Set a target of 80 runs to win, Simon's team put up a dogged fight but were all out for 62. The early finish to the match meant extra time for drinks and the repast the hosts had laid on in the specially erected tent. Toasts were drunk to the Queen, the Governor, and the teams' captains. It was almost sunset when the wagon bearing the Umzinto team began the two-hour journey home.

Arriving back at Dewsbury after nine that night having forgotten to buy the cake he promised for Cynthia and feeling quite inebriated, his reception was anything but pleasant. “I am very disappointed in you, Simon Prescott!” Cynthia bellowed as he headed for the bathtub.

****

Long before sunrise on Monday Eric and Sarika set off in Eric’s carriage for Alexander Brander’s homestead three miles south of Umzinto. Their arrival shortly before the appointed time of 7 o’clock seemed to take Brander by surprise as if he had not expected Sarika to pursue her intended land acquisition.

Greeting them brusquely he made it clear to Eric that he disapproved of the assistance and shelter Sarika was being given on Woodhouse Lea. Eric ignored his attitude and asked that the meeting commence at once as he had a busy day ahead. But the atmosphere worsened when Eric insisted that he intended to sit in on the meeting. “It is none of your business what I discuss with this coolie friend of yours,” fumed Brander. Eric objected to his derogatory reference to Sarika and countered by pointing out that she had asked him to be part of the discussion. Ushering them into his office, the first question Brander asked was why Sarika wanted to acquire land.

“I am a settler in this colony just as you are, Mr Brander, and therefore I have as much right as you do to own a piece of land,” she replied.

“So what are you going to do with a plot that you buy?”

“I intend to set up a business and have residential accommodation for myself.”

“What sort of business do you intend to establish?”

“I aim to establish a general dealer store.”

“What makes you think Umzinto needs another coolie store? There are already half a dozen, all selling the same things and making a mess of our main thoroughfare.”

"Mr Brander, I take exception to your insulting description of my commercial ambition as being *another coolie store*. I intend to compete commercially with the existing white-owned stores, Archibald's and Knox's, offering an even wider range of goods. Moreover, I intend to employ white colonists as store assistants."

"Suit yourself, but I am telling you that the newly formed Alexandra County Association, based in Umzinto is unlikely to grant you a licence to trade."

"You're wrong there, Alex," said Eric. "That Association is not your toy to manoeuvre into supporting your opinion. As a resident of the County and a property owner, I am automatically a member of the Association. Until I am consulted and the opinions of others are canvassed, you cannot presume anything. Anyway, the granting of trade licences is the task of the magistrate."

"The magistrate is unlikely to ignore the opinion of the County Association," riposted Brander.

"Mr Brander, are you aware of how many white colonists are regular customers of the established Indian shops? Are you aware that the number of Indian settlers in this County is growing at a faster rate than the number of white settlers?"

At a loss as to how to respond to Sarika, Brander promptly declared the meeting over. "You will be notified in writing of my decision in due course." But determined to have the last word, Sarika asked how he could make any decision without having inquired about the location and extent of the land she wished to purchase. Typically, Brander ignored her query and curtly hastened them out of his office.

****

CHAPTER 2

Despite the near drought conditions, the 1876 sugar crop in Alexandra County was a bumper one. Added to that was the prospect of higher prices on the overseas market as a result of the failed sugar beet crop in Europe. On Dewsbury, Simon was delighted with his first coffee crop of 5,000 pounds.

A negative development, however, was the winding up of the Alexandra Shipping Company. Its formation in July 1874 had heralded the promise of a breakthrough in communication, trade and transport between Durban and the County. But economics had dictated the fate of the Company. Lower overland wagon prices and the often-hazardous conditions in ferrying goods out to the waiting steamer beyond the breakers at Scottburgh had resulted in the ship frequenting Port St Johns and East London instead.

As Charles Sinclair remarked at the Cutty Sark, "Well, folks, here we are facing 1877 with the same challenges we had more than 15 years ago. No proper roads, no bridges and shipping ventures that just never get going. Even the grand Welborne scheme of a railway line down to Port Shepstone fizzled out when the plans were revised so that the line would reach no further than Isipingo. Then, the British government scrapped the scheme in its entirety because of its financial implications for the colony."

"Cheer up, Charles. Every county has its challenges and drawbacks. The Mhloti River on the North Coast is a transport rider's headache. In the Richmond/Ixopo area and in Umvoti County, stock theft is rife. A report tabled in the Legislative Council stated that farmers in those areas lost over 1,200 sheep this past year. At least we don't have that problem in Alex County thanks to our cordial relations with the neighbouring native location" observed David Aiken.

****

Simon decided that the best way to abate Cynthia's frosty relationship with him after disappointing her with his all-day cricket outing in Scottburgh when he had returned late and inebriated, was to treat her to a dinner at the Royal Hotel. Having his assistant Peter Richardson as a tenant in the cottage on Dewsbury meant that the Prescotts could go away to the coast or to visit Victoria and Gordon in Durban and not have to worry about the security of the estate and feeding Rex, their dog. It also meant that once in a while, Peter could be asked to babysit George and James.

To smooth the way to the outing, Simon suggested she visit the new Archibald's store and pick out a smart outfit. The Saturday evening following the Scottburgh disappointment found Simon and Cynthia seated in the dining room of Umzinto's Royal Hotel. Simon had informed proprietor William Thornton beforehand of his intended visit and the reason for it. In turn, the proprietor had enquired what dishes he could add to the menu to appeal to Cynthia. Without hesitation Simon had told him: roast lamb and for dessert - Crème Brulée.

Having complimented Cynthia on how glamorous she looked in her new dress with its low-cut front, her smiling response made him feel somewhat assured that he was redeeming his status in her eyes. A pre-dinner gin and tonic had also helped to relax her. The clincher was when Mr Thornton personally presented the dinner menu. Cynthia smiled and licked her lips. "Oh, this is so delightful. My two favourite dishes on the menu," she exclaimed to Simon who pretended to look surprised while sharing her pleasure. To lubricate the situation a little further, Mr Thornton presented the Prescotts with a chilled bottle of Cape Rose wine.

Sipping their wine after having despatched the light seafood hors d'oeuvre, Simon's confidence in how the evening was proceeding increased when in response to his hand reaching under the table and caressing her thigh, she grinned at him.

The main course, its presentation and succulence followed by the Crème Brulée, topped with raspberries and the complimentary Irish coffees on the Hotel veranda, rounded off an outing that clearly had rekindled Cynthia's affection for her husband. She showed it by kissing him passionately after they had boarded their carriage and rested her head on his lap as he steered the horse back to Dewsbury. She was also pleased that she had a surprise waiting for him.

After thanking Peter Richardson for having looked after George and James who had behaved well and were asleep, Cynthia repaired to the bathroom while Simon undressed in their bedroom. Minutes later she tip-toed into the bedroom. Simon gasped when he saw her. She had loosened her hair so that it hung over her breasts which were visible under the loosely crocheted negligée which left nothing to the imagination.

Like the courting lovers they had been before their marriage, they embraced and caressed each other before getting into bed. Amid words of endearment, Simon heightening her passion until she gasped in ecstasy.

****

Almost two weeks after meeting with Alexander Brander, his response to Sarika's inquiry about purchasing land in Umzinto was in the Harrisons' mailbox. Characteristically, it was terse and devoid of motivation: "Your request to purchase land is denied."

Although the Harrisons were livid at Brander's response, Sarika took it in her stride. The discrimination and persecution she had suffered as a consequence of her relationship with Michael inured her to colonial attitudes concerning ethnicity. "I don't and won't accept Brander's response. It is purely vindictive based on his rejection of my relationship with Michael," she said.

"I agree. But we need to tread warily in proceeding to challenge his decision," said Eric. "Known as the 'Father of the district,' he is a popular figure and held in esteem by most. So, the consensus of the community would side with him. The Alexandra County Association, for what it's worth, is purely an advisory body which he would use to justify his opinion."

"Of course, what we don't know is how our new Resident Magistrate, Captain Mr Lucas, would respond. It is his prerogative to award trading licences and to rule on land applications. As a military man he may prove less prone to be being swayed by civilian sentiments. On the other hand, however, Brander's position in the Alexandra Mounted Rifles as Quarter-Master and as County Field Cornet may incline him to support the decision against you," ventured Eric.

"I think the situation calls for some outside, neutral assistance. What about getting hold of Martin Pryce, Simon Prescott's brother-in-law?" suggested Frances. "His legal expertise secured the insurance money Sarika was paid as a result of Michael's death. I think we should write to him at Goodricke's law office in Pietermaritzburg and apprise him of the situation."

****

With Christmas of 1876 approaching, plans for family gatherings were made. Simon, Cynthia and their two boys had been invited to spend the festive season with his sister, Victoria, and her husband, Gordon Snell, and their daughter, Lily, on the Berea in Durban. Edward Hawksworth was anxious to see his grandchildren, so Frances, Eric and their two boys were to spend Christmas on Beneva estate. Frances' uncertainty about whether Sarika would want to accompany them to her father's estate was solved when the neighbouring Harrington family invited Sarika to join them for the occasion. Emily Harrington had met Sarika when she had brought her daughter, Priscilla, to Woodhouse Lea for piano lessons with Frances. Chatting with Sarika while Priscilla was having her lesson, Emily discovered that she and Sarika had a shared experience: both had lost infants to dysentery.

For Sarika, the hospitality of the Harringtons, John and Emily, was a welcome development since apart from Frances and Eric, she had no other social links within the district. At lunch on Christmas Day, Sarika was asked for details as to how she had arrived in the Umzinto area. "It's a story that began when I was 12 and was indentured to an estate in the Illovo area. Fortunately, I was assigned to household duties and spared the drudgery of working in the fields. I was also exceptionally favoured by my very kind mistress who provided basic education on weekends. On the completion of my five-year indenture in 1866, she asked me not to re-indenture. Instead, she employed me to do secretarial and administrative work on the estate. In 1871, when my father had completed his ten years of indenture, we moved to Umzinto and made a living as hawkers."

"Was your mother not indentured?" Emily enquired.

"Yes, she was. But when we disembarked from the ship in Durban, my mother and brother were assigned to a different estate from that of my Father and me. No provision was made for family members to be kept together. So, we never saw or heard from them again."

"Oh, that is awful. I am embarrassed that such heartlessness was practised by our colonial authorities!" exclaimed Emily.

"Since the resumption of indenture in 1874, however, that practice seems to have abated. Anyway, it was while I was in the hawking trade with my father that I met Michael who was Eric's assistant on Woodhouse Lea. Unfortunately, our relationship was scorned by the white community with only Frances and Eric showing any sympathy and support. I was even treated as a pariah by my fellow Indian traders. But on reflection, I think their attitude was based on business interests. You see, they were only too happy to snap up the white customers we lost on account of my relationship with Michael. On advice, we left Alex County and moved to Isipingo where Michael managed a small sugar estate. There we found a more relaxed social atmosphere. But sadly, our contented situation was short lived when Michael was killed in a boiler explosion on Reunion estate."

"Yes, I remember hearing gossip about the accident. What struck me as quite heartless was the ambivalence in the expression of feelings. While the tragedy was regretted, at the same time, it was coupled with scorn for your relationship with Michael," remarked John.

"I am not surprised. Social convention runs very deep in this community which is why I am indebted to Eric and Frances for resisting the disdain of the community because socially it has cost them. You might have realised it from the fact that Eric no longer frequents the Cutty Sark because of the criticism levelled at him for supporting my relationship with Michael."

"We saw a few liaisons like yours when we lived in Victoria County. Some of them involved high-profile colonists and proved embarrassing for the families involved. But I don't recall any bitter recrimination. Possibly, in your case, what you have experienced is because Umzinto is a relatively small white community whereas in Victoria County the communities of Umhlanga, Verulam and Tongaat are large in comparison," John noted.

"I think the ostracism you have experienced has been greater because Michael was the son of the resident magistrate, Mr Moodie. Consequently, there was a tendency to express solidarity with the Moodies as the family expected to uphold social convention," said Emily.

"So, Sarika, do you have any plans for the new year?" asked John. Responding, Sarika related her intention of acquiring land on which to build a store and accommodation for herself and how it had been rejected by Land Commissioner Brander. "Thanks to the initiative of Eric and Frances, legal advice is being sought from the lawyer who fought my case for compensation following Michael's death. I feel confident he will overturn Brander's decision."

****

Martin Pryce headed Goodricke's legal team in Pietermaritzburg, the colonial capital. Educated in England, he had qualified as a barrister and worked at the courts of Grays Inn in London before intending to immigrate to Australia. But fate had caused him to remain in Durban after his ship bound for Melbourne docked in the port. A chance meeting with the founder of Durban's first law firm, Mr John Richardson Goodricke, resulted in the offer of a position in the firm. Martin's decision to accept the post had a beneficial consequence: he met the Prescotts of Umzinto and married the lady of his dreams – Anne Prescott. At the urging of her sister, Victoria Snell, an arch critic of colonial social conventions, Martin had taken up Sarika's claim against the powerful sugar syndicate De Pass, Spence for compensation insurance as a result of the death of her common-law husband Michael Moodie on the Reunion estate in 1875.

Upon receiving Sarika's letter explaining her intention to buy a plot of land on the north end of the Umzinto thoroughfare and Land Commissioner Brander's blunt denial of her request, Pryce immediately consulted case law files. They revealed several precedents of permission to rent Crown land as well as instances where white landowners had sold off plots to Indians. Armed with those precedents, he addressed a letter to Brander supporting Sarika's right, as a subject of Her Majesty, Queen Victoria, to purchase land. Brander's response was prompt. He cited the opinion of the Alexandra County Association opposing Sarika's request. Eric was furious when he received copies of this correspondence. "Brander is lying when he claims the ACA opposes Sarika. There hasn't been a public meeting on the issue to canvass opinion, so he has no grounds to make that claim. I am going to demand a public meeting to gauge opinion."

True to his word, Eric confronted Brander and demanded the holding of a public meeting. Within the week notices were placed in Umzinto, Umkomaas, Scottburgh, Park Rynie and Ifafa advertising the ACA's public meeting on land acquisition. "Are you going to attend the meeting?" Eric asked Sarika. "No," she replied. "I would like to but feel that my presence would just exacerbate emotions. Better that you defend my right, Eric."

On the appointed afternoon at the Umzinto school, a crowd of 40 Alexandra residents assembled to express opinions on the issue. Speaking first, Brander justified his denial on the basis that there were already about half a dozen Indian stores in Umzinto. "If we condone another coolie store, history will hold us to account for having turned Umzinto into a coolie town," he thundered to applause.

Eric was next to address the meeting but struggled against heckling and barracking. Unable to present his case coherently, he left it to John Harrington. Comparatively unknown in the County, Harrington was accorded a fair hearing citing examples of Indian commercial enterprise in Victoria County where he had lived for almost 16 years. "Verulam has several Indian-owned stores premised on Indian-owned land. Those Indian stores enjoy a growing number of white customers. Is that not also what is happening in Umzinto? Whether we like it or not, an Indian settler has as much right to own land as we do. If you look at the immigration figures, it is obvious that Indian immigration to Natal is outstripping white immigration. And that does not take into account those Indians currently indentured. The majority of them will remain here when their contracts expire around 1879/1880."

Responding to Harrington's address, one of the hotheads from the Cutty Sark told Harrington to go back to Victoria County. "If Victoria County wants to become a coolie county, that's their business. But we don't have to put up with that trend in Alex County." When the vote was taken, it was clear that although John Harrington's words had had some impact, 25 of the 40 men present supported Brander. Barely concealing his delight at the outcome, Brander announced that he would be advising Magistrate Lucas to make a declaration denying Sarika's land purchase request. Before he had finished his announcement Eric was on his feet demanding to know what Brander would do if a white colonist hired his land to her. "You can't stop a white resident leasing his land as he pleases," he shouted as the meeting broke up noisily.

****

Returning to Woodhouse Lea after the meeting, Eric knew what the next move had to be in order to keep Sarika's hopes alive. Informing her and Frances of the outcome of the meeting, he said it was vital to reach Martin Pryce urgently. "It is so annoying that there's no telegraph service in Alex County because Martin needs to be apprised immediately of the situation before Brander tries to influence Magistrate Lucas's decision. If we post Martin a letter it could be three days before he receives it in Maritzburg. I think what I have to do is get to Durban tomorrow by hiring a speedy spider carriage and going directly to Goodricke's office where Martin can be telegraphed."

Late the following afternoon Eric arrived at Goodricke's Durban office. A telegram was hastily prepared for transmission to Martin Pryce. Within the hour Martin had replied: "Will check on Lucas's record affirming land sales to Indians." His strategy delighted Eric as it would place Lucas in a difficult position if there was evidence that as a magistrate in Ladysmith, he had sanctioned land purchases by Indians. Hoping to receive news from Martin the next day, Eric spent the night in the Royal Hotel. The following afternoon, after browsing around some shops to pass the time in the hope that Martin would be able to find the evidence he needed to secure Sarika's case, Eric returned to Goodricke's office. At length, a telegram arrived from Goodricke's Pietermaritzburg office. It read: "Evidence found. Details to follow."

Since it was too late in the day to return to Umzinto and, in any case, time was needed to prepare a legal brief, Mr Goodricke advised Eric to spend another night at the Royal Hotel. But by 10 am the next day, Eric was on his way back to Umzinto armed with Goodricke's letter to Magistrate Lucas. Arriving back at Woodhouse Lea that evening, Sarika and Frances were eager to read what Martin Pryce had researched on Lucas's tenure regarding land purchases by

Indians in Klip River County. Four cases were cited along with reference to Indian trading stores in Ladysmith. "I'd love to see Brander's face when he hears of this!" exclaimed Sarika.

The next morning Eric rode to Umzinto to see Brander who smugly informed him that Magistrate Lucas would be issuing his decision shortly. Without mentioning Goodricke's letter to Lucas, Eric set off to the Magistrate's office. It was the first time he had met Lucas and was impressed by his military bearing and directness. Broaching the issue concerning Sarika's desire to purchase land, Lucas indicated that Brander had apprised him of the meeting held by the Alexandra County Association.

"My view on the matter is that there needs to be acceptance of the reality laid down by the Secretary of State for Colonies regarding the rights of settlers irrespective of their ethnicity. I am not prepared to be swayed by public meetings at which emotions transcend reason and reality. I will be declaring that this Indian lady, Sarika, like any settler, is free to purchase land. I believe it is important to avoid a situation where every time an Indian seeks to purchase land or apply for a trading licence, the likes of the ACA attempts to stir up emotions. Once the legal details of her property have been finalised, I foresee no difficulty in granting her a trading licence," said Magistrate Lucas.

Thanking him for his time and his frank views on land applications, Eric was eager to return to Woodhouse Lea with his news. Predictably, Sarika and Frances were thrilled at how things had turned out. "Perhaps I should have gone directly to Magistrate Lucas in the first place. It would have saved having to travel to Durban and engage Martin's resources," said Eric. "When Lucas was telling me how he resented what Brander had done, I felt both embarrassed and relieved that Goodricke's letter in my pocket was quite unnecessary. Anyway, Sarika, now that we know Magistrate Lucas's view, I think you should deal directly with him in making your land purchase application. I would think he would then instruct Brander as Land Commissioner to draw up the plot details which would then be conveyed to the Surveyor General's Office for registration. I am going to enjoy seeing Mr Brander eat humble pie!" exclaimed Eric.

****

CHAPTER 3

Sarika followed Eric's advice and had a cordial meeting with Magistrate Lucas the outcome of which was that Brander was instructed to meet with Sarika on the site she wished to purchase. Eric accompanied her on the appointed day eager to observe Brander's interaction with Sarika. His courteous conduct suggested that Magistrate Lucas had given him a bit of a lecture on how he was to carry out his duties.

She selected a two-acre plot near the intersection of the Umzinto thoroughfare with the wagon route to Park Rynie. The land sloped gradually upward from the road which would facilitate a commanding view from where she intended her house to be constructed. Eric advised that before committing herself to the site, its proximity to a source of borehole water should be established, a task Brander undertook to investigate. A few days later, after Brander reported the presence of underground water at the top end of the property, Sarika signed the purchase papers for her property for which she paid £8.

Her next challenge was to find a builder to construct her house and shop.

****

At the Cutty Sark, Brander found himself subjected to criticism. "At that public meeting, Alex, you said another coolie store could not be condoned. Now you tell us this Sarika woman has bought land in Umzinto. What's going on, Alex? Did she bribe you?" charged Charles Knox indignantly. Before Brander could respond, Charles Paglar wanted to know why the vote taken at the County Association meeting had been disregarded.

"Gentlemen, things are no longer as they were. Magistrate Lucas told me that it is now a principle within the Empire that all settlers have the same rights regardless of their race. I was instructed to co-operate in accepting Sarika's application and surveying the plot she has chosen. I am afraid the opinion of the County Association against having another coolie store has no legal standing," said Brander.

"Are telling us that we just have to accept more and more coolie commerce? Surely there must be ways to deter or frustrate that process?" asked one of the hotheads.

"Yes, there certainly are ways we can put a spoke in the wheel of that trend. In Sarika's case, who is going to build the premises she wants on her plot? Through subtle means, we can frustrate that process. If Umzinto was an established municipality, we could prescribe various building and health regulations, but, of course, Umzinto has yet to achieve that status. Nevertheless, in the long term, the only legitimate means we have to frustrate this process is to discourage our fellow colonists from trading with Indian businesses. To apply that realistically, our stores need to undercut the Indian stores in pricing which would require negotiating with the suppliers of goods and transport," Brander declared.

"I'm in the transport business, as you all know. But to reduce transport prices significantly means risking going out of business. Maintaining wagons and carriages along with cattle and horse feed costs a great deal. Some of you may have noticed that there are now several native-owned transport businesses. They are charging their own people at least a shilling less on journeys to and from Durban. They make up that cost simply by having more passengers. It is also quite likely that Indian shop-owners would provide some incentive to a transporter to lower his prices," Charles Sinclair advised.

****

Sarika's land purchase was also the topic of discussion at the Royal Hotel bar. "I am very pleased for Sarika. Magistrate Lucas upheld her rights and ignored Brander's efforts to intimidate him. I have no doubt that had James Moodie still been the Magistrate, Sarika's land purchase bid would have been bogged down in red tape and procrastination," said Eric Harrison.

"I agree. Magistrate Lucas demonstrated decisiveness which bodes well for the County's endeavours to get the government to address the roads and bridges issue," remarked Dr Lancelot Booth.

"Her next hurdle is going to be constructing her intended residence and store. Eric, do you have anyone in mind who can undertake that task?" asked John Harrington.

"No, but I recall my Father-in-law, Edward Hawksworth, hired some very capable builders and carpenters to renovate Woodhouse Lea before Frances and I moved in. However, that was nearly ten years ago when bankruptcy was threatening planters and compelling some of them to resort to other means in order to survive."

****

St Patrick's Anglican Church in Umzinto had long been an established meeting place of the local community. Averaging some 60 members of the congregation each Sunday, the turnout was as much to honour the Sabbath as it was an occasion for social interaction. As new settlers in the district, the Harrington family was welcomed by Reverend Joseph Barker. He had been the serving prelate since 1861 when services took place in a barn before the church building, described as "very ecclesiastical" by Mercury's editor, was completed in 1869.

Over the years, Reverend Barker had developed a sharp perception of issues that sowed potential discord amongst his flock. Although he did not frequent public places like the Cutty Sark, he was aware of the latest controversy that had surfaced there. At Michael Moodie's funeral, he had preached a sermon exhorting reconciliation to abate the ostracism generated against Michael's relationship with Sarika. Ecclesiastically correct, his words had failed to modify adherence to social conventions. Rejection of Sarika continued to manifest itself beyond the death of her common-law husband.

In his first sermon of 1877, the theme of Reverend Barker's sermon was tolerance. "The Head of our Church, Her Majesty Queen Victoria, has decreed that all her subjects enjoy the same rights. She has appealed in earnest for tolerance and acceptance of that principle. She understands that we dwell in societies that are evolving. She regards diversity as one of the great strengths of the Empire." To premise his case, Reverend Barker cited a passage from the Book of Acts in the Bible (10: 35): "God accepts men from every nation who fear him and do what is right."

Following the conclusion of the service when social interaction took place amongst different groups, Charles Paglar queried the thrust of Reverend Barker's words. "It seems obvious that Barker was referring to Magistrate Lucas's disregard of Land Commissioner Brander and the County Association's opinion on land purchases by Indians. The problem I have with his Biblical quote is that it presumes people from other nations are Christians. But where Sarika is concerned, that is not the case."

Gathering separately from the adults were members of the younger generation. Some attended Umzinto School; others received tuition from governesses. Apart from parading in their Sunday best, the unexpressed interest amongst the teenagers was in the opposite sex. At fifteen years of age Priscilla Harrington attracted attention from one of the few boys present. Her auburn locks, deep green eyes, creamy complexion, ready smile and graceful disposition appealed to Lawrence Paglar. But he was too shy to introduce himself.

****

William Joyner, owner of Ellangowan sugar estate until he sold it in 1871, was known in Alex County for his building proficiency. Assisted by his industrious sons, he had built a commodious house on Ellangowan as well as the structure that housed his steam-powered mill. In 1862 he collected £61 in subscriptions and built a classroom and an adjoining cottage for a teacher and his family in the Ifafa district. Since the death of his wife, Joyner was known to spend time prospecting for gold and doing odd jobs.

The topic of Sarika's building intentions came up in conversation at Beneva where Frances, Eric and their boys were spending a weekend with her father, Edward Hawksworth. "Joyner and his sons did a great job on Woodhouse Lea. From what I hear they would be available to undertake Sarika's construction because they are struggling to make a living," said Edward.

"Joyner makes his bricks and has all the necessary carpentry tools so he is independent. He won't brook any intimidation because of who he is working for. I remember back in 1862 when he objected to Magistrate Moodie's imposition of a £10 fine for obstructing the passage of some native cattle that were being taken to the pound because they may have trespassed on his property."

Back at Woodhouse Lea, Sarika said she was looking forward to discussing the plans, terms and conditions of her intended buildings with William Joyner.

****

Since 1863 the Park Rynie Fair, held over a weekend every year in July, had been the highlight of Alexandra County's social calendar. It attracted people from Durban, horse racing punters, the young and the old who relished an outing to the coast and an opportunity to experience the fun and excitement of traditional English entertainment. Its popularity had seen it progress into a commercial success with fully catered tents for hire relieving visitors of the need to bring their own or to settle for accommodation in wagons.

Peter Richardson, Simon Prescott's assistant on Dewsbury, was anxious to experience the spirit of the Fair. Since moving to Alex County his social life beyond Dewsbury had been limited to occasional visits to the Cutty Sark. Tall and handsome, at 23 years of age he hankered after some female company. Recognising that his lonely life needed spicing up, Simon and Cynthia insisted he takes Friday off so that he would have a full weekend at the Fair. In advance, they had reserved a catered tent for him on the site.

Upon arriving at the Fair and having located his tent, Richardson lost no time in heading for the bar. After his ride from Dewsbury on a warm morning, he wanted a cold beer while he relaxed and hoped some young female talent would drift into view.

Emma Johnson worked as a governess for the Crookes family at Ellingham estate, situated then in the Scottburgh area. She was born in Natal in 1854 following the arrival of her parents from London. Having been employed as a governess in Pietermaritzburg and in Howick, in 1876 she decided to move to the coast. The opportunity presented itself when she noticed an advertisement for a governess in the *Natal Witness* placed by the Crookes family of Ellingham estate. The isolated, frontier character of Alexandra County appealed to her as an adventurous, developing area which she would like to sample. Although her tasks at Ellingham were not onerous, she had come to feel constrained by the role governesses were expected to play. At the age of 23 she longed for a life beyond looking after and educating other people's children. Like Peter Richardson, she found herself socially insulated and isolated. So she was elated to be given the weekend off to attend the Park Rynie Fair. Improbably proportioned, voluptuous and outgoing in character, she hoped the weekend would stimulate and change the horizon of her life.

Since it was a warm July morning, ideal for the beach, Emma was wearing a low-cut, sleeveless, summer dress which displayed a beguiling swell of her femininity.

Looking for some refreshment before she made her way to the beach, she passed the bar on her way to the tea and coffee counter. For Peter Richardson, her sudden appearance put him on high alert as he watched her ordering tea and then sitting alone at a table sipping it. When confronted with a challenge, hesitation, he had learned, invariably spelled disappointment or failure. Intuitively he got up, beer in hand, and sauntered over to her table.

Her instant smile and response to his introduction triggered a wave of elation in him. The attraction was mutual and spontaneous. While she chattered away about herself, Peter found himself mesmerised by the way her pale brown eyes accentuated her facial expressions along with her full, sensual lips and dark hair that hung casually over her shoulders. At length, she paused and asked: "So, Mr Richardson, what can you tell me about yourself?"

Aroused from his reverie, Peter avoided answering her question. Instead he suggested a walk on the beach where the conversation could be continued. Arriving on the beach, Emma removed her slippers relishing the soft sand underfoot. Feeling more relaxed, Peter briefly related his background growing up in Victoria County before moving recently to Alex County and landing the position of assistant to Simon Prescott on Dewsbury.

After strolling some distance along the shore, Emma suggested they take a rest and sit down. Stretching out on the sand with her head resting on her hands, Peter found himself staring at a rare sight: the publicly exposed shoeless feet and ankles of a Victorian woman. Aware of Peter's interest, she playfully nudged his arm with her toes. Unable to resist the surge of desire he experienced, he leaned over and kissed her. Panty-melting chemistry was kindled.

That evening, having had supper, a mug or two of punch and explored the various attractions of the Fair, Peter invited her to his tent. Without hesitation she accepted saying she first needed to fetch her possessions from the tent she had hired. "She's moving in," said Peter to himself, scarcely able to comprehend his good fortune. What followed was a night of unleashed, uninhibited, erotic fulfillment. Two sexually frustrated people had found each other and mutually satisfied their cravings.

The rest of the weekend was a blur of inexhaustible togetherness. On the Sunday afternoon before the Fair closed Peter and Emma sat on the beach and pondered their future. Both felt the weekend portended a significant change in their lives. "As far as the immediate future is concerned, I am committed to Ellingham as governess until December. So that gives us time to establish our relationship." Dreamily, Peter agreed. "I just hope the Crookes family give you time off on the weekends so we can be together." Emma said she thought they could be accommodating but would enquire.

Leaving the Fair ground, Peter rode alongside her carriage to the gates of Ellingham, where they exchanged passionate farewells after promising to write to each other.

Cynthia was the first to greet him when he arrived back at Dewsbury. "Well, Peter, did you have fun? Did you meet somebody nice?" she asked teasingly. His blushing smile answered her question. "Then you can tell us all about it at supper time," she said giving him a saucy grin.

A while later after George and James had gone to bed, Peter joined Simon and Cynthia for supper. After listening nostalgically to his weekend experience, they both remarked how the Park Rynie Fair had influenced and affirmed their relationship. "It was also where my young sister, Anne, met the love of her life and married him," remarked Simon. "I recall Frances Hawksworth telling me that it was at the Fair she realised that Eric Harrison was the man she wanted to marry" said Cynthia reminiscently.

With those good omens on his mind, Peter Richardson went to sleep a happy man. But the next day he heard news from Park Rynie that was tragic.

****

The Harringtons and the Paglars had also spent the weekend at the Fair. John and Emily were aware that their daughter, Priscilla, was attracting male interest and so were quite happy when they saw her chatting to Lawrence Paglar. His family was regular in Sunday attendance at St Patrick's. Since 1870 Charles Paglar had been employed as the custodian of the Umzinto prison and storekeeper of the gunpowder magazine.

Lawrence, the Paglars' only child, was 15 years of age and seemed destined for a clerical job in the government service in a few years' time. At the Fair he had plucked up the courage to speak to Priscilla while she was at the book stall. Her response had been warm and friendly. On the first evening of the Fair, their families had sat together at supper time. Later, asked by her parents what she thought about Lawrence, she said she found him interesting because of their shared interest in reading.

As the weekend progressed their respective parents were content to leave the two teenagers to their own devices. Exploring the rock pools at the beach during low tide proved a mutual interest. Permission to swim and frolic in the surf was granted provided there were other adults bathing. But disregard of that provision was to have tragic consequences.

Late on the Sunday afternoon when the Fair was closing and many had departed for their homes and destinations, Priscilla and Lawrence decided to have one last swim in the sea while their parents packed their tents. Arriving at the beach, they found it deserted and the tide was in. Priscilla was hesitant to enter the surf as the waves on the shore seemed quite big and powerful. Lawrence, however, plunged in. Within seconds he found himself out of his depth and being drawn away from the beach into deeper water. Having little swimming experience or ability, his plight was immediately desperate. Priscilla's screams at him to return went unheard above the crash of the waves as he drifted further away. Her panic increased when she noted that he had ceased frantically waving his arms. Then she lost sight of him altogether.

Totally distraught she continued to scan the water in the hope he would reappear. Sobbing in desperation she ran back to the camp and told her parents what had happened. Immediately Charles Paglar and John Harrington dashed off to the beach only to find Lawrence's body floating partly submerged as it drifted slowly towards the shore some distance down from where Priscilla said he had entered the water.

After about half an hour his drowned body was washed ashore. Grimly the two parents retrieved it and carried it back to the camp. A weekend of fun and friendship had given way to a funeral and a burial.

A very sombre, tearful crowd gathered at St Patrick's two days later. Priscilla was inconsolable. She was wracked by guilt for having agreed to go to the beach for a last swim and her mind was fixated on those final images of Lawrence drowning. Charles and his wife were grief-stricken. As their only child, they had lavished him with love and care. The void that his warm-hearted and cheerful character would leave in their home was too great to contemplate. Leaving the cemetery and heading back to their carriage, Charles turned to his wife and said: "I can't live here anymore. We have to move away from Umzinto. To continue living here will be a daily reminder of our dear son."

Within three months the Paglars had moved to Pietermaritzburg. Charles had applied for the post of manager of Grey's Hospital and his wife for the post of matron. Reverend Joseph Barker and former Alexandra County Magistrate, James Moodie, provided glowing testimonials of Charles' character and proficiency.

****

CHAPTER 4

Following an exchange of correspondence between Sarika and William Joyner, a day was agreed upon when they would meet at Sarika's plot in Umzinto. Eric had agreed to be part of the meeting.

Joyner had brought measuring tape, stakes, and a sketchbook. Noting the incline of the top end of the plot, he pointed out that it would require recessing to create a platform on which Sarika's residence could be built. Having a basic idea of the size she wanted, he marked the area out with stakes repeating the process on the lower end of the plot where her shop was to be positioned.

The three of them then went to the Royal Hotel where over a light lunch Sarika provided specific details of the layout she desired for her residence: a main-en-suite, one other bedroom, an office, a bathroom, a pantry, and an open area comprising kitchen, sitting room and dining area. Having noted the square yard measurements she requested; the discussion then proceeded to the layout of the shop where Sarika's main concern was the provision of a storeroom. "The internals of the shop will be more about shelving and counters, I would think."

After noting details about the type of roofing, windows, doors, cupboards and ablutions, Joyner said he would produce a detailed sketch plan of the buildings and a costing of the project including materials and labour. Asked what he estimated the full amount would be, he thought a sum of between £90 and £110 would suffice but cautioned that a porcelain bath, a Mott cast iron, coal-fired stove along with other appurtenances would increase costs. To get started, he asked for a deposit of £20.

****

At the Cutty Sark, one of the hotheads remarked how he had observed Joyner measuring Sarika's plot and hammering stakes into the ground. "It looks like the building is going to start soon. Maybe it's time to frustrate their efforts." Another of the anti-Sarika groups asked what was envisaged in that regard. "Well, removing the measured stakes would be the first thing. Then once Joyner starts stockpiling bricks, some of them could disappear. What do you think, Field Cornet Brander?"

"All I will say is that I did not hear this conversation," Brander responded.

****

Priscilla's visits to Woodhouse Lea for her piano lessons served a dual purpose: taking her mind off her tragic experience while at the same time being therapeutic. Sarika was able to empathise with her having experienced the loss of Michael. Sitting quietly in the drawing room at Woodhouse Lea with her arm around Priscilla, Sarika was able to get her to unburden herself emotionally.

"Try to accept, Priscilla, that it was not your fault that Lawrence was irresponsible in plunging into the surf without having considered the conditions and his lack of swimming skills. The fact that you had decided not to take the risk should have cautioned him. While it is undeniable that you were both irresponsible for thinking of swimming when your parents had instructed you not to do so if the beach was deserted, apart from that, you cannot blame yourself for Lawrence's impulsiveness."

"I have experienced much anguish over the death of my common-law husband, Michael. I have asked myself over and over how things might have been different if he had arrived earlier or later at the sugar mill on that day instead of being there just when the boiler exploded. But there's no answer to that. Subsequently, I have had to endure the loss of my baby. Life, however, goes on remorselessly. You are still very young, and the scars of this tragic experience will fade in time. Lawrence would not want you to spend the rest of your days in mourning for his sake."

****

About ten days after the Park Rynie Fair a letter arrived in the Dewsbury post box addressed to Peter. Hoping it was from Emma, he was not surprised.

To My Dashing Lover

I am still in awe of our weekend and miss you terribly. I find I struggle to concentrate on the lessons I am supposed to be giving to the Crookes' children because you preoccupy my thoughts.

It appears the only time I can take leave from Ellingham is on a Saturday after my morning chores. On Sunday I am generally expected to accompany the children to church with their parents, which does not leave much of the rest of the day free.

Please, Peter, come around on Saturday morning. Take me to the beach. Take me in your arms. My loins long for you!

Your Emma

At supper that night, knowing that Peter had received a letter which, she presumed, was from Emma, Cynthia asked how the romance was going. Coyly, he related her desire for them to spend some time together but that it seemed only Saturdays were available. "Oh! That is a pity," exclaimed Cynthia, "because it doesn't give you much leeway to fetch her, bring her to your love nest in the cottage and return her to Ellingham by sunset." Smiling ruefully, Peter pointed out that Emma's contract as governess expired only in December.

"Is she not entitled to leave during the Michaelmas break?" asked Simon. "When my sister, Victoria, was a governess for the Greenacres' children in Durban, she was permitted a week's break over Michaelmas."

The next day Peter posted a letter to Emma in which he promised to fetch her from Ellingham on the forthcoming Saturday. He also asked her to enquire about having time off over Michaelmas. Reciprocating her libidinous desires, he said he was salivating at the thought of exploring her loins again.

****

In terms of Clause 18 of the Natal Charter, a member of the Legislative Council was obliged to resign his seat in the event of becoming an insolvent debtor. In April 1877 the South Coast's lone representative on the Council, James Aiken, resigned when his Maryville estate was declared insolvent. A by-election was scheduled in June but attracted only a single candidate, William Hawksworth, who was then duly declared the new MLC for Alexandra and Alfred counties.

In the months leading to the scheduled general election of 1877, politics dominated discussions in the Royal Hotel bar. Proprietor William Thornton remarked how ironic the mood in Alex County had become. "Before Aiken became our first public representative in 1873, there were petitions and protests about how this County was politically neglected. Yet when he resigned in April, the fact that no one challenged his potential successor, William Hawksworth, to an election contest shows how complacent and indifferent people have become."

"That seems to have been the case across the Colony with several candidates having been unopposed," noted Dr Lancelot Booth. "William Arbuthnot's challenge to Hawksworth in the general election at least gave us a sniff of a contest with the end result proving a cliffhanger."

"Indeed! Hawksworth's victory by a single vote was probably the ballot he cast for himself!" chortled James Ross.

"The *Natal Witness* claims our election here was a 'spirited contest.' I think that's a gross exaggeration considering only 69 electors on the voters' roll of 179 bothered to vote. That's barely 40%. No wonder the South Coast is fobbed off in the Council and our calls for roads and bridges are ignored," fumed a disgusted John Redman.

"Although he is no longer our representative, James Aiken's call for a port to be developed on the Mzimkulu is the sensible solution to much of our transport isolation. Hawksworth needs to harp relentlessly on that so that Port Shepstone can come to reflect the reality of its name," opined Eric Harrison.

****

Within a week, Joyner returned with the sketches he had promised. "You will note there are no windows on the south-facing side of the buildings because that is mostly where our rain comes from. I would recommend solid doors for the front and back entrances of the buildings rather than stable doors which are not as secure. An item I omitted to mention earlier is the provision of water tanks to harvest the run-off of rainwater from the roof. You will need one at the shop as well."

Delighted with the plans, Sarika thanked him and urged him to start digging the foundations. "My sons and I certainly will, Sarika, but first we have to excavate a large section at the top of the plot to create a platform on which your house will stand. By the way, have you thought of a name for your house? I always feel that naming something gives it character."

"Yes, I have, Mr Joyner. My house will be called 'Michaelhouse' after Michael Moodie. His death resulted in an insurance award by Reunion Estate to me as his common-law wife. That money is financing what you are going to build."

****

At 10 am on Saturday Peter Richardson was at the gates of Ellingham. A short while later Emma was in the carriage snuggling up to him as he held the reins. “I hope we are going to the beach as I have brought towels.” Nodding his head he kissed her. Heading for Park Rynie beach, conversation was substituted by close physical contact. They parked the carriage in the shade outside the tavern near the beach where the horse was fed and watered. Then, wasting no time, Peter and Emma strolled along the beach until they located a shady, private, sheltered spot above the sand dune. Spreading their towels out, they lay down next to each other.

Within minutes both were almost naked as they gave way to the desires they had expressed in their letters. Emma was insatiable and exhausted Peter. An hour after their physical workout, Peter suggested having lunch at the tavern. “Hunger and thirst are my needs,” quipped Peter as he led Emma towards the tavern. “Didn’t I feed you enough just now, darling? Emma inquired provocatively.

Hungrily they devoured the Shepherd’s pie they had ordered and followed that up with fruit salad and cream. “As the afternoon is still young, may I suggest we hasten to my love nest at Dewsbury,” said Peter. Within an hour they arrived. Emma was introduced to Simon, Cynthia and the two boys. After an early afternoon tea, the Prescotts discretely retired to their bedroom leaving the lovers to retreat to the privacy of Peter’s cottage. Locked in each other’s arms they savoured what separation and distance had denied.

“So, Emma, what do you have in mind once your governess contract ends at Ellingham?” “I don’t know, darling. There’s not much a single woman can do to earn money. It’s a man’s world out there.” “Have you thought about teaching? Umzinto School is quite well established. Cynthia taught there before George and James were born.”

"It's a possibility, I suppose. But it's a very constrained form of employment: rules, regulations and poor remuneration. I'm outward going and don't enjoy being confined as I am now as a governess. Being a teacher would be no different. Anyway, let's not get anxious about what I will do after December. I'm sure something exciting will turn up. Just as exciting as Peter Richardson," she said as she mounted him and began to unbutton his shirt.

****

Spade work was all William Joyner and his sons did during the first two days on Sarika's site as they dug into the upward section of the plot to develop a recessed platform or terrace. Once the excavated soil had been cleared, Joyner hammered stakes into the ground marking the actual positioning of the house. But when they arrived on the third day to begin digging the foundations, they found the stakes had been removed and the spots marking their positions had been filled in.

Joyner was furious. "This is sheer vindictiveness on the part of an element in this community that opposes Sarika being able to own a piece of land and build on it. I hope this is not the beginning of ongoing harassment," he said as he began to measure out the dimensions again.

While he was thus engaged, his sons were wheeling uploads of bricks. Fortunately, in excavating the terrace, they had inadvertently come across a small natural spring that would relieve them of having to bring their water for mixing the lime and sand for the brickwork. After a delayed start, the Joyners made good progress in digging the foundations to a depth of about thirty inches and to the width of three bricks. Before leaving the site at the end of the day, a count was made of the stockpile of bricks.

Arriving the next morning, it was immediately apparent that several bricks had been removed – 30 in all as a count revealed. "This is not only harassment. It is theft. It also means that replacement of materials is going to play havoc with our budget if this pilfering continues. I am going to report this to Field Cornet Brander," declared William Joyner.

Leaving his sons to begin laying the bricks, Joyner went off to find Brander. Accosting him at the post office, he related the two incidents that had occurred. Responding, Brander weakly suggested that materials left in the open would tempt thieves. "I don't agree with that excuse because it does not explain the removal of the stakes and the measurements I had marked out. Whoever is responsible for these actions is not a thief. This is beginning to look like a deliberate attempt to sabotage work on the site because of who owns it," fumed Joyner as he turned and walked away.

That night at the Cutty Sark the anti-Sarika hotheads boasted of their depredations. Responding, Brander informed them of his meeting with Joyner and asked that they cease their actions as they placed him in a difficult situation.

For the next few days work proceeded on the site without any further incidents. Having completed the foundations, bricklaying of the walls commenced. By the end of the first week, the height of the brickwork required Joyner to mark out where the windows and front and rear entrances would be. But it would be a task he would have to repeat as when he returned on the Monday morning, two sections of the brickwork had been sabotaged. Broken bricks lay scattered on the ground.

Once more, Joyner reported what had occurred to Brander. "What are you going to do about this, Field Cornet?" he demanded.

"It is not within my brief to protect private property. That is your responsibility," replied Brander weakly.

"Very well, then. Together with my sons, I am going to apprehend these louts who are trespassing on private property. And when I do, I expect you to charge them with malicious damage. Furthermore, I will expect Magistrate Lucas to punish them severely."

That night at the Cutty Sark Brander informed the regulars of Joyner's visit and intended course of action. For the week that followed no further incidents occurred and substantial building progress was made on Sarika's site. As a precaution, Joyner's sons took turns to sleep on-site in the hope of encountering trespassers. That occasion arose the following week.

Two of the Joyner sons had arranged their sleeping bags within a section of the developing building which sheltered them from the wind. Around midnight they heard voices. "These Joyners don't seem to get the message," said the one intruder to the other. "We'll have to keep smashing it up until the cost of replacing materials forces them to pack up and leave."

"Is that so?" shouted Murdo, the eldest of the Joyner sons, armed with a crowbar, as he confronted the intruders. Taking advantage of their shock and surprise, Murdo swung his crowbar at the lead intruder's ribcage while his brother, Donald, hit the other intruder on the back of the head with a mallet then tackled him to the ground. With both intruders lying on the ground writhing in pain, having fetched lengths of rope, the Joyner brothers then securely trussed up the intruders. "This is how we treat your type. When my father arrives in the morning, he will give you a thrashing before we drag you off to Field Cornet Brander and see you locked in gaol," raged Murdo.

Following his arrival in the morning, William Joyner interrogated the intruders in an attempt to find out who else was involved in their vendetta against Sarika's building. Then he administered several lashes to each of them using his horse whip. "Now we will take you to Mr Brander and make sure he gaols you until your case is heard by the magistrate."

Brander found himself in an awkward situation. He knew the two intruders from the Cutty Sark. To project his authority while simultaneously deflecting attention from his legally compromised predicament, he attempted to reproach Joyner for having thrashed the two intruders. "You had no right to take the law into your own hands," he declared.

"What I do on private property is my business, Mr Field Cornet, especially when people trespass with the intention of sabotage. You told me it was my responsibility to protect that property, so now don't try and tell me how I must go about that," shouted William Joyner.

That night at the Cutty Sark, Brander tried to defend himself by reminding the anti-Sarika hotheads that he had told them to cease their vendetta. "That may be so Alex, but the impression we got was that it was just a temporary measure. Now, two of our gang are in gaol."

"I did warn you. Joyner was insistent that your two friends be gaoled until their trial. When there is a risk of a felon absconding, gaoling is standard practice."

****

Magistrate Lucas exhibited his military background and discipline in dealing with the culprits charged with malicious damage to Sarika's property. Having established that they would plead guilty, he dispensed with having to call a jury. The only issue would be the punishment to which he would sentence them.

Present at the court proceedings were the Joyners and Sarika as joint plaintiffs. In support were Eric Harrison and John Harrington. The Cutty Sark hotheads were conspicuous by their absence. Having acknowledged their guilt in the light of the Joyners' statements relating to the incidents of damage, Magistrate Lucas said that before he sentenced the culprits, he needed to make some comments.

"The maintenance of law and order is the first duty of a magistrate. It requires timely and judicious application of the law. Wrongdoing cannot be allowed to flourish and must be punished when those responsible are apprehended."

"The crimes to which you have pleaded guilty are unacceptable in any decent society. But beyond them, your expressed aim of continuing to inflict damage on the private property of Miss Sarika Singh, as Murdo Joyner has recounted to the court, is what I find extremely disturbing. That is because it reflects an attitude of intolerance towards a fellow settler based purely on the colour of her skin. As an officer of the law, I am pledged to uphold Her Majesty the Queen's noble principle of tolerance and recognition of diversity. Consequently, I find your attitude in that regard more repugnant than the crimes you have perpetrated."

"Accordingly, therefore, I sentence you each to 12 lashes which will be administered by Field Cornet Brander. In addition, you will return the 30 bricks you pilfered from the building site. In conclusion, I hereby issue the following warning: should there be any further damage caused to private property, the culprits will receive one year's hard labour in addition to 12 lashes. This case is closed."

But in one respect the case was not closed. Magistrates had to await the Governor's assent for whipping or flogging. If permission was declined, a jail sentence would apply.

****

Whereas comment on the sentence passed was extremely critical at the Cutty Sark, at the Royal Hotel bar opinion was on the side of magistrate Lucas.

Field Cornet Brander found himself in an extremely awkward position. He had failed to nip the actions of the hotheads in the bud by his initial comment when he had pretended to be unaware of what they intended. All along he was aware of the identity of the culprits. He could have arrested them long before the Joyners thrashed them and trussed them up. Now he found himself possibly having to administer their sentences of 12 lashes each. Given his predicament, he stayed away from the Cutty Sark.

"Interesting that Brander is not here tonight," remarked one of the hotheads "I hear he has appealed to the magistrate to change the sentence to a fine. That's what generally happens with sentences involving settlers. Lashes are administered to the natives and Indians."

At the Royal Hotel bar, the consensus was that Brander had been placed in a difficult position. Never before had he been required to administer lashes to fellow colonists. Dr Lancelot Booth offered some perspective when he elaborated on Lucas's military background. "Flogging, as it is called in the military, is a common punishment for refractory soldiers. When I was in Pietermaritzburg, there were times when I was called to Fort Napier which was where Captain Lucas was stationed prior to his appointment as magistrate in Klip River County. At Fort Napier I witnessed soldiers being flogged. Some of my cases involved treating infection as a result of flogging. So, for Lucas to sentence those two miscreants to 12 lashes each would not be exceptional. For medical reasons, however, I would have to be present when the lashes are administered, that is, if the Governor grants permission."

"I was particularly impressed by his stand on the principle of tolerance. Our previous magistrate, James Moodie, hedged on that principle. We saw it directly with Sarika. He failed to treat her civilly at his own son's funeral and never responded when she informed him of the death of his six-month old grandchild," said Eric.

****

CHAPTER 5

With the threat of theft and property damage having abated, Joyner and his sons made rapid progress on Sarika's residence. By the end of September, the roof had been erected and construction was focused on the internal aspects of the building. In addition to the rainwater tank, water from the natural spring was gravity-fed into a second tank. While some of Joyner's crew were busy with the carpentry aspects of the house, the others began digging the foundations of the store.

Situated on flat ground, its construction was a lot easier, as apart from the storeroom and small office which Sarika required, the internals involved only shelving and counters. By late November 1877, the roof of the shop had been erected, gutters attached, and a downpipe in place above the rainwater tank.

William Joyner's estimates proved accurate. Expenditure had come to £95 with an additional £20 for the Mott stove and porcelain bath. But that excluded furnishing the house and items such as curtains and linen. Thanks to Frances, who helped out with some of those items that were not required on Woodhouse Lea, Sarika was able to fund the balance of her needs inexpensively. Nonetheless, she vowed that 'Michaelhouse' was a work in progress. In time, with profits she hoped to make from the store, she intended to make it more decorative.

Shortly before Christmas, work on the store was completed. Double doors and glass windows graced the roadside front of the shop above which hung a simple sign – 'Sarika's.' Her next challenge was to source stock for her shop. Her aim was to carry a variety of merchandise that would set her store apart from the existing Indian-owned shops while at the same time rivalling

Umzinto's two main European-owned stores - Archibald's and Charles Knox's.

At the Royal Hotel bar, talk of the debut of Sarika's store was batted about. In response to Eric's question about where Sarika could source merchandise, proprietor, William Thornton, proved helpful. "A hotel needs everything a home and a store needs. So I will make a list of the merchants I deal with in Durban who will be able to supply Sarika with all she needs to start with. Obviously, in time, she may source from other suppliers. The other important aspect is transport. Some of those wagon operators are unscrupulous and unreliable. I use Charles Sinclair a lot although I know he is one of the Cutty Sark regulars. What I could offer, though, would be to include Sarika's orders with mine so Sinclair would not be aware."

****

In the knowledge that Victoria and Gordon Snell would be overseas with their daughter Lily during the Christmas period, Simon's other sister, Anne Pryce, invited the Dewsbury Prescotts to spend the last week of 1877 with the Pryces, Martin and baby Eleanor, at their Pietermaritzburg home in Taunton Manor. It was only the second time since her birth in June 1876 that the Dewsbury Prescotts had seen their niece who was named after her late grandmother, Eleanor Prescott.

It was also the first time the Dewsbury Prescotts had visited Anne and Martin's home in Taunton Manor and immediately recognised its likeness to Victoria and Gordon's Berea home. For George who was seven years old, the wooded ten-acre plot was fun to explore while the two toddlers, James Prescott aged 19 months and his cousin Eleanor aged 18 months, found compatible amusement in the playroom.

For the two couples Cynthia and Simon, Anne and Martin, it was an opportunity to catch up with each other's lives. Beaming with delight, Anne announced that she was pregnant again and was looking forward to another June baby. Cynthia cheerfully mentioned that their cottage had become a love nest since their assistant, Peter Richardson, had met Emma Johnson. "They are housesitting Dewsbury for us while we are here, so we know the property is in good hands." Martin enquired after Eric and Frances at Woodhouse Lea but carefully avoided mentioning anything about Sarika because he knew that Simon and Cynthia were prejudiced towards her.

Since the commencement of construction of the railway line from Durban to Pietermaritzburg, almost two years earlier, Martin said referrals by the Attorney General's office of cases of land transfer, arbitration, and expropriation to Goodricke's Pietermaritzburg branch had kept him busy. "The engineering involved in routing the line is challenging because of the topographical gradient in parts. Inevitably, legal challenges arise from landowners seeking compensation. I am told that construction is costing £9,000 per mile and will take at least another two years before the iron road reaches Pietermaritzburg. But look on the bright side: the end result will enable you to travel to us by train in comfort and in a much shorter time than a carriage takes. George and James will love it."

****

Much of the first month of 1878 saw Sarika busy ordering merchandise, pricing it, and packing it on shelves. William Thornton proved most helpful in providing reliable suppliers and in using Charles Sinclair's transport to deliver orders. It was Sarika's intention before officially opening the store to have as full a range of goods on sale as possible to ensure that her first customers became regulars. It also occurred to her that she would need an assistant and mentioned that to Frances and Eric. "The Indian traders are not keen to provide any help because they see me as competition. Besides, I want to project an image of tolerance and colonial togetherness. So, I need to have a white male or female assisting me in the store," she said equitably.

“I suppose Emily Harrington could be approached if only on a short-term or temporary basis,” Frances suggested. “Estate owner’s wives are quite committed to their own households. But there’s no harm in enquiring.”

On a visit to the Harringtons’ Preston estate to see whether Emily might be available to provide assistance, Sarika found the response was a qualified one. “I can be on hand only for the first week of the store’s opening. Maybe among your first customers, you’ll find someone willing to take on the position full time. I say full time with caution because working on Sundays when, I presume you will be trading, will not appeal to church-going colonists.”

On Wednesday, January 23, Sarika’s officially opened. Handbills advertising the occasion had been placed on the post office notice board as well as on the notice boards of the Congregational and Anglican churches. However, the initial response was disappointing. Reviewing the first week of trade with Sarika, Eric wondered whether resistance amongst white colonists was a result of residual ethnic prejudice towards Sarika. “In spite of those circumstances, I think the solution is to appeal to the pocket. Marketing is you forte. Slash prices on key items that households need, even if you sell them almost at cost. The important thing is to get people into the shop,” advised Eric.

His suggestion proved successful. Whatever misgivings existed in the wider community dissipated as a steady stream of customers came into the shop to benefit from the bargains on offer. Among them was Peter Richardson. Dispatched by Simon to check on mail at the post office, to obtain a selection of seeds for Dewsbury’s vegetable plot and a bottle of household disinfectant, Peter decided to see if he could source those items at Sarika’s. In making his purchases he fell into conversation with Emily Harrington. Although they had not previously met, Emily explained that she was helping only temporarily because she could not afford to neglect her chores on Preston estate as a wife and a mother.

Emily's conversation with Peter germinated an idea in his head. Would being a shop assistant at Sarika's appeal to Emma? Her contract as governess at Ellingham had expired a month earlier and since then she had not been able to find employment that suited her. Thrilled at the prospect, he was anxious to get back to Dewsbury to discuss it with Emma who had moved into the cottage with him since leaving Ellingham.

Emma was busy helping Cynthia in main house where she had also been providing a bit of necessary schooling for George. "I have some interesting news for you, darling," said Peter to Emma. "How would you like to be an assistant in the new store in Umzinto called Sarika's?" Explaining how he found out about the job, he said he thought it would appeal to Emma's desire to be exposed to and involved in wider social interaction which she had missed while being a governess.

Cynthia's ears pricked up at the mention of Sarika. "I know it's been nearly three years since my brother's death and even longer since his relationship with Sarika, but I can't see myself buying anything from her store." Not wishing to contest Cynthia's views since he was an employee at Dewsbury, Peter diplomatically acknowledged her statement and dropped the subject.

That evening in the privacy of the cottage, Emma agreed to be taken to Sarika's for an interview the next day. The two women took an immediate liking to each other. While Emily dealt with customers, Sarika and Emma exchanged life stories in the store's small office. Their interests were mutual: Sarika wanted a convivial white colonist who was comfortable in projecting the image of racial diversity and female enterprise. A bonus was that Emma was very attractive. For Emma, the prospect of being Sarika's shop assistant addressed her desire to interact with a variety of people in a vibrant environment. On that basis Sarika requested Emma to commence her role as shop assistant on February 1.

****

At the Royal Hotel bar in the late summer of 1878, talk centred around colonial security. Dr Lancelot Booth remarked that a circular he had received had drawn attention to health issues regarding laagers. "The government is going to construct defence laagers in Richmond, Umzinto, Verulam, and near Dundee this year. It seems things are not going well between the British authorities and the Zulu kingdom. As you may have read in the press, the confederation policy of the Disraeli government involves the British annexation of the Zulu kingdom and the disbanding of the Zulu army. Obviously, the Zulu king is opposed to those requirements. So things are looking a bit ominous."

"Are you suggesting that there could be a war involving the colony with the Zulu?" asked John Redman.

"Yes. That's the reason for these defence laagers," said Dr Booth. "They are fortified structures in which settler women, children and the elderly can shelter in the event of an attack. From a medical point of view, as the district surgeon, I would need to deal with injuries and the health hazards that would arise if many people were confined in a laager for any length of time."

"Although I respect the authorities for recognising the possible danger posed to the settler population, I really can't see that in Alexandra County we could be in danger from a Zulu attack. We are surely more than 120 miles from the Zulu kingdom," averred proprietor William Thornton.

"That's true, William, but I think there are other concerns about settler vulnerability. First of all, if a war broke out, a number of our local men would be required to leave the County and join the fighting front. That would leave the Alexandra Mounted Rifles depleted. Another threat to consider is the possibility of a local uprising of the natives or an attack by the Pondos on the southern boundary. Remember, gunrunning from Pondoland has been a troubling issue for several years. It is also possible there are elements who might view our vulnerable situation as an opportunity to plunder," observed Eric Harrison.

"Nonetheless, I find it very unlikely that our local natives would rise up. Unlike other counties, the native population here is placid and passive. We have scarcely any livestock theft here, unlike Umvoti County where it is rife," said William.

"Militarily, things must be brewing as I notice our magistrate, Captain Lucas, is out of the county and that we have an acting magistrate in the form of Thomas Reynolds, brother of the late Lewis Reynolds," noted James Ross.

****

After her first week as an assistant in Sarika's store, Emma felt quite exhausted. Lazing on the sofa in the cottage with her feet resting on Peter's lap, having downed a glass of rum-infused punch, she recounted her experience. "I am still getting accustomed to the location of things in the store – from thimbles to pots of glue. Sarika has a very comprehensive stock. Then, of course, some items must be weighed as they are sold in pounds and ounces. Cotton materials, which are sold by the yard, must be measured and cut. Serving one customer can take quite a while and might involve having to climb the ladder to fetch an item off the top shelf."

"But apart from those factors, I am enjoying the work. It is interesting to see which items are in demand and to follow up with new orders for them. Customers are mostly the younger generation which pleases Sarika. She says it reminds her of the tolerance shown towards her relationship with Michael when they lived in Isipingo."

"Did Sarika remark on how the store was coping financially?"

"Yes. Its turnover has improved but it is too early to project how it will fare in the months to come. For that reason, she is going to pay me £3 a month until the shop's profits increase."

****

The opening of Sarika's drew critical remarks at the Cutty Sark. "Who does this coolie think she is? I mean, first of all, she cohabited with that white lad who was killed in Isipingo. Now she is employing a white girl as her assistant," fumed one of the hotheads. "What has become of the mentality of white colonists in that they not only buy from coolie shops but are now prepared to work for a coolie?"

Noting their animosity, Field Cornet Brander pointed out the predicament white colonists faced in Natal. "It is imperial policy that all settlers enjoy equal rights. So, we have to accept that types like Sarika are free to have their own businesses. The only course of action we could take would be to require conformity to recognised standards. Unfortunately, the difficulty we have in Umzinto is that we have yet to establish a local government structure or municipality. If we had such a structure, we could enforce bylaws regarding building plans, health and hygiene standards, trading hours, noise levels, and such like issues. We could also demarcate commercial and residential zones so that Indians could not simply have shops wherever it suited them."

"I think we also have to accept that a good number of our fellow colonists live very frugal lives. That's the reason you won't find them here at the Cutty Sark. Economic reality dictates that they buy what they need from a coolie store because it is cheaper," remarked David Aiken.

"So what's the solution?" asked another of the hotheads.

"There isn't one. Even if the standard of living improved for white colonists, the increasing Indian population means that, over time, more Indian businesses will be established. This Sarika is a shrewd woman. Not only is the physical location of her shop well placed but her added advantage is that she owns her two-acre plot. Most of the other Indian stores are on rented property," said Brander.

"But who is renting land to coolies? Can't they see that they are the cause of this unsightly bazaar that has developed in our village?" raged a hothead.

"For a landowner, rental money is welcomed regardless of who pays it. That is an economic reality. Unless there were laws that prohibited an Indian from renting land in a specific area or zone, a landowner is free to rent to whomever he likes," declared Brander.

****

Since Sarika had moved into her house – Michaelhouse, as she had named it – Eric had not seen or spoken to her. Besides wanting to see her store and meet her assistant, Emma, he wanted to discuss the issue of security. Relating the essence of the recent discussion of which he had been part at the Royal Hotel bar, he pointed out that in the event of a security scare, all women, children and elderly folk would be confined in the laager the government was going to build.

"My concern is that your property would be vulnerable to vandalism, theft and even to being set on fire. Although I feel this is highly unlikely because I cannot imagine a Zulu impi marching 120 miles to little Umzinto. I also feel that a local uprising is highly unlikely given the sound relations we have with the neighbouring native location. Nonetheless, Sarika, in the light of possible risks, do you have insurance on your property?"

Somewhat embarrassed, she admitted that having been engrossed in stocking the shop she had neglected to address the issue of insurance. "Thank you, Eric, for your concern and timely reminder. My original £200 insurance award is almost exhausted. Stocking the store has required a huge financial outlay. If the store had to be looted or set on fire, I would be penniless without insurance."

Promptly after Eric's departure, she posted a letter to Natal Bank in Durban enquiring about the monthly cost of an insurance policy valued at £400 through the Glasgow Insurance Company.

****

In the cottage at Dewsbury that night, Emma told Peter of her meeting with Eric Harrison. "Sarika owes a great deal to Eric and his wife Frances for her social rehabilitation after the tragic death of Michael. What struck me in seeing her interact with Eric is the sad fact that apart from the Harrisons and Harringtons, you and me, Sarika has no social circle. Yet here we are, tenants on the Prescott estate of Dewsbury, and the subject of Sarika is taboo. I'm not comfortable with that. Cynthia and Simon just don't want to engage on the subject. I can understand the social convention that Michael breached at the time. But, good heavens, he has been dead for nearly three years. Anyway, Sarika is a settler just as we are. More than that, by her initiative and enterprise, she puts us to shame because both of us are merely assistants: I am dependent on her; you are dependent on Simon."

"How very philosophical and thoughtful, Emma! You surprise me! So what do you have in mind?" enquired Peter as he massaged her feet.

"Sarika told me about Simon's older sister, Victoria, who lives in Durban. She said that Victoria was very sympathetic towards her and Michael when they were being ostracised by the Umzinto settler community and had advised them to move away. Apparently, Victoria is a fearless proponent of social reform and is part of an outspoken group of women who lobby for voting rights and against the social constraints to which we women are subjected. Perhaps I should write to her and see what she might suggest in trying to transform Cynthia and Simon's attitude towards Sarika."

Emma was not a procrastinator. There and then she penned a letter to Victoria in which she asked how Cynthia and Simon could be approached on the subject of Sarika. Within a week Peter fetched Victoria's response from the Umzinto post office.

Dear Emma

I am delighted to make your acquaintance as one who espouses reformist thinking by your desire to enlighten Cynthia and Simon towards social tolerance.

I realise that as tenants, you and Peter do not wish to jeopardise the goodwill of your landlords! So, before making any suggestions, you need to be aware of Cynthia's situation at the time of her brother's relationship with Sarika.

As the daughter of the Resident Magistrate of Alexandra County her family was placed in socially very awkward circumstances. Her Father was severely embarrassed in the Cutty Sark when his son's sexual liaison with Sarika was crudely disclosed. At the school where Cynthia was teaching, she was subjected to awkward questions by some of her pupils. On one occasion, when her family was attending the Sunday service at St Patrick's, the sermon on miscegenation was pointedly directed at the Moodie family.

Simon, my brother, is a traditionalist. He stood stoutly with Cynthia throughout the unhappy Sarika saga. Like me, he is outspoken but not necessarily where social convention is concerned. He may be somewhat inflexible in that regard, but I have an idea. He and Cynthia are respectful towards Eric and Frances going back more than ten years. If Cynthia and Simon's feelings towards Sarika can be moderated, Eric and Frances would be the ones to achieve that.

I would suggest, therefore, that the Harrisons invite the Prescotts for a visit during which the Sarika subject could be delicately addressed.

I look forward to hearing from you on this matter.

I have the honour to be...

Victoria

"I'll show Victoria's letter to Sarika tomorrow and see what she says," said Emma. Although appreciative of Victoria's remarks and her suggestion, Sarika felt the approach to Eric and Frances should come from Emma and Peter. "Given your connection with me, Emma, and the fact that you and Peter are tenants on the Prescott's estate, you have a mutual interest in seeking to promote a civil accord between myself and the Prescotts," Sarika advised.

In that context, Emma wrote to the Harrisons relating what Victoria and Sarika had advised. She was pleased to receive a prompt response from Frances endorsing the idea and promising to expedite it.

****

CHAPTER 6

The South Coast is a beautiful wilderness wanting in all aspects of civilised settlement – Natal Almanac, 1863.

In April 1878 the overland telegraph from Grahamstown reached Pietermaritzburg linking the colony with Cape Town. As the *Natal Mercury* commented, "Natal is henceforth of South Africa, not in it." The news delighted Gordon Snell as he remarked to Victoria, "This speeds up the pace of commerce. Within a few hours, I can have the response of wine merchants in the Cape to orders from E Snell & Co in Durban instead of waiting up to ten days. This is real progress. I understand that sometime in 1879 we will be connected to London via Aden. What a revolutionary prospect!"

"It is progress indeed, darling. But it seems to me like putting the roof on a building before the doors and windows have been constructed. Having speedy communication by a wire outside of Natal is at odds with the basics of our internal communication – roads and bridges. The absence of that infrastructure continues to retard us and to isolate counties from each other."

At the Cutty Sark communication was also the topic of conversation.

"Have you heard about the newly arrived ship from England called the *Somtseu*?" asked David Aiken. "It's a 47-tonne steamer with a very shallow draft enabling it to enter our two big rivers – Mkomanzi and Mzimkulu. Its owner, TN Price of Durban, deserves our praise for recognising the potential of Alexandra County if it has a reliable coastal shipping service."

"Well, I hope you're right, David. The Alexandra Shipping Company promised us the same service but failed within two years. However, I feel that if the mouth of the Mzimkulu proves reliably navigable, Port Shepstone can live up to its name. Although it's about 25 miles from Umzinto, it's half the distance Umzinto is from Durban," said Charles Sinclair.

****

"We have a letter from the Harrisons which is unusual. I wonder what the occasion is," remarked Simon to Cynthia having just returned from the village. "Apart from inviting us to lunch on Sunday and catching up with each other's lives, Frances says Nicholas and George might enjoy each other's company being almost the same age," said Cynthia.

"Well, that's nice of them. I've never been to Woodhouse Lea. I'll leave a note accepting their invitation at the Royal Hotel bar which Eric and John Harrington frequent. Eric visits the post office only once a week, so sending a letter would not reach them in time."

Simon mentioned to Peter that the Prescotts would be visiting Woodhouse Lea on the coming Sunday and asked him and Emma to stay on Dewsbury for the day as a security measure. When Peter told Emma, she was delighted.

****

There had been little contact between the Harrisons and the Prescotts since Michael Moodie's funeral nearly three years earlier when circumstances regarding social convention had strained relations between the two couples. However, Nicholas Harrison's pleasure in having George's company immediately relaxed the situation upon their arrival. After having had tea, Eric showed Simon around Woodhouse Lea's estate while Frances showed off the improvements her father had made to the residence. The Harrisons aimed to re-acquaint the couples with each other on a one-on-one basis which they hoped would facilitate the actual objective of the meeting.

Before repairing to the dining room for lunch, Eric served drinks on the patio which was basking in warm autumn sunshine. Frances and Cynthia chatted animatedly about domestic issues while keeping an eye on two-year-old James Prescott as he played with some toys Frances had brought from the playroom. In response to Cynthia's enquiry as to the whereabouts of the older Harrison son, Edward, Frances said he was spending the weekend with his grandfather on Beneva. "He turns eleven in June and is a budding farmer. He's the apple of my Father's eye and loves being with his granddad especially as Beneva has one of the largest sugar mills in the colony." Since Eric was the leading producer of coffee in the county, Simon was interested to attain first hand insights on plantation maintenance and production which would enhance Dewsbury's coffee enterprise.

With little James taking his scheduled afternoon sleep after Cynthia had fed him while George and Nicholas had their lunch on the patio, the four adults had the dining room to themselves. Eric had agreed to let Frances initiate the conversation which would lead to the subject of Sarika.

"You are so fortunate to have an assistant who lives on Dewsbury. At least you can afford to take a break or go away secure in the knowledge that your property is not left unattended," observed Frances.

"Yes, it really is handy having Peter Richardson living in the cottage. He's good with George and James as well. We noted that recently when we left them in his care so Simon and I could have an evening out at the Royal Hotel," said Cynthia.

In his usual jocular vein, Simon pointed out that the presence of Peter's lady friend, Emma Johnson, who had moved in with him, probably accounted for the ease with which George and James had been managed in the absence of their parents. "Emma was a governess at Ellingham, so she is experienced in working with children."

"So, does she do a bit of governess work with George during weekends when she's not working at Sarika's shop?" asked Eric, adding quickly that he had met her at the shop and, to keep the conversation light-hearted, said he found Emma very attractive.

"Eric, you never told me that!" exclaimed Frances. "I am going to have to keep a check on my husband visiting Sarika's shop!" she jested, smiling at Cynthia and Simon.

"Have you been to the shop at all?" asked Eric. "It's as well-stocked as Archibald's and reasonably priced. What's novel about it is that the merchandise is spread around the shop on shelves making it accessible to customers instead of being stowed away behind the counter as is usually the case."

Frances and Eric knew this was the moment in the conversation that could be the turning point. Simon looked momentarily at Cynthia and then spoke.

"Emma sure is an attractive lady but beyond that, I don't see any reason to have to go Sarika's shop. Peter goes there only because Emma works there. I can get all we need for Dewsbury at Archibald's."

Cynthia then joined the discussion. "My brother's relationship with Sarika placed my father and the Moodie family in a very difficult social position. I feel Michael would still be alive if that whole business with Sarika had never happened. After all, Eric, he was your esteemed assistant here on Woodhouse Lea."

"Cynthia, we understand your position in this matter. As you and Simon are aware, Eric and I had a great deal to do with Michael and Sarika. We did so out of compassion when they were in socially difficult circumstances. As a result, we saw a side of your brother that you and the wider community did not see. He confided in Victoria and poured his heart out to her in a letter. She counselled him and advised him to move away from Alex County. As you are probably aware, having been in the Prescott family for over ten years, Victoria is a very perceptive and shrewd judge of character. Michael and Sarika were in love. Sadly, the way they were depicted in the community was purely in terms of immoral lust. But the adversity they experienced strengthened their love. Victoria recognised that even though she had never met Sarika."

To keep the momentum of the case for Sarika going, Eric continued. "By encouraging them to move away from Alex County, through Victoria's initiative, Gordon was prepared to offer Sarika a job at E Snell & Co. After Michael's death, Victoria asked Martin Pryce to lobby De Pass, Spence for compensation which is how Sarika obtained the money to buy her property and have her shop built."

By his silence and body language it was apparent that Simon was processing the fact that his sister had played a background role of goodwill in the whole saga. He and Victoria shared a Prescott characteristic of being unafraid to speak up on issues. His conscience told him that she had done the right thing. His memory reminded him that they had seldom disagreed with each other.

A momentarily awkward silence pervaded the room which Frances interrupted apologising for delving into an issue that occurred almost three years ago and quickly changed the subject enquiring how Cynthia's parents and her sister, Ruth, were enjoying life in Ladysmith.

"My Father says he preferred his Alex County caseload to what he has to deal with in Klip River. He says he is bored with stock theft cases! My Mother has joined the tennis club and is active in the Anglican Church. It pleases me to say that Ruth is engaged to a young farmer."

They exchanged further news about each other's families over coffee in the drawing room until Cynthia heard James's crying, indicating that his afternoon nap was over. While she fetched him from the bedroom, Simon and Eric went out into the yard to summon George and Nicholas. A short while later, after thanking the Harrisons for the lunch invitation and agreeing to have more frequent get-togethers, the Prescotts were on their way back to Dewsbury.

Simon was uncharacteristically quiet as their carriage plodded its way back to Umzinto. It occurred to him that his stand on the Sarika/Michael issue had been premised on his unquestioned loyalty towards Cynthia and the Moodie family. Victoria, as he reasoned, could afford a detached, impartial outlook because she was not directly involved. Having arrived at a new perspective on the whole subject, he saw merit in being socially civil to Sarika and visiting her shop. But first, he would have the delicate task of persuading Cynthia to have a change of heart.

****

There was great excitement at St Patrick's that Sunday with the announcement by Reverend Joseph Barker that a church camp would be held for the youth at the Congregationalist Amahlongwa mission station inland of Scottburgh. Emily and John Harrington were particularly pleased as their children had not had the opportunity for such an outing since their move from Victoria County four years earlier. With Priscilla's help, Emily compiled a list of the basic requirements for the camp before they set off to Sarika's shop to make their purchases.

For Stewart, Priscilla, and David, it was their first visit to Sarika's store. Not having seen them since taking up residence in her own home, Michaelhouse, Sarika was delighted by their presence. While she chatted with Emily, assisted by the Harrington youngsters, Emma sourced the various camping requirements from Emily's list. "Once Reverend Barker has told us what specific amenities will not be available at the mission, we may have to make some additional purchases," said Emily as they left the shop. Apart from extra blankets which were advised as the camp was taking place in the middle of winter, no further purchases were necessary.

In the days leading up to the three-day camp, speculation was rife as to new acquaintances they might make. Reverend Barker had mentioned that youth from the Congregationalist Church in Umzinto would be attending as well as from the new Anglican Church at Sezela.

They were not disappointed. In all twenty teenagers attended the camp – nine girls and eleven boys. Morning sessions saw them separated, boys from girls. An American female Congregationalist missionary led discussions with the girls' group while her counterpart did the same with the boys. Afternoon sessions were open to all and included games and team sports after which the campers were free to do as they pleased. That was the time to which Stewart and Priscilla looked forward. Both had seen members of the opposite sex they found attractive. Stewart had his eye on a girl from Sezela called Lucy. Priscilla fancied Luke, the son of the American Congregationalist missionary. Held in the commodious dining room, mealtimes afforded an opportunity to foster relationships by being seated in close proximity to whoever was deemed desirable.

At 16 years of age, Lucy was a little overweight but her bubbly character, infectious laughter, blonde hair, and sparkling brown eyes captured Stewart's attention. During the first afternoon's outdoor free time, Lucy and Priscilla attempted a game of tennis on the crudely marked outfield against Stewart and Luke. Lucy proved quite agile in returning shots and grinned sportingly at Stewart when she failed. He thought her facial expression seemed to say more than the moment suggested.

At length, tired of fetching the ball out of the grass, interest in the game waned. Anxious to initiate a conversation with Lucy, Stewart formally introduced himself. With the introductions over, Lucy invited Stewart to join her on a bench in the courtyard where they could relax and talk. It soon turned out they had much in common, apart from living on sugar estates.

“I’m an outdoor girl,” said Lucy. “I like horse riding and exploring the outdoors. The idea that I’m expected to spend my time sewing and cooking does not appeal to me. My younger sister likes that which suits me. Do you see yourself doing anything beyond Preston estate, Stewart?”

“No. I like it there and as my father’s assistant our aim is to increase cane production and have a distillery installed which will bring in more money.” After engaging in more banter about their lives, Lucy said she needed to return to the dormitory but looked forward to seeing Stewart at supper time. Back in the girls’ dormitory, gossip was already rife concerning Stewart and Lucy. “Do you fancy him, Lucy?” she was asked. Shyness, not being one of Lucy’s traits, she riposted, “So what if I do? Jealousy will get you nowhere!”

Unlike Stewart or Lucy, Priscilla was reserved. Although she fancied Luke, she hoped he might take more notice of her. That moment came at supper time when they were in the queue to be served their meal. Luke asked her if he could keep her company at the table. Later, sitting next to each other, feeling somewhat overwrought, Priscilla’s efforts in making conversation were disappointing. Nonetheless, sensing her nervousness, Luke was patient and understanding. Rising from the table when supper time was over, he patted her wrist and said he looked forward to seeing her the next day.

****

Upon their return to Dewsbury after their visit to Woodhouse Lea, Peter and Emma thought the Prescotts looked pensive, so they dispensed with small talk and returned to the cottage. “I wonder how their day with the Harrisons went?” Emma inquired. “Perhaps Eric will visit the store tomorrow and provide some news.”

In the main house, after having bathed the two boys, had a light supper, and put the children to bed, Simon took Cynthia in his arms and said: “We need to talk.” Holding her close while sitting on the sofa and stroking her hair, Simon could feel Cynthia was emotional. “Darling, I think there is something to be grasped from Victoria’s role that we heard of this afternoon as well as her perspective regarding your brother, Michael. At the time, our commitment to social convention denied us appreciation of the personal aspect involved. We could not afford to be indifferent because of the position in which your father was placed by his son. But, now three years after those troubled and tragic days, should we not allow bygones to be bygones? Michael loved Sarika. For his sake, I don’t think he would want us to continue to distance ourselves from her.”

When Cynthia looked up at her husband’s face her eyes were glistening with tears. “I miss my brother and in my heart I now feel a sense of guilt that we did not recognise his love for Sarika. I admire Victoria for seeing what we were blind to see. I regret that social convention divided us. Eric and Frances deserve great credit for their goodwill towards Michael and Sarika. You are so right, my darling Simon. Michael would not want this uncivil barrier to persist. It shames me that someone like Emma treats Sarika as the fellow colonist she is and is content to be employed by her, while we allow the past to dictate the present.”

“That is so brave of you. Since hearing what Eric and Frances told us, I have been worried about how you would feel. I know you are loyal to your father which is why your change of heart is so admirable. I have to admit that my thinking on this subject changed when they told us about Victoria’s role. I just felt we had to reconsider our attitude,” said Simon as he kissed Cynthia. “Tomorrow I am going to write to Victoria and thank her.”

A wave of emotional relief swept over them as they held each other closely in bed. Thinking of how death had deprived Michael and Sarika of their physical bond, Cynthia whispered: “Make love to me, Simon.”

****

By the time the church camp at the Amahlongwa mission ended, at least one new acquaintance had become a romantic one. Stewart and Lucy were seen kissing passionately on the last evening of the camp. At the supper table, beneath the oversized table cloth, he had caressed her thigh. Although they had promised to write to each other, the chances of spending time together were almost zero because of the distance between Stewart's residence on Preston estate in the Park Rynie district and the Lucy's on the Hart estate in Sezela. But there was one bright prospect: the forthcoming annual July fair at Park Rynie.

For Priscilla, the camp had meant an introduction to Luke as a friend. Like his missionary father, he was a Biblical student who aimed to propagate the faith. As a result, Priscilla agreed to attend the Congregationalist services in Umzinto instead of St Patrick's. Emily and John Harrington were pleased that their two older children had succeeded in starting new friendships. In the Umhlanga district of Victoria County where there were more than 20 sugar estates, they had had several friends. But since moving to Alex County which had far fewer estates and was thinly populated, social contact for youngsters had been minimal.

****

Having written the letter to Victoria that he promised, Simon decided that instead of going alone to the village to post it or sending Peter to do so, the Prescotts, as a family, would visit Sarika in her store and post the letter on the way.

It was an emotional occasion, as Emma observed. Sarika had just emerged from her office when the Prescotts arrived. Hand in hand, Simon and Cynthia walked up to her. "Sarika, we have come to apologise to you for how we have treated you. We should have done this long ago but we hope you can forgive us." Tears welled up in Sarika's eyes as she embraced first Simon and then Cynthia who had also become teary-eyed. Emotions set free expressed more than words as the Prescotts experienced the liberating effect of repentance. For her part, Sarika was gushing in recognition and thanks. “We have so much to talk about. I want to invite you to have dinner with me as soon as it is convenient.” Emma, who was standing nearby, assured Simon and Cynthia that Peter and herself were available to babysit George and James whenever the Prescotts required.

Before returning home Simon and Cynthia were shown around the store by Emma and made a few purchases which, as a token of her gratitude to them, Sarika insisted were free of charge. Arriving back at Dewsbury, Simon and Cynthia felt that a weight had been lifted from them. “I feel a new social chapter has opened for us in Umzinto,” he confessed.

****

For Stewart and Lucy, being together at the Park Rynie Fair that July was fun, but it also confirmed that their relationship had no long-term prospects. Having had the opportunity to be alone from the company of their respective families, they indulged in some passionate kissing and groping, but when their conversations became less frivolous, it was clear that their paths would deviate. Lucy made it clear to Stewart that she could not wait to leave her parents sugar estate and seek employment in Durban. “I see that as a start in life before going overseas,” she said. For Stewart whose ambition was to take over Preston estate from his father later, Lucy’s ambitions would not feature in his life. Nonetheless, they parted amicably, the Park Rynie Fair, once again, having been a determinant of relationships.

****

CHAPTER 7

Hope for a revival of coastal shipping glimmered late in June and July 1878 when the *Somtseu* anchored off Scottburgh beach, discharged cargo onto lighters and loaded sugar. But it made no subsequent visits, its owners preferring to service Port St Johns. At the same time, however, interest in developing the mouth of the Mzimkulu seemed to be increasing. Captain West of the *Somtseu* and the ship's owner, TN Price, had examined the river mouth during a spring low tide. They found a single slab of rock in the channel which, in their view, could be cheaply demolished by blasting. They also noted that the river was navigable upstream for possibly five miles.

News of this lifted hopes in the Royal Hotel bar. The Reynolds brothers, Frank and Charles, were particularly encouraged as their growing sugar enterprise comprising around 9,000 acres needed transport solutions. David Aiken informed the patrons that he had written to the colonial secretary, Charles Bullen Hugh Mitchell, urging that an official enquiry into the physical changes was needed to make the entrance navigable. "If shipping could be established on the Mzimkulu it would promote trade in lime, marble, sugar, coffee, fish, mealies, hides, and timber." It worried him that by procrastinating, Natal could lose trade to Port St Johns which the Cape government was looking at as a lucrative development prospect.

Unfortunately, in the weeks and months ahead, events in the colony concerning security superseded focus on river port shipping prospects. Determination on the part of the British High Commissioner in South Africa, Sir Bartle Frere, to impose the policy of confederation had disrupted the hitherto peaceful relations between Natal and the Zulu kingdom. The policy required the Zulu to be subservient to Britain by accepting annexation and disbanding their army. In Frere's view, Zulu king Cetshwayo was a bloodthirsty tyrant, and his army was a menace to the region. In that context, during the latter half of 1878 tensions rose as Frere found reasons to justify a looming military confrontation. The tension reached a high point when an ultimatum was issued to Cetshwayo on December 11, 1878, giving him until January 10, 1879, to comply with ten demands.

Besides the hurried construction of laagers, the government ordered an audit of the availability of weapons in stock for defence as well as enrolment of local defence detachments. That topic was earnestly discussed at both the Cutty Sark and the Royal Hotel bar. "Field Cornet, what do you make of the pathetic voluntary enrolment response the mayor of Durban managed to secure for his Borough Guard?" enquired one of the Cutty Sark hotheads.

"The fact that the mayor could summon only 106 men in a big place like Durban seems to suggest one of two things. Either the locals don't see a war breaking out with the Zulu or they are very confident that the Zulu army would be defeated long before it got near Durban," replied Brander.

At the Royal Hotel bar, the availability of arms drew concerned comment. "I wonder what our Captain Lucas thinks about the weapons audit of just 50 carbines with which, as Commandant, he is supposed to defend both Alex and Alfred counties," ventured William Thornton.

"Although most of us have our own rifles and arms, it's a bit presumptuous of the authorities to expect us to cater for what is supposed to be the government's duty to protect colonists, particularly as it seems they are the ones who look set to start a war," opined Robert Anderson.

"The seriousness of the government's need to raise a force of colonists is well illustrated by the response George Clarence of Delta Estate in Isipingo received from the colonial secretary. Clarence asked to be exempted from the Isipingo Mounted Corps because he is the manager of the estate which employs 150 indentured Indians. He was told that under the circumstances he could not be exempted," said Dr Lancelot Booth.

Thus, a feeling of anxiety and uncertainty pervaded the colony as the end of the year approached.

****

Some months earlier, the Prescotts had taken up Sarika's invitation to have dinner with her. It turned out to be a gastronomic and heart-warming occasion. Michaelhouse, Sarika's residence, was tastefully furnished reflecting her artistic character. Cynthia admired the draped curtains and carpets, and the warm colours of the cushions scattered about on the chairs and the sofa. "As I came to know your brother, I recognised his zest for life and his warm-heartedness. The décor you see is meant to reflect his character," said Sarika. Her reverence for Michael's memory caused Cynthia to experience another pang of regret at how she had treated him in the last months of his life.

Dinner was a Western and Indian culinary fusion: a rice and lentil-based salad served with small portions of butter chicken and avocado pear, followed by a vegetable biryani with side dishes of chutney, dhal and papadum. Dessert was a fruit salad rich in mango, banana, loquat, and gooseberries smothered with cream. Relishing the repast, Simon earned a provocative stare from Cynthia when he suggested she would have to upgrade the menu at Dewsbury.

Conversation during the meal concerned speculation about the security situation with Simon saying that as a member of Alexandra Mounted Rifles, he would be obliged to do duty wherever the group was required. Regarding personal matters, Sarika conceded that she still felt socially isolated. "I encounter a social barrier even where my fellow Indians are concerned. That is why I am so grateful to enjoy your company and that of the Harrisons, the Harringtons and of course Emma and Peter. Someone I would like to meet is

Victoria. Her counsel in matters concerning me proved so prudent and exceptional."

"I think that could be arranged. Gordon, her husband occasionally comes to Alex County to sample and purchase supplies of rum. He's due for a visit. Maybe Victoria can accompany him. It's about time she paid Umzinto a visit anyway because it's been years since she was last here. I think what will incentivise her to come is the outlook you share with her on social reform," opined Simon.

****

Simon's suggestion to Victoria that she accompany Gordon on his scheduled visit to Alex County's rum distilleries in order to see her nephews and to meet Sarika, received a positive response. During the five-day period that the Snells were in the County, they stayed at the Royal Hotel. Gordon had three distilleries to visit which took roughly a day each to reach, then to sample their produce before returning to write reports concerning recommendations.

Victoria divided her time between visits to Dewsbury and to Woodhouse Lea to see Frances and Eric. For Sarika, however, meeting Victoria was a social highlight. Leaving Emma to run the store, Sarika took Victoria up to Michaelhouse for refreshments and the discussion she had been looking forward to having.

Sarika was not disappointed. Victoria's ardent pursuit of social reform was the badge she wore convincingly. "I can't overstate how impressed I am by your initiative and enterprise in establishing your store despite attempts to discourage you. Given your circumstances, I don't know of any colonial women who would have pursued what you have done. Without exception, the ones I meet are all too comfortable living in the shadow of their wealthy husbands to challenge the status quo regarding the position of women in society. That's why, Sarika, you are the great exception to the rule. What is astounding about your achievement is that only a dozen years ago you were just an indentured servant. I think your remarkable will to rise above that stigma is what colonial society disdains to accept because it perceives your success as a threat to its welfare and privilege."

Deeply honoured by the lavish praise Victoria had heaped upon her, Sarika modestly contended that she owed an enormous debt to the wife of the estate owner in Illovo where she had been indentured. "She gave me the only education I have ever had, teaching me the three Rs and then entrusting me as her secretary. Since the establishment of my shop, I intended to thank her and invite her here but have been informed that recently she passed on."

"Oh, that is a shame because I was going to include her in what I want to establish. It's one of the other reasons I decided to accompany Gordon to Alex County. I want to establish a loose association of reform-minded women. By challenging the constraints to which we are subjected, identifying issues where women are overlooked for posts such as pound mistress, ferry keeper, librarian, post mistress and, of course, exposing the unfounded nonsense by which we are denied the right to vote. All four of our major newspapers rely on local correspondents for news of the country districts. Volunteer to be a local news and views correspondent. There is ample scope for more county and country news. By being accepted as a news correspondent you grow the field of responsible tasks women can manage and hasten the day when we are finally recognised for our capabilities that go far beyond household chores."

"In that, I am passionate about tolerance being the cornerstone of social reform, I regard it as crucial to have your involvement as an Asian – that's the reformist term I want to popularise in place of 'Indian,' which is viewed pejoratively. Already you have turned Simon and Cynthia's attitude around. That's a significant achievement which is not going to go unnoticed in this community. Emma, it pleases me to say, is very enthusiastic to be involved in our quest. Importantly, she was born here and does not have the heritage of the old country engrained in her. Like you, she is also young. For me, that's another advantage in shaping our future."

"Are you intending to have some kind of newsletter by which we keep in touch?"

"Certainly! It will provide addresses of other women in the colony; news of developments; examples of issues that ought to be pursued and relevant news from England and the Australian colonies. One of the activities I recommend is to have tea parties to which you invite just a few women to gauge their leanings. I have found in Durban that many women are afraid to disclose their feelings. But when gathered in small groups they tend to relax and unburden themselves."

Before concluding their meeting, Sarika invited Victoria and Gordon to dinner at Michaelhouse. "I would like to meet Gordon. After all, he was prepared to offer me employment at E Snell & Co when Michael and I were set on following your advice to leave Alexandra County as a consequence of the ostracism we were experiencing here."

Victoria was delighted to accept the invitation. On the last night of their five-day stay, Sarika put on a repast for Victoria and Gordon as good as any served in the best dining venues in Durban. Returning to the Royal Hotel afterwards, Gordon remarked how impressed he was by Sarika's business acumen and her general sophistication. "She is such a cultured lady."

****

The uncertainty and anxiety which gripped the settler population late in 1878 at the prospect of war with the Zulu army was not helped by changes in the defence structure of Alexandra County.

At the Royal Hotel bar during the last week of 1878, Dr Lancelot Booth disclosed that Captain Lucas had been transferred as Commandant from

Alexandra County to Victoria and Durban County. "His impulsive manner soured relations with the various defence groups in the County. Also, that his defence plans were incomplete. An unofficial source described his bearing as 'impolitic.' So, the defence of Alex County now falls under Alfred County's magistrate, Major Giles, based in Harding. It baffles me how Giles is supposed to co-ordinate defences here when he is 50 miles away and we have no telegraph service. It also means Alex County is going to have an acting magistrate for the foreseeable future."

Frank Reynolds said he had heard that the authorities were calling up the Alexandra Mounted Rifles along with other defence groups for border duty. "While I can understand the need to have a stout defence of the border along the Tugela River, it bothers me that the authorities do not appear to appreciate that our southern borders with the Griqua and the Pondo are troublesome at the best of times. With most of our manpower concentrated on the Zulu threat, what's to stop elements from across our southern borders plundering our farms and estates?"

His question was greeted by a pensive silence. Early in January 1879, Simon and Eric were amongst the 30 men the Alexandra Mounted Rifles (AMR) despatched to the Zululand border.

****

Fortunately, the colonial contingents like the AMR played only a passive role in the early part of the Anglo-Zulu war having been restricted to defence of the border with Zululand. As such they were spared inclusion in the monumental tragedy suffered at Isandlwana on January 22, 1879, when 1,329 were killed by the Zulu army including the officer commanding, Colonel Durnford. But it was not until March that the AMR was stood down and the men returned home.

The absence of men in communities as a result of the military requisitions was promptly recognised by Victoria as affording opportunities for women to assert themselves. In a newsletter she circulated to her small group of reformist ladies she advised them to encourage women to join the ranks of the existing defence groups that were depleted by the needs of the war. As a result, Cynthia, Frances and Emma were amongst the ladies from the Umzinto district who attended the drills of the AMR.

Although Peter had not been drafted by the AMR, in Simon's absence, he was fully occupied running Dewsbury which involved sheep, poultry, vegetable crops, the coffee plantation as well as the distillery. Consequently, Emma and Frances, like many other women, had to perform tasks usually carried out by the menfolk such as harnessing the horses and driving the carriages on excursions to fetch supplies for their estates.

Heartened by the responses she received from ladies in outlying districts, Victoria lost no time in propagating the role women were playing in the maintenance of everyday life in the colony during this time of peril. Her penned remarks were published in the *Natal Witness* and the *Colonist.*

While attention is rightly focused on the role our menfolk are bravely playing in defending the colony, cognisance needs to be given to how life in our villages and farming areas is being maintained.

It is commendable that women have shown initiative by coming forward to learn shooting skills in the various rifle groups whose ranks have been depleted by military requisitions. On many estates, women have abandoned their kitchens and their sewing and taken to the fields to supervise livestock, crop maintenance and harvesting.

Where transport is concerned, women are boldly and proficiently fulfilling the role that men traditionally play, thereby ensuring that supplies are delivered and disruption of the economy in the counties is minimal.

Although war is cruel and causes much sadness, it also produces circumstances that promote change. It is fervently hoped that as a result of this present conflict fresh appreciation for the abilities and potential of women will colour the thinking of society.

I have the honour to be -

Victoria Snell

Durban

A few days after the publication of Victoria's letter, a letter from controversial cleric Bishop Colenso was published which indirectly tilted at Victoria's praise for the role of women by commending the native population for its peacefulness and co-operation with the colonial authorities.

****

CHAPTER 8

In the wake of the disaster at Isandlwana public opinion was unanimous that Britain had to strike back. By July that had been achieved when the Zulu capital of Ulundi was overwhelmed. After eluding his pursuers, Cetshwayo was captured and exiled to Cape Town. However, despite the months that the war persisted in Zululand, life in Alex County returned to normal.

In February Sarika held a *soiree* at her store to celebrate her first year in business. The occasion was well advertised using notices and handbills. Dewsbury supplied a cask of rum-infused punch which appropriately augmented the array of snacks Cynthia, Frances, Emma and Sarika had prepared. All the regulars from the Royal Hotel bar attended with their wives. But apart from Field Cornet Brander, the Cutty Sark company was conspicuous by its absence. Brander felt obliged to attend as the sole representative of officialdom in the absence of magistrate Captain Lucas who was very much involved in the war.

Addressing the gathering Sarika thanked everyone for their presence and their patronage of her shop. "This is truly a memorable occasion. When I look back on the months before this building was completed, I had doubts whether my ambition would materialise. But it has and that is thanks to all of you particularly Eric and Frances Harrison, Emily and John Harrington, Simon and Cynthia Prescott, Emma Johnson and Peter Richardson. Although they are unable to be here, I also owe much to the encouragement and counsel of Victoria and Gordon Snell of Durban."

Eric then came forward to offer some thoughts. "Our celebration here marks a significant milestone in our journey as settlers and colonists. Not long ago, such a gathering would have been most unlikely. Deep-seated social conventions would have militated against it. But acceptance of Her Majesty, Queen Victoria's principles of tolerance and diversity is what our presence here reflects. Unspoken, however, is another principle that Sarika has observed and implemented and that is conformity to standards. For that she deserves admiration and respect because it not only sets her apart from others of her race but serves as an example to us all that from lowly beginnings social elevation is possible."

Frances was very proud of her husband's speech. "It's such a pity Victoria was not here to hear it and to witness the occasion because the ambience reflected exactly what she is striving to achieve socially." Thanks to Frances' initiative, a report on Sarika's celebration together with Eric's tribute appeared in the country news column of the *Mercury.* Victoria's newsletter also featured it.

Not surprisingly, negative reaction to Sarika's celebration was noted the following day at the Cutty Sark. "This coolie is getting too big for her boots. She's now got all these people eating out of her hands. Next thing she's going to want to buy out or takeover Knox's store. She's too darned ambitious," fumed one of the hotheads.

In a similar vein, a letter was published in the *Mercury* warning the people of Umzinto to be wary of the growth of Indian commercial influence. "Come to Durban and see the extent to which Indian commerce is challenging white business," stated the anonymous letter writer.

****

A month after celebrating her first year in business, Sarika was awakened one night to the sound and smell of fire. Looking out of her bedroom window she saw her shop was burning. Hastily pulling on a gown and shoes, out of a sense of hope that somehow, she could stop the blaze, she rushed down the pathway. But there was nothing she could do. The contents of the shop were feeding the flames. Then it occurred to her that all her business records were in her office which was engulfed in flames. Helplessly she witnessed her livelihood reduced to ashes. She also noted that there was no one about. Whoever had set fire to her shop had made sure that he was not in the vicinity to watch it being destroyed.

Bitterly upset, Sarika returned to Michaelhouse once the flames had died out leaving just the shell of the building and the smouldering remains of the comprehensive range of stock the shop had housed. Too upset to return to bed, she made herself a cup of tea and contemplated the meaning and the consequences of what had occurred. It was clearly a case of arson. Someone or some people despised her so much that they sought her ruin through fire. But thinking back on how she had been persecuted for her relationship with Michael, gave her courage. "The ostracism and discrimination I experienced made me stronger. I confronted magistrate Moodie and his wife directly when I told them I was pregnant with their grandchild," she ruminated. "I will not give up. I can't afford to. What else could I do?" In a positive state of mind, she welcomed the first rays of daylight. Her first priority was to report the fire to Field Cornet Brander.

She didn't have to. He was at the smouldering site before eight o' clock that morning. Evidently, he had received the news earlier which surprised Sarika as nobody had been around when her shop was burning. In greeting her he expressed perfunctory commiserations at her loss. "In trying to track down who was responsible for this, I will rely on gossip. Invariably some loose talk provides a lead," he said. After some discussion about how the fire had started, he concluded that a rolled-up bundle of cloth soaked in molten wax was set alight and thrown into the shop after breaking one of the front windows. "Unfortunately, in a situation like this there are no clues." Significantly, he offered no thoughts on the motive for the fire.

Reaction within the community to the destruction of Sarika's store was akin to the difference between night and day. At the Cutty Sark the consensus was that fate had intervened. Unfortunate though the situation was for Sarika, it was a signal that "coolie" stores were not welcome in Umzinto. Oddly, there was no speculation as to who might have caused the fire. Instead, one hothead suggested that Sarika might have caused the blaze herself. His reasoning was that she could benefit from the insurance award.

At the Royal Hotel bar, outrage was unanimously expressed. There was sympathy for Sarika's loss and hope that she would re-establish her business. "I know she was substantially insured," said Eric, "but until the store is rebuilt, she will not be able to earn any money. And that goes for her assistant, Emma, as well."

"I am convinced that fire was caused by one of those types who tried to sabotage the construction of Sarika's property. I reckon Brander must have an idea who would have been likely to start that fire," declared William Thornton. "Apparently, he is waiting for some loose talk in the hope of finding a clue. Very passive police work, I think."

"You're right, William. He should be interrogating that Cutty Sark bunch individually, finding out where each one was on the night of the fire and getting alibis to prove their whereabouts," opined James Ross.

"Has anyone considered whether someone in the Indian community could have started the fire? After all, some of them resent the success she has made of her life besides disapproving of her affair with Michael Moodie," ventured John Harrington.

Two weeks passed before Natal Bank sent out an assessor from Glasgow Insurance to certify Sarika's loss. In the meantime, William Joyner had provided a quote on the cost to rebuild the store. The absence of records concerning the value of the stock lost posed a problem. But between Emma and Sarika it was possible to list most of the items and their approximate costs. After some haggling, Glasgow Insurance agreed to award £135 to replace the building and its contents.

****

Although he was no longer the MLC for the two South Coast counties, having revived the aim of shipping on the Mzimkulu in 1876, by 1879 James Aiken was the foremost proponent of that scheme. In the opinion of William Bazley, whom Aiken had hired to inspect the mouth of the river, at a cost of between £300 and £350, the rocks impeding the entrance could be dynamited thereby providing a clear 30-yard passage. But Aiken's appeal in June to colonial secretary Mitchell for government funding was dismissed as "not feasible at this time."

Nonetheless, a boost for the project was given by Governor Henry Bulwer later that year when he toured Alexandra and Alfred counties. His observations were warmly commended by the Royal Hotel bar regulars. "The fact that he singled out the Umzinto district for what he termed 'the rapid extension of sugar cultivation' is overdue recognition of our enterprise," said Frank Reynolds of T Reynolds & Sons, the largest landowners in the county. "The unspoken implication of his comment is that it emphasises our need for transport solutions."

A further hint that the government was finally tilting towards developing the Mzimkulu for shipping came in Bulwer's opening address to the much-delayed 1879 session of the Legislative Council. He said he hoped that by "some means" the river mouth could be improved as he believed there was huge potential for trade. His intentions were reflected in the colonial engineer's undertaking to recompense Aiken once Bazley had completed the job of removing the rocks from the river mouth.

****

During the last weeks of the momentous year of 1879 a quiet aura of confident expectation pervaded the residents of Alex County that after nearly 20 years, a solution to their transport woes seemed in the offing. Reflecting that outlook in addition to the demise of the Zulu military threat (which adherents of Bishop Colenso believed was never a threat), a well-attended public celebration took place at the Royal Hotel. At ten shillings a head, the hotel laid on a sumptuous spread. Dewsbury supplied a five-gallon cask of rum punch. Mrs Archibald pounded out the well-loved tunes of the day on the piano. Apart from a brief welcome by hotel proprietor William Thornton, it was an informal occasion where all and sundry could mix socially and generate a bit of community spirit.

Since Sarika's store had re-opened it had enjoyed greater patronage than before the fire, so when Eric asked if she would be attending the function at the Royal Hotel, she had no hesitation in replying in the affirmative. Leaving Peter and Emma to babysit George and James, the Prescotts along with the Harrisons and the Harringtons ensured that Sarika was in good company. That was until one of the Cutty Sark hotheads, under the influence of rum punch, made derogatory remarks to Sarika. Incensed by this outrage, Simon punched the hothead in the face causing him to lose his balance and stumble to the ground. Immediately, however, Simon found himself accosted by three of the hothead's allies. Sensing that a brawl was about to take place, Eric Harrison and John Harrington intervened and prevented any further altercation.

Although the rest of the evening continued without any incident, it was apparent that there were those present who resented Sarika's presence and physically distanced themselves from her. But there were also several ladies who made a point of chatting to her and making her feel welcome and they weren't necessarily all her customers. With her lustrous, shoulder-length, ebony colour hair contrasting with the bright colours of her traditional sari, Sarika was conspicuous not only for being the only Asian present.

Towards the end of the occasion, as people were making their way to their carriages, Field Cornet Brander came up to Simon and said he had some fearful news. "I was in the shadows of the carriage park area when I saw the lout you punched talking to his mate. I overheard him saying it was time Prescott and Harrison were taught a lesson for supporting the coolie bitch."

Responding, Simon enquired whether the two that Brander had mentioned could be the arsonists who had set fire to Sarika's store. "It's possible, but without witnesses, there's no case. However, we now have two strong suspects. I will have my men watch them closely particularly as they have named you and Eric as targets."

****

Hugh Lawson managed Crofton Estate in the Park Rynie area on behalf of its owner who resided in Pietermaritzburg. At 30 years of age, he was unmarried and relatively new to the district since relocating from Victoria County. Socially detached, occasionally he visited a bar in Park Rynie when meals were at half price. Having seen the notice advertising the function at the Royal Hotel, he decided to break his lonely routine and attend the celebration which for just ten shillings would buy him a meal and some free punch.

As a stranger at the function, he could afford to observe those in attendance while he nibbled on the snacks and sipped a glass of punch. Eyeing the women in attendance, he realised they were all either wives or had partners. The conspicuous exception was the only Asian woman present. In Victoria County he had had a brief liaison with a young Asian girl and was not intimidated by social convention in that regard. What attracted him about this Asian woman was her obvious beauty, maturity and sense of deportment. In his eyes, that was what elevated her above the other ladies present. Eavesdropping on a conversation, he gathered that she was the owner of a store called Sarika's in Umzinto. Having had his fill of the food and punch on offer, Hugh decided to head for home. At the first opportunity, however, he resolved to return to Umzinto and to visit the store called Sarika's.

That opportunity came a few days later. Prominently placed, facing the route he had just travelled from Park Rynie, Sarika's store was conspicuous. Since the function at the Royal Hotel, Hugh had been debating how he should approach her. If at the outset it was clear that she had no interest in him, then he might have to accept that his pursuit was futile. Nonetheless, he believed that persistence has its rewards. If he found she was socially receptive, his dilemma was how and where he could have some time with her. Upon walking into the store, he asked the assistant, Emma, if Sarika was present. As if on cue, Sarika emerged from her office and enquired how she could help. Although feeling somewhat overwrought in her presence, Hugh managed to sustain his aplomb and asked if he could talk to her in her office.

Happy to oblige, Sarika led him into her small office. After introducing himself, Hugh made a brief reference to the celebratory function at the Royal Hotel where he had seen her. That afforded Sarika the opportunity to comment on the occasion which, she said, was her first social foray in the district. "I can appreciate how you felt as I had a similar experience in Victoria County where social convention was the standard," he said. While Sarika digested the significance of his remark, he reached across the desk and placed his hand on her arm. "Sarika, I really would like to have dinner with you and exchange details about our respective life journeys."

Confronted with such a proposal from a stranger she had met scarcely five minutes earlier, Sarika said she needed to think about his request and would write to him when she had come to a decision. Thanking her for her response and her time, Hugh promptly left the store.

Emma was curious as to who the stranger was and what he wanted. Coyly, Sarika related the details of the encounter then returned to her office and closed the door. She found herself in a quandary. Was her life to be lived in memory of Michael or to venture forth towards new romantic horizons? Before her encounter with Hugh Lawson, she had not given any thought to seeking a new romantic liaison. Certainly, there was no one in the Indian community she would consider. Besides, they had ostracised her as a result of her relationship with Michael Moodie. Regarding the white colonist community, the predominance of social convention and the attitude among some that still prevailed towards her, four years after Michael's death, provided a clear answer. While most of the white community accepted her commercially with some being loyal customers, Sarika had no illusions about her place within the broader ranks of Umzinto society.

Nonetheless, she found Hugh Lawson's sudden intrusion into her life intriguing and maybe even exciting. She had to admit she found him attractive. He was fairly tall, well-built, had blue eyes, thick sandy-coloured hair, and was clean-shaven. She guessed he was about her age. Weighing up the situation, she came to the conclusion that he deserved a positive response. In the social context within which they lived, he had shown courage and initiative in wanting to meet her. There and then, she decided to write to him and invite him to dinner at Michaelhouse. Since Emma passed the post office on her way home to Dewsbury at the end of the day, she asked her to post the letter.

Riding back to Park Rynie, Hugh reviewed his impressions of his brief meeting with Sarika. Having not heard her voice before, her spoken English betrayed not a hint of her Asian identity. Her pale skin pigmentation contrasted with the lustrous condition of her ebony hair. Her ample breasts, he noted, were evident beneath the maroon-coloured sari which adorned them. The fact that she had responded with equanimity to his dinner request he interpreted as a positive signal. Although he had not come to make any purchases, he noted that her shop was very comprehensively stocked. "She strikes me as a shrewd and competent business lady who is also very beautiful," he told himself.

At Dewsbury, Emma told Peter of the brief meeting the stranger had with Sarika and that he had enquired about the possibility of having dinner with her. "From the way you relate Sarika's response, that letter, to Hugh Lawson of Crofton estate in Park Rynie, is the dinner invitation," reasoned Peter smilingly.

****

Cynthia and Frances were both alarmed when told by their respective spouses of the threats Field Cornet Brander had heard uttered against them for supporting Sarika. Both speculated on what form the threats might take. "My biggest fear is fire," said Simon to Cynthia, recalling the fire on Beneva in 1867 which had destroyed half of Edward Hawksworth's sugar crop. "I just hope Brander's men in his security detail have their ears to the ground."

On Woodhouse Lea, Eric expressed similar fears to Frances. "Besides the threat of fire, what worries me is your isolation here in the house when I am out on the estate or have travelled to Umzinto. I would hate to have to deal with a hostage situation such as the Prescotts experienced when Anne was kidnapped. When I am not here, I want you to have that firearm handy all the time. Hopefully, though, it won't be necessary to apply the training you and Cynthia had with the Alexandra Mounted Rifles back in February."

****

Two days after Sarika's letter to Hugh Lawson was posted, he fetched it at the Park Rynie post office. It was nothing more than a brief note in which she looked forward to dining with him at Michaelhouse and specified the date and time. Hugh was elated at what the prospect might hold in terms of romance.

On the appointed evening, he arrived at the scheduled time. Sarika wore a turquoise colour sari which exposed the small bead ring she wore in her navel and was barefoot, explaining that she liked to feel the rugs under her feet. Entering her sitting room area, Hugh smelled the aromatic scent given off by the burning of joss sticks. Having poured two glasses of fruit cordial, Sarika adopted a lotus-like posture on the couch opposite Hugh. Initiating conversation, she related how she came to be in Umzinto after having started life in Natal as an indentured child at the age of twelve. Listening to her account of the ostracism she and Michael had experienced, his tragic death followed by the death of their six-month-old child, Hugh rapidly came to appreciate her resilience and strength of character.

He then detailed his origins which began with his birth in 1849 aboard one of the Byrne immigrant ships sailing to Natal. His father's expertise in mechanics enabled him to gain employment in the harbour until the early 1860s when maintenance of the sugar mills in Victoria County proved more lucrative and resulted in the Lawsons moving to the Umhlanga area. By 1870, Hugh was employed as an estate assistant in the Umhlanga district. Following the deaths of his parents through illness, without any other family, he decided to make a fresh start in life by taking up an offer to manage Crofton Estate in the Park Rynie district.

Over dinner which commenced with a chicken salad starter, followed by a mild vegetable biryani and a dessert of rhubarb tart, their conversation topics ranged from local conditions and the economy of the colony to personal interests and ambitions. It was apparent they had much in common: both had lost their parents and had no other family; both were trying to pursue new lives in the county; both had experienced love across the racial divide.

After having rounded off the meal with cups of coffee, Hugh said it was time to ride back to Crofton Estate. Sarika found herself considering whether to invite him to sleep over. Finding him very attractive and not having slept with a man since Michael's death, the opportunity was very tempting. But on second thoughts she decided her needs could wait for a subsequent occasion. Thanking Hugh for his company, she embraced and kissed him saying she hoped to see him again soon.

Appraising his evening with Sarika, Hugh felt he may have met his soul mate. There was nothing about her that he could fault. She had a tastefully furnished house and a successful business. She was very attractive, eloquent, and worldly-wise. Was he falling in love with her or was he just infatuated?

PART TWO

CHAPTER 9

It was mid-morning some ten days before Christmas. Eric had left early in the carriage to make a series of purchases in Umzinto. Frances was busy with household chores. Edward and Nicholas were in the courtyard playing but had stopped when they saw a man walking towards the barn where Woodhouse Lea's coffee crop was stored. Reasoning that a strange situation was developing, twelve-year-old Edward called his mother. By the time Frances came to the courtyard, smoke was billowing out of the barn as she caught sight of the intruder going towards the shed where farm implements were stored.

She shouted at him to leave the premises at once. But he took no notice. Instead, he emerged from the shed with an axe and was moving towards the house shouting "You Harrison coolie lovers are not wanted here." With that, he began to smash the windows of the closest outbuilding. Having heeded Eric's plea to have the firearm handy at all times, Frances raised the gun and shouted to him to desist at once or face injury. He ignored her warning. So she fired a loose round as an indicator of her intentions. In response, he laughed at her and shouted, "You don't scare me, woman!" With the coffee barn on fire, the intruder smashing windows with the axe, and moving defiantly towards the house, Frances feared for what he might do to her and the children as well as to the house. So, she screamed: "Stop now and leave us alone!" But the intruder ignored her and laughed derisively. When he was just twenty yards from her, she shouted a final warning: "Get away from us now, or else!" With a smirk on his face, he advanced towards Frances brandishing the axe. Shaking in fear she raised the gun, focused on his torso, and pulled the trigger. At such close range, the impact of the bullet felled him to the ground. A dark stain of blood spread rapidly across his chest. The only sounds in the silence that followed were gurgling noises from his throat. Trembling in fear and shock, Frances moved forward to take a closer look at what she had done. The intruder was dead.

Hastily returning to the house, she closed the rear entrance and told the children they were not allowed out until their father gave them permission. Feeling distraught and in a state of horror at what the intruder might have done, Frances made herself a cup of tea mentally thanking the drill officer of the Alexandra Mounted Rifles for the training he had given her.

A while later Eric returned in an anxious state. From a distance, he had seen a cloud of smoke hovering above his estate. Pausing to note the smouldering remains of his coffee barn after stabling his horse, he hastened towards the house. As he neared the kitchen entrance, he saw the dead body of the arsonist. Horrified, he sprinted into the kitchen and immediately took Frances into his arms. She had heard him arriving and was waiting for him. Tearfully she related what had happened. Holding her close and kissing her, he found himself trembling in the realisation of what might have occurred if she had not undergone a firearm drill after the Isandlwana massacre. Then, as a wave of relief replaced his dark thoughts, he smiled at her and complimented her on her marksmanship. She attempted to return his smile but could not dismiss the grim implications of the morning's events. "What do we do now?" she asked.

"First of all, I need to place the intruder's body in the shed. We don't want our boys to see it. Then I shall have to return to Umzinto and fetch Field Cornet Brander. He will want a statement from you when he removes the body."

It was mid-afternoon before Brander arrived in a carriage. In the interim Frances had produced a detailed written statement. After reading it, he said the important aspect of the experience was that she had given the intruder three warnings. His disregard for them while verbally threatening her and behaving menacingly with an axe, exculpated Frances from any wrongdoing. Besides, the intruder had committed an act of arson. Regarding the intruder's identity,

Brander said: "He is definitely not someone I have seen at the Cutty Sark. But between what my men will pick up from gossip in the district and any loose talk in the Cutty Sark, his identity is bound to emerge." Wrapping the intruder's body in some sheeting, Eric helped to load it onto the carriage. Burial in a plot in Umzinto reserved for paupers and the likes of the intruder would take place the following day.

That evening at the Cutty Sark, Brander initially did not comment on what had occurred at Woodhouse Lea, hoping to see if one of the hotheads would raise the issue and thereby possibly provide a clue as to the identity of the intruder Frances had shot. When nothing was forthcoming, Brander disclosed the details of his call at Woodhouse Lea. Judging by the looks that were exchanged among some of the hotheads, he discerned a degree of prior awareness. Feigning curiosity as to the identity of Frances' victim, one of them asked for a description of the intruder's body. "Seems like it was that tramp from Ifafa called Ginger," was the response to Brander's description.

What intrigued Brander was the absence of any chatter amongst the hotheads about how brave Frances had been in confronting the axe-waving arsonist or any discussion about the motives of the attack. Instead, a subdued silence prevailed on the matter. Consequently, he deduced that the attack on Woodhouse Lea was part of an organised plot. Having reached that conclusion, he realised his first priority the next day was to warn the Prescotts on Dewsbury.

Within a day, however, the news of what had occurred at Woodhouse Lea was widespread. Simon and Cynthia were horrified by Frances' experience. "Thank heavens Frances proved a crack shot, Cyn. I hope you would be equally capable if you needed to be," said Simon as he hugged his wife. At the Royal Hotel bar that evening Frances' experience was the sole topic of conversation. As John Harrington later related to the Harrisons, Frances was praised for her bravery and marksmanship under dire circumstances.

Five days after the attack on Woodhouse Lea, Brander's men made two arrests. Both were traders in the Ifafa district. Interrogated by Brander, they confessed to hiring the tramp called Ginger to commit arson on Woodhouse Lea for a payment of £3. One of the arrested men was the one Simon had punched in the face during the public celebration at the Royal Hotel earlier in the month. Under interrogation, they implicated others in the plot to commit acts of arson on Woodhouse Lea and Dewsbury. As a result, a further five arrests were made. All five were regulars at the Cutty Sark. The spate of arrests also led to the unmasking of the arsonist who had set fire to Sarika's shop. Since Christmas was only two days away, the seven were held in the Umzinto gaol until acting magistrate Frederick Baker could preside over their case scheduled for Monday, December 29.

****

Since his transfer as postmaster from Umzinto to Howick, it had been a while since Ralph Harrison and his wife Mary had travelled to Alexandra County to see their grandsons, Edward and Nicholas. But at the invitation of Edward Hawksworth to celebrate Christmas 1879 along with Frances, Eric and their boys on his Beneva estate, the occasion facilitated a Harrison family gathering. "My house is commodious. There's plenty of room for you all," Hawksworth had beckoned. As ever, he was delighted to have his two grandsons on the estate, particularly as he recognised Edward as the future assistant manager of Beneva.

Sipping a cold beer before lunch, Eric felt at ease leaving Woodhouse Lea unattended for the two days they were away. "The gaoling of those seven criminal conspirators gives me confidence that Woodhouse Lea is safe," he quipped to his father-in-law. "The loss of my coffee crop and the barn that it housed together with smashed windows of the outbuilding is a small price to pay for the safe survival of my family."

At the Christmas lunch, Edward expressed thanksgiving for an occasion that might otherwise have been marked by grief. "I am so proud of you, dear Frances. As my only child, you are not only a wonderful daughter, wife and mother but a brave and exemplary colonist. And Eric, I could not wish for a better son-in-law. It also pleases me to have Ralph and Mary here. As grandparents, we need to have regular contact with our grandchildren. Let's raise our glasses and give thanks for our blessings."

Over at Dewsbury, the company of Peter and Emma, as light-hearted as ever, lifted spirits and banished thoughts of what Frances had faced on Woodhouse Lea. It was a warm day ideally suited for the cold buffet Cynthia and Emma had prepared. After a leisurely lunch, they all strolled up the stream which flowed through Dewsbury. "There are some fine pools ahead where George and James will enjoy cooling off," said Simon winking at Cynthia as he recalled how they had skinny-dipped in those pools one summer's day before they were married.

At Taunton Manor, above Pietermaritzburg, Anne and Martin Pryce hosted Victoria and Gordon Snell. Preparing Christmas dinner in the kitchen, the Prescott sisters reminisced about the Christmases they had celebrated at Dewsbury. "I miss Mum and Dad," said Anne. "Dad's death from dysentery at just 50 years of age when we were still teenagers was such a loss. Mum never got over his untimely passing. Christmas without Dad's spirit was just never the same." Putting a comforting arm around her younger sister, Victoria agreed, saying it was important for family gatherings to take place frequently so that the new generation involving her daughter Lily, Anne's daughters, Eleanor and Elizabeth, and Simon's sons, George and James, would grow up to value family spirit.

The Harringtons had the company of Sarika and Hugh on Christmas day at Preston estate. Not wanting Hugh to spend the day in a local pub for want of company, Emily Harrington had readily agreed to Sarika's request for Hugh to accompany her. It proved a convivial occasion. Although John Harrington had not previously met Hugh, having both relocated to Alex County from Victoria County, their mutual interest in the sugar enterprise stimulated discussion, particularly as regards distilleries and transport issues. Eagerly listening to their conversation was young Stewart who had just commenced as his father's assistant on Preston. Priscilla, who was very fond of Sarika, enquired when it might be possible to help out in her shop.

Heading home after a sumptuous Christmas lunch, Hugh invited Sarika to his residence on Crofton estate which she had not previously visited. Having not had a private moment with Hugh since their dinner together at Michaelhouse, she did not hesitate to accept. Once indoors, they could not keep their hands off each other. Within minutes Sarika had discarded her sari. Hugh led her to his bedroom where their respective pent-up libidinous desires were liberated. Fuelled by passion, they passed the night in mutual ecstasy.

****

The Umzinto courtroom was crowded on Monday, December 29 when the seven accused in the plot against Eric Harrison and Simon Prescott were led in by Field Cornet Brander's security detail. As all the accused had acknowledged their crimes, acting magistrate Baker had dispensed with calling up a jury since the only issue was the extent of their punishment.

Brander read out the charge sheet: all seven had conspired to inflict damage on the properties of Eric Harrison and Simon Prescott. The two from Ifafa had paid £3 to a tramp called Ginger to commit arson on the Harrison estate. One of the remaining five accused was also responsible for the arson attack earlier in the year which totally destroyed the shop known as Sarika's. All were motivated by antipathy towards the Indian lady known as Sarika and sought, through depredatory measures, to dissuade Messrs Harrison and Prescott from flouting social convention by their social relations with her.

Noting that the evidence before him was irrefutable, acting magistrate Baker sentenced all seven to one year in prison for conspiracy to intimidate and inflict damage on the private properties of Messrs Harrison and Prescott.

"Regarding the two who hired the tramp called Ginger, I hold you accountable not only for the destruction he caused on Woodhouse Lea but also for his life-threatening actions regarding Mrs Harrison and possibly her children. For you two conspirators, I am imposing a prison sentence of three years in addition to the one year already imposed."

"For the accused responsible for burning down Sarika's shop, a major act of arson, I hereby sentence you to four years in prison in addition to the one year already imposed."

"I hereby reiterate what Magistrate Lucas emphasised in the earlier case involving the property of the Indian lady, Sarika: he sentenced the accused to twelve lashes each for their intolerance towards a fellow settler. The convicted should consider themselves fortunate that magistrate Lucas is not presiding today as undoubtedly, he would have included lashes in his sentencing."

"I also find that the crime of those convicted here today is based on an attitude of intolerance that led to intimidation, arson and even the loss of life. Mrs Harrison would not have had to kill the arsonist sent by two of the convicted if they had not filled his mind with intolerance and paid him to act as he did. As settlers we depend on each other in this community for a variety of goods and services – from labour to food and produce sourced locally and from Durban and overseas. It is unacceptable that violence is plotted against fellow settlers based simply on intolerance. This case is closed. Field Cornet, please return the convicted to the gaol."

****

Over at the Royal Hotel bar, toasts were drunk to acting magistrate Baker for the sentences he had handed down. "That element at the Cutty Sark is a disgrace to our community. If you go back three years, they were the plotters against Sarika buying a piece of land and building on it. Then some among them tried to sabotage the building process. Now we know that it was one of them who set fire to Sarika's shop. Good riddance, I say!" declared proprietor William Thornton as he offered everyone a half-price round.

Since five of the regulars at the Cutty Sark had been convicted and were in prison, the ranks at the pub were somewhat depleted. But it allowed the owners to re-brand the watering hole. As one of the owners remarked, a fringe element within the community had regarded the Cutty Sark as its exclusive turf. "Now that five of them are serving gaol sentences, by implication, the name 'Cutty Sark' is associated with a bunch of felons. So, to dispel that image, we are renaming the pub the 'Wiltshire' and hope to attract a better class of colonist as a result."

****

Developments in Umzinto were the main features of Victoria's next newsletter to her small group of reformist ladies. Frances Harrison's despatch of the intruder on Woodhouse Lea who had threatened her with an axe was cited not only for the bravery she displayed but also for the ability of a woman to defend herself. "How does that square with the repeated refrain that women are weak and incapable of exercising responsibility?" was the question Victoria posed in her editorial.

Regarding social integration, Victoria cited Sarika's attendance at the celebratory function held at Umzinto's Royal Hotel. "Since we are increasingly commercially dependent on our Asian fellow colonists, we need to embrace them socially as well. I urge you, Ladies, to widen your social networks. There must be other Sarikas out there who need to be nurtured within our communities. Remember the exhortation of our illustrious monarch, Her Majesty Queen Victoria, to appreciate diversity as a significant reality of the Empire."

In advertising a forthcoming event, Victoria advised that Sarika would be addressing the Berea Reformist Ladies group in Durban in January 1880.

****

As the re-branded watering hole, the Wiltshire attracted six new regulars, all of them property or estate owners. Bunting Johnstone, owner of Ida Vale, was Umzinto's original resident. He claimed to have settled in the district in 1848. James McMillan was the owner of Umzinto Lodge which was founded in 1858 by the late James Arbuthnot. Charles Reynolds of T Reynolds & Sons became a regular as the Wiltshire was closer to his Esperanza residence. William Pigg, Captain Tucker and George Quick made up the balance of the new regulars and lent credibility to the pub's owners that the Wiltshire should reflect a better class of colonists.

News that Natal would start 1880 with telegraphic contact through to London via Aden and across the Mediterranean Sea to Europe was welcomed by Charles Reynolds. "This long overdue development will greatly benefit the colony's economy."

"Well, that's fine for you, Charles, as your firm conducts its business from Durban. What irks me is the total neglect of the southern counties. The majority of our roads are impassable – no bridges, no weirs – and those conditions not only slow down travel but drastically increase the price of transport," fumed Captain Tucker. "That was made clear by Governor Bulwer in his address to the legislative council in November. Besides the telegraphic links northwards from Durban, the North Coast as far as Stanger is now also telegraphically linked. But south of Durban – no provision is made for telegraphic linkage – not even as far as Isipingo. Yet in the same speech Bulwer acclaimed the 'rapid extension of sugar cultivation' in Alex County. If that is the case, how does he expect us to flourish when our infrastructural needs are ignored?" inquired Captain Tucker indignantly. His question was greeted by silence.

To lift feelings, George Quick said that progress in preparing the entrance to the Mzimkulu River was encouraging. "I understand from James Aiken it is possible that by June the *Somtseu* will be paying regular visits."

****

"Compatibility within diversity" was the topic of Victoria's January 1880 meeting of her reformist ladies' group. In correspondence, she arranged for a speedy spider carriage to transport Sarika to Durban and for her to stay at the Snells' Berea residence. In turn, Sarika arranged for Priscilla Harrington to assist Emma in managing the store in her absence.

Arriving the day before the meeting, Victoria and Gordon were thrilled to have Sarika as their guest, recalling how much they had enjoyed their evening with her at Michaelhouse. Gordon was curious as to how Sarika intended to make her case for diversity. "As much as I recognise and accept the broad reality of diversity, I am at a loss as to how there can be a kind of one-size-fits-all approach. In the first place, amongst white colonists there are categories that are not compatible. I don't see myself as a wealthy businessman having much in common with the white stevedores down at the harbour. Amongst the Asian population, Sarika, you have elevated yourself above the indentured and hawker class of which you were a part just six years ago."

"Your observations are correct, Gordon. Class is the reality that needs to be understood. Within that framework, it is possible to cultivate compatibility. Commercial interests and needs are proving it. You probably don't see that in your business because of legislation that discriminates against Asians concerning the sale of alcohol, but in retail commerce, diversity is compatible. I see it in my shop, and I saw it when I was in the *dukahwallah* trade."

Later when Victoria and Gordon had retired to their bedroom, he commented that following the first occasion when he had met Sarika, he had described her as a very cultured lady. "Now, I have to admit, she is also very perspicacious. Your meeting tomorrow, darling, is going to make headlines for your brave reformist movement."

****

At almost 18 years of age, Priscilla Harrington had blossomed. Tall and adorned with long, lustrous, auburn hair, deep-green eyes, and having a willowy figure, she proved more than just a competent assistant at Sarika's store. As word got around about this attractive new shop assistant, new customers gravitated to Sarika's store.

Priscilla's social life had stalled. Her relationship with Luke whom she had met at the Amahlongwa church camp, had thrived while she frequented the Congregational church services. But it ended when Luke returned to the United States with his missionary parents. Sarika's agreement to employ her as a shop assistant had gladdened her since she had no desire to pursue a vocation as a governess. Her parents, Emily and John, were also relieved that their daughter had found gainful employment as they had become concerned at her languishing on Preston estate.

In Priscilla, Emma recognised a recruit for Victoria's reformist movement. Like herself, Priscilla eschewed the conventional route women were expected to take by being governesses, school or music teachers. Working in Sarika's shop facilitated contact with the wider community and nurtured business skills. Given the success of the store, Emma felt that, in time, Sarika might consider opening a branch of her enterprise elsewhere on the Alex County coast. If that occurred, Emma hoped that she might be appointed as manager. For Priscilla, meanwhile, the attention she was receiving from some of the young estate assistants who frequented the store provided prospects for social engagement.

****

CHAPTER 10

Sarika's appearance at the meeting of reformist ladies held in the Anglican Church Hall on Durban's Berea on a warm January morning destroyed the stereotype perception of Indian females. Of average height, pale-skinned, her lustrous ebony hair neatly coiffed, resplendent in a dark blue sari, and speaking the Queen's English without a hint of Asian accent, Sarika's presence and presentation had her audience in awe.

Introducing her, Victoria briefly outlined Sarika's vintage from serving indenture on an Illovo estate to how she came to be the successful owner of a retail store after the death of her common-law husband and their infant child. "Sarika is the role model of a resilient, determined, and enterprising colonist who merits more than recognition. She merits accolades."

Good morning, Ladies!

Thank you, Victoria, for that introduction but the truth is I would not be here if it was not for your initiative and the guidance you afforded me in the journey that has brought us here today.

Ladies, I am deeply conscious of the significance of this occasion. It has no precedent and so it is an honour accorded to me not merely for being here, but to address you on a topic that few are prepared to consider – compatibility within diversity.

Her Majesty, Queen Victoria implores us to accept and to recognise cultural and ethnic diversity. She has declared that diversity should not discriminate regarding the rights to which a settler is entitled.

Last night in discussing this issue, Victoria's dear husband posed a very pertinent question. He asked how one applies what he termed 'a one-size-fits-

all' approach. He rightly pointed out that compatibility is not even possible amongst white colonists. As an example, he cited the white stevedores at the harbour as not being compatible with him as the executive head of a successful commercial company.

My response to him was that compatibility needs to be understood within the framework of class. But on reflection, the more practical route to compatibility is simply by conformity to standards. If a white stevedore conformed to standards of dress and conduct his presence in the smoking room or the bar of Durban's Royal Hotel should be acceptable to those of the business class who frequent such premises.

Regarding compatibility with those of different ethnicity, it is a reality within the retail field. I see it in my shop in Umzinto. I employ two white ladies as assistants. Many of my customers are white colonists. A common need for supplies and services infuses compatibility.

Unfortunately, that compatibility does not extend beyond my shop because of laws that discriminate against non-Europeans. Here in Durban, you have curfew laws that seem to apply only to Indians and natives. Just over a year ago, a prominent Indian property owner and businessman, Aboobaker Amod, was fined for violating the curfew hours. Yet in the world of commerce, Amod is more affluent than many of the white businessmen in this town.

To my mind what impedes compatibility is the social convention that all Indians are just coolies. That is as grave a misconception as believing that all white people are educated and civilised. Thus, the one-size-fits-all phrase ensures that compatibility is a casualty of social convention. Unfortunately, what is enforcing and perpetuating that social convention is the trend in the passage of discriminatory legislation. What is exacerbating that trend is the increasing number of free or non-indentured Indians – like myself. And the motivation behind it is fear of race domination, which is amplified by social commentators and authors, like Charles Dilke, who propagate non-European races as being inferior.

Social relations are inherently complex even amongst people of the same race. Distinctions based on religion, politics, affluence, inherited titles, education, rank, location, and gender conspire in different ways to frustrate compatibility. Based on that reality, we could only aspire to compatibility within our diversified circumstances by acknowledging conformity within established standards. Such an outlook inevitably would produce different classes of people, irrespective of ethnicity, but each class conforming to the criteria prescribed by convention and thereby jealously preserving it.

What I am arguing is that by conforming to standards, people of different races can be allied in upholding standards. Such compatibility would generate social stability instead of the social barriers that are being erected by discriminatory legislation and the infusion of prejudice and intolerance as a result.

That is the reformist horizon I project. Sadly, however, under our present circumstances, it is idealistic, particularly when we have yet to eliminate what dear Victoria Snell aptly terms 'the suffocating constraints' to which women are subjected.

Sarika's address was acknowledged by hearty applause. Victoria was gushing in thanking her for advancing a practical approach in confronting social convention issues that were vexing social relations. Having opened the floor to questions, Sarika was asked to spell out her standpoint on the Durban Municipality's curfew bylaws.

"Whilst the purpose of the curfew is to deter and to limit the mobility of criminals and ne'er-do-wells, it needs to be applied with discretion. As they stand, the curfew bylaws constitute thinly veiled discrimination against non-

Europeans and as such, project the image that only non-Europeans are lawbreakers."

Asked whether the recent Zulu threat to colonial security had generated social compatibility, Sarika gave two examples. "At the Canonby estate where 200 Indians are employed, the Alexandra County home defence commander, Stephen Bent, supplied 100 firearms and ammunition for use by those Indians in the event of a Zulu attack. In Durban, in the wake of the disaster at Isandlwana, Indian merchants requested permission to form a reserve town guard. Both instances reflect an allegiance to standards and security. Both illustrate that diversity and differences in race need not deter common alliance."

A week after Sarika's address, a report appeared in the *Times of Natal* under the headline – 'Indian speaker attacks social conventions.' Despite the notes Victoria had forwarded to the paper, its account of Sarika's address criticised her suggestion that conformity to social conventions would eliminate the need for racially discriminatory laws. "It is utterly presumptuous for the previously indentured to attempt to lecture colonists on the maintenance of our customs and traditions. It is up to each group to abide by whatever their culture prescribes," opined the *Times.* The report also deprecated Victoria's reformist group for indulging in what it dismissed as "political frippery."

****

The new year of 1880 was hardly underway when tragedy struck the Harrington family. Aged fifteen, David, their youngest child, had been attending the Sunday service of the Congregational Church in Umzinto with Priscilla. While he had welcomed the news that a summer camp would be held at the Amahlongwa Mission, at eighteen years of age, Priscilla felt she had outgrown such ventures and declined to attend. In any case, she was committed to her role as an assistant in Sarika's store which she found socially more exciting than a church camp.

Geographically, the Amahlongwa Mission was closer to the Umpambinyoni River than to the Amahlongwa River. Consequently, the children spent much of their free time splashing about and playing in the Umpambinyoni. As a result of previous floods its 40-yard breadth in places was mostly a shallow, boulder-strewn expanse since the bulk of its water flowed in a deep, narrow channel below a high rock wall.

Usually, one of the adult supervisors was on hand to curb any irresponsible behaviour among the children as they swam in the pools, clambered over the boulders or dived into the deep water of the channel. But a danger lurked deceptively beneath the outer parts of the barely wet expanse of the riverbed – quicksand.

David had wandered away from the splashing and horseplay of the others to the outer expanse, curious to see if any fish were confined in the odd surviving pools since the recent heavy rain. Initially, he ignored the mild suction that he felt underfoot as he plodded along until suddenly, he found his stride immobilised when he could not extricate his feet which had sunk into the muddy silt. Alarmed he began to struggle but his movements caused his legs to sink deeper into the ooze. Alarmed, he began to shout for help. But his cries went unnoticed by the frolicking children. Meanwhile, his frantic movement served only to suck him deeper into the quicksand. At length, his cries were heard, and some children came running across to see what was wrong. By that stage, he had sunk up to his waist and was powerless to extricate himself. With no adult present, one of the children took the initiative to run back to the camp to summon help.

Several minutes passed before one of the missionaries arrived. By that time David, who was short in stature, was up to his chest in the quicksand. Quickly assessing the situation, he realised that there was no point in trying to wade in to free David as he too would then become a captive of the quicksand. Frantically he searched the fringe of the riverbed for a strong branch or part of a tree that had been swept down during the recent flooding. But what he found was neither long enough nor strong enough. If he had been aware, he would have told David to keep still as that would have stopped his descent into the mire. He would also have told David to take deep breaths to give his body some buoyancy. Sadly, however, such advice was not dispensed.

Wriggling to get his hands up to grasp the slender branch the missionary was holding out, served only to cause David to sink even deeper. Anguish enveloped the situation as David became hysterical. The missionary was praying loudly and desperately. The children present were crying. If the assistance of another adult had been available, it would have been possible with the aid of a rope to manoeuvre David gradually out of the clutches of the quicksand. But fate denied that possibility as David's air passages became choked with the mud. Gurgles and bubbles signalled that asphyxiation was ending his life.

All present were overcome with grief. They had witnessed a horrible death which would scar their memories indelibly. Marking the spot of the tragedy, the missionary and the children returned to the camp with their tragic news. After a brief discussion, carrying a rope, a spade and a ladder three of the missionaries returned to the site of the tragedy. One of them thought that by digging around the spot where David's body was encased might loosen the suction of the quicksand. The effort proved partially successful in that the dead boy's head became visible. By extending the ladder over him while two of the missionaries counter-weighted it, the lighter of the three crawled along it with the rope to attempt to fasten it under David's armpits so that his body could be pulled out.

With great exertion and patience, they managed eventually to manoeuvre David's body sideways which reduced the suction of the quicksand and enabled them to haul it out of its temporary grave. Wrapping it in a sheet they carried it back to the camp. Seeing as it was almost dusk, it was decided that nothing further could be done until the next morning. That evening all present at the camp attended a prayer and requiem service for David Harrington.

Many of the children were inconsolable. He had been a quiet yet respected member of the youth group of the Umzinto Congregational Church who was regarded by the church leadership as having the potential to pursue a vocation in missionary work.

First thing the next morning one of the missionaries rode to Umzinto to convey the sad tidings of David Harrington's death and to put out the word that the camp had been closed as a result which required children to be fetched by their parents. One of the other missionaries transported David's body in a carriage to Preston estate. Understandably, the Harrington family was devastated to learn of the horrific circumstances which had ended David's young life. His death was the second the family had suffered having lost a child years earlier to dysentery.

After the initial shock and grief had subsided, John Harrington became obsessed with how this tragedy could have occurred. He wanted answers. The following day, leaving Stewart to manage the estate, he rode to the Congregational Church in Umzinto and requested to meet with the pastor and the missionaries who had been at the Amahlongwa camp. In an uneasy atmosphere, he ascertained that adult supervision of the children on that fateful afternoon had not been scheduled and that nobody seemed able to account for that reason. Dismayed by their response, John said he would arrange to have David's funeral conducted at St Patrick's Church of which he was a member. Furthermore, in all likelihood, Priscilla would no longer be attending services at the Congregational Church.

Two days later a small, sombre group of mourners gathered at St Patrick's where Reverend Joseph Barker conducted a memorial service. The loss of a young life in such a dreadful manner cast a pall over all present. Determined to keep David's memory present in their daily lives, the grief-stricken Harringtons buried his body on Preston estate.

****

When the topic of young David's death was raised at the Wiltshire, Bunting Johnstone, as the veteran of the district, reminded those present of the more dangerous hazard that lurked in rivers. "When I moved here 30 years ago, crocodiles were a real danger in most of these rivers, particularly the Mkomanzi. In 1853 a missionary was attacked by a crocodile while fording the Mkomanzi on his horse. The brute grabbed his leg but mercifully did not succeed in pulling him off his horse. Amazingly the horse was not attacked. The missionary survived but lost a lot of blood."

"Those children playing in the Umpambinyoni would not be at risk as crocodiles prefer the lower reaches of rivers which tend to be deeper, particularly the estuaries where fairly large fish abound," commented Charles Reynolds. "Anyway, the gradual development of lands and human encroachment has eradicated the crocodile menace to a large extent. However, sharks in the Mkomanzi and Mzimkulu River mouths are quite common when the tide is full."

****

Interest in the development of the Mzimkulu for shipping was stimulated at the Royal Hotel bar thanks to a visit by David Aiken. He disclosed that his brother, James, had signed a contract with William Bazley in July 1879 to develop the river mouth for navigation. Although the government had rejected his appeal for funding, he remained confident that in due course it would recognise its obligation. "I was told that the only public works that could be considered were those concerning defence," said David. "There was no appreciation of the fact that if trouble broke out on our southern border, shipping access via the Mzimkulu could land military support within hours whereas wagon transport would take up to ten days."

"Having been part of the negotiations that led to the design and construction of the *Somtseu,* my brother James has pledged to see that works on the river mouth are undertaken. Since last August William Bazley has persisted, often under difficult conditions, to rid the river entrance of patches of rock. That task is almost complete and will be followed by the construction of a pier or training wall which, hopefully, will result in a navigable channel of deep water."

"James Aiken certainly deserves the highest praise for his initiative and enterprise," commented Frank Reynolds. "Opening up the Mzimkulu for trade is urgently needed to counter the growing trade and shipping traffic at Port St Johns. Reports in the *Natal Witness* indicate that the *Adonis* is making regular voyages there."

"So when may we expect the *Somtseu* to make its first entry into the Mzimkulu?"asked Eric Harrison. Responding, David Aiken said the ship's owner, TN Price, had drawn up a schedule which prospectively would commence in May.

****

Sarika regarded her employment of Priscilla as an adroit decision. Not only was she competent and reliable but her attractiveness was drawing some of the younger male customers away from the two European-owned stores in Umzinto – Archibald's and Knox's. That was how Priscilla met Geoffrey Southam. He was an assistant on Ellangowan estate. Aged 25, he had grown up in the Isipingo district and had recently moved to Alex County preferring to work for a privately owned sugar enterprise as opposed to one of the large, corporate-owned ones in Isipingo.

The cottage he rented on Ellangowan was lacking in bed linen and cooking utensils. Riding from Ellangowan, which was south of Park Rynie, Sarika's was the first shop in Umzinto that greeted a traveller arriving from the coastal route. Entering the store his attention was immediately drawn to Priscilla's presence. She was arranging some stock on a shelf as he approached her. Momentarily captivated by her slim figure, peaches and cream complexion, deep green eyes, sensual lips and gracious disposition, he barely managed to acknowledge her greeting. Smiling as she tossed back her cascade of auburn hair, she enquired how she might be of assistance. Although he verbalised what he had come to buy, libidinous thoughts were running riot in his mind.

Resourceful in procuring his domestic needs, Priscilla was not shy to engage him in conversation which is how she learned about his circumstances and role on Ellangowan. Enamoured by her charm and eager to spend time with her, on impulse Geoffrey asked her if she had any plans for the coming weekend as he would like to invite her to go boating with him on the Mkomanzi. Priscilla did not hesitate in accepting his invitation, saying her parents were unlikely to object.

At dinner that evening John and Emily were delighted to agree to their daughter's outing with Geoffrey Southam. "I've heard that boating near the Drift Hotel on the Mkomanzi is very popular on weekends. I just hope the weather will be kind to you. Anyway, I look forward to meeting Mr Southam," said John.

Grateful that her parents had not demurred in the matter, Priscilla was elated at the prospect of a change in the routine of her socially restricted life on Preston estate. From her brief meeting and interaction with Geoffrey at the store, she had felt a spontaneous frisson of excitement. She perceived a hint of derring-do in him which appealed to her in addition to his physical appearance and long, dark brown hair. Emma, who had been present in the shop that morning and discretely observed the interaction between the two of them, expressed positive thoughts about him. "He seems a solid, likeable lad who reminds me of Simon Prescott on Dewsbury," she remarked.

Arriving early on Saturday morning at Preston, Geoffrey made his acquaintance with the Harringtons before he and Priscilla set off in a two-seater carriage for the Drift Hotel. During the almost two hour journey their conversation topics varied between family issues and future prospects. Upon arriving at the hotel, they ordered refreshments before setting off to the small jetty and climbing into the river craft Geoffrey had hired.

It was a pleasant autumn day. The surface of the river was smooth as Geoffrey plied the oars heading upstream. “There’s a spot further up which has a small beach on the same side of the river as the hotel where we can come ashore almost without getting your feet wet. I understand there’s a pleasant glade in the vicinity where we could relax for a while before returning to the hotel for a late lunch.”

In due course they came ashore, secured the craft and set off a short distance to an open area with a park-like lawn. Settling down next to each other, Geoffrey thanked her for her assistance in selecting the linen and bedding he had bought for his cottage and amorously suggested that she might like to try it out. To his surprise Priscilla said she looked forward to it and kissed him. In response, he took her into his arms. “I love your beautiful auburn hair. It is so unusual,” he said stroking it. An hour passed rapidly as the lovers plied each other with endearments and embraces until a sudden change in the weather interrupted their passions.

A strong wind had churned up the surface of the river. “It’s going to be a challenge rowing back to the hotel,” remarked Geoffrey. His words were no understatement. The gale whipped the river surface into small waves and showered them with sheets of spray. Geoffrey became alarmed for two reasons: he was barely making any headway rowing into the wind and water was beginning to splash into the craft. Without any means of reducing the inflow of water, he realised that there was a risk of the craft sinking. On that basis he decided to return to the small beach, haul the craft safely out of the water and return on foot to the hotel.

Struggling against the howling gale while trying to negotiate the uneven ground strewn with stones and rocks from previous floods, Priscilla managed to twist her ankle. Holding onto Geoffrey for support as she hobbled along, the return journey to the hotel took a lot longer. But at length, after explaining to the hotel proprietor, Mrs Nelson, where he had left the river craft, Geoffrey had Priscilla seated in the dining room with her painful ankle elevated on a chair. While waiting to be served their meal they sipped glasses of sherry Geoffrey had ordered from the bar.

"I am afraid you will have to miss a few days at Sarika's because the treatment for a swollen ankle requires rest and keeping your foot elevated. It should also be tightly bandaged," he advised. "Thank you, Dr Southam!" jested, Priscilla. "Are you going to visit your convalescing patient daily and exercise your bedside manner?" she enquired teasingly. Geoffrey's response was to lean over and plant a kiss on her forehead.

Advertisement in the *Natal Mercury*

****

On Saturday May 8, 1880, the *Somtseu,* carrying 50 tonnes of cargo, became the first vessel to navigate the entrance of the Mzimkulu. Years of speculation, lobbying and frustration seemed finally at an end. However, the occasion was not without drama. A hawser rope from the lighter which the *Somtseu* was towing, fouled one of her propellers which inhibited steerage and caused the little ship to brush up against a rocky outcrop. Returning to Durban resulted in the *Somtseu* being out of commission for a month as the damage to the plates in her bow required considerable attention. In her absence, TN Price despatched the *Buffalo* to Port Shepstone in fulfilment of his undertaking to provide a regular service.

Advertisement in the *Natal Mercury*, May 10, 1880

Besides the work carried out in the mouth of the river to remove rocks, at wagon drift, almost three miles up the river, a warehouse was under construction alongside a wharf where incoming and outgoing cargo could be stored. In the months that followed, records showed that an average of sixty tonnes of cargo a month was successfully delivered to the warehouse.

Back in the Umzinto district after spending a month with his brother James at the warehouse, David Aiken provided the regulars at the Royal Hotel bar with details of the sea carriage taking place on the Mzimkulu. "The most significant aspect is the saving in time and transport costs. It means that within

12 hours of the ship leaving Durban, goods that would take eight to ten days by wagon to reach Port Shepstone would be packed in the warehouse. In terms of costs, it works out to a saving of £4 per tonne." Asked to provide details about the nature of the cargo, he said groceries, flour and rice made up the bulk of the imports. The balance comprised construction materials and native goods. "At the moment, the *Somtseu* is ferrying only wool, hides, lime, fish and timber to Durban. But soon sugar, fruit and dairy products will be part of her return cargo."

In response to the bullish sentiment in the bar, proprietor William Thornton provided a round of free drinks for all. "The *Somtseu's* voyage is the best news we have ever had in Alex County. The significant thing about it is that it has been achieved by private enterprise – not the government," exclaimed James Ross heartily.

Addressing David Aiken, Frank Reynolds said he understood that the demolition work Bazley had done on the river mouth was paid for by David's brother, James. "I hope you are claiming that back from the government," he advised.

"Yes, we have been badgering the colonial engineer, Albert Hime, since last October for payments. His response has been that the government will consider payment only once Bazley has completed the job. Now our total expenses amount to £548 of which we have paid Bazley £348. But the work on constructing the training wall is going to take many months. We are hoping that with elections coming up in September political pressure can be applied as we cannot afford to be out of pocket to that extent," replied Aiken.

Despite the jubilation at the relative ease of the *Somtseu's* maiden voyage to the Mzimkulu, the months ahead proved that it was not all plain sailing. Of 17 trips the *Somtseu* made between May and November that year, conditions in the river mouth forced her to abort nine of them and to return to Durban without having discharged her cargo.

CHAPTER 11

In several respects, 1880 certainly proved to be a watershed year in Alexandra County.

Chatter amongst patrons in the Wiltshire following the establishment of shipping on the Mzimkulu concerned changes in the official ranks within Alexandra County. William Pigg noted that Resident Magistrate Lucas had been granted twelve months leave to visit England. "We have hardly seen him in office since the winter of 1878. John Hathorn is the latest acting magistrate in the County. Before him we had Frederick Baker and Thomas Reynolds."

"Well, at least our law-and-order department has grown," observed Bunting Johnstone. "For years it was left to Field Cornet Brander to have his own security detail. Now we have an actual police force headed by Constable JC Whitwell. I see the colonial government has also increased the salaries. Whitwell will be earning £84 a year, the same as our new gaoler, Christopher McGuiness. Constable Whitwell is assisted by two Indian constables each on £24 a year and twelve native constables each earning £12 annually."

"Although I am fully in favour of white control of all aspects of government, I have to question the extremely low remuneration levels of employment for the Indian and native constables," remarked Captain Tucker. "They are unrealistic and are going to encourage bribery as those policemen illicitly seek to augment their salaries. To my mind, such niggardly pay structures suggest that our rulers don't care too much for the maintenance of law and order. Besides, there is also a personal risk factor in police work."

“I don’t agree,” countered Charles Reynolds. “It’s not a full-time job for those native constables. They are each given a full uniform, and their duties are assigned by means of a roster. By their liaisons within the native location potential criminal elements can be checked thereby making our neighbourhoods more secure and the cost of maintaining order minimised.”

“A perceptive comment, Charles, which reminds me of what I read about how our little island homeland runs its empire: on a shoestring! We see it clearly in Alex County where they have yet to pay the Aikens for making navigation possible on the Mzimkulu and, of course, in the provision of funds for bridges and proper roads,” ventured James McMillan.

****

Distance was the only impediment in Sarika and Hugh Lawson’s relationship. She was reluctant to sleep over at Crofton which meant that Hugh had to risk being away from the estate at night if he wanted to be with her in Umzinto. A solution that occurred to her was to ask Emma if she and Peter would sleep over at Michaelhouse. They agreed without hesitation as facilities in Sarika’s residence were vastly superior to those in their cottage on Dewsbury.

Sarika’s cooking was an additional benefit for Hugh spending a night with her. But it meant stocking Crofton’s kitchen with utensils, condiments and the food sources that Sarika needed to prepare her signature dishes. As their love affair deepened, Sarika found she was spending nights more frequently on Crofton than in Michaelhouse.

Her shop was thriving and posting increasing profits. She had long since increased Emma’s salary to £5 a month. Priscilla’s competence was such that she could run the store singlehandedly. Perhaps, she speculated, it was time to progress in a new direction.

Relations between Geoffrey Southam and Priscilla Harrington had blossomed. While convalescing from her twisted her ankle she had enjoyed almost daily visits from him. Her parents were delighted with their relationship and anticipated wedding bells in the not-too-distant future. Match-making in Alexandra County in 1880 was difficult because of the population disparity between white males and females: 263:206.

****

The key issue in the 1880 elections was whether Natal should remain governed by officials appointed by London or become self-ruling within the empire. A lively meeting held in Umzinto by the Alexandra County Association had indicated a preference for self-government. Challenging the sitting council representative, William Hawksworth, for the sole South Coast seat on the council was Thomas Reynolds. Since 1877, as the largest sugar estate owners in the County, Thomas and his sons, Frank and Charles, had become a significant economic force.

Following the announcement of his candidacy, Thomas held a public meeting at the courthouse in Umzinto. Apart from indicating his support for the policy of self-rule, he boasted of the tram rail network that was being erected in the fields of his largest estate. A first of its kind in the county, its innovation would accelerate the dispersal of harvested cane to his mill as well as proving labour-saving. To emphasise his financial stature, he said his company had "a substantial balance on the right side."

As a vote sweetener or what he termed a "harvest home celebration," he invited all those present at the meeting to a free lunch at the Royal Hotel where, as a press report phrased it, "a capital cold collation was served" and drinks flowed freely.

Chatter at the bar afterwards was about Thomas's election prospects. "It looks as though my father will win the seat," said Frank Reynolds. "He received 40 candidate endorsements to Hawksworth's 36. Notably, Field Cornet Brander has endorsed the Reynolds ticket. Samuel Crookes of Ellingham and William Bazley are backing Hawksworth."

"Another significant indicator of support is that of the *Natal Mercury.* Owned by John Robinson who is campaigning for self-government, media support increases the prospects of winning," noted district surgeon Dr Lancelot Booth.

"That's true. Although Hawksworth also supports self-government, the *Mercury* has shown preference for Reynolds because Hawksworth's performance in the council has been lacklustre. As a long-standing council member, Robinson's opinion of Hawksworth is undoubtedly reflected by the *Mercury's* endorsement of Reynolds," remarked William Thornton.

"While most candidates are calling for railway construction in their manifestoes, I think Reynolds is being sensible by prioritising roads and bridges over railways. Alexandra County will get railroads eventually. But our first need has always been bridges and proper roads," observed John Redman.

****

A major fun sports day hosted by the Alexandra Mounted Rifles was advertised for Thursday and Friday, September 9th and 10th, at Park Rynie. Since Priscilla's ankle had righted itself and she was back at Sarika's store, Geoffrey enquired whether she would be allowed to take the day off and accompany him to the sports day. Sarika was only too happy to oblige.

On the appointed day, Geoffrey fetched her from Preston estate but instead of heading to the sports ground, he pointed the horse southwards in the direction of Ellangowan. "I have a surprise for you. We'll spend the day at Ellangowan instead," he informed Priscilla whose spontaneous kiss on his lips indicated her approval. Arriving at the estate after their brief detour, they headed directly to Geoffrey's cottage. "You said you would like to test the bed linen you advised me to buy, but first please put my new kitchen utensils to work by making tea," he said as he hugged her.

Seated side by side in the small open-plan area of the cottage having enjoyed their tea, Priscilla wasted no time in venting her libidinous mood. Within minutes she had removed Geoffrey's shirt and was groping him. In turn, he loosened her bodice and was caressing her substantial bosoms. In that half-undressed state, they lurched into the bedroom and completed disrobing.

Consumed by desire and feeling totally uninhibited, the next hour passed in a blur of erotic pleasure. Although it was Priscilla's first sexual experience, the vigour of her assault on Geoffrey's erogenous zones dispelled any indication of her novice status. Presently, hunger of a different kind beckoned. "I'm famished and am going to see what I can prepare in your kitchen to eat," announced Priscilla. To Geoffrey's amazement she bustled through into the kitchen still naked. Minutes later she returned to ask if an omelette would be to his liking. Suddenly feeling recharged, he joined her in the kitchen and commenced a fresh round of foreplay in between her tending the cooking of the omelette.

They passed the afternoon in bed together until Priscilla said she had better be returning to Preston. "As the advertisement promised, we have had a fun sports day, but at Ellangowan - not Park Rynie!" she jested as she dressed and tidied her hair into shape for her return home.

****

Frank Reynolds' prediction of his father winning the election proved correct. By the end of September, the results from Alexandra and Alfred counties were finalised: Reynolds – 62 votes; Hawksworth – 27. With his sons, Frank and Charles, living and working full time on their Alex County sugar estates and with no meeting scheduled for the colonial legislature until the New Year, Thomas spent most of his time on his Oaklands estate in Victoria County. His absence from the constituency was criticised by Hawksworth.

In the Wiltshire, Charles Reynolds claimed Hawksworth was displaying a case of sour grapes. "Of the 36 endorsements Hawksworth received for his candidacy, the fact that only 27 of those voted for him, should caution him to keep a low profile. Besides, there's a political situation brewing in the Transvaal, so once again, as we saw last year, sittings of the legislative council are suspended. Anyway, between Frank and myself, we can monitor things locally in the absence of our Father."

****

Sarika's thoughts about opening a second store gained momentum following the two-day fun gathering in Park Rynie. Hugh had spent some time there chatting to the locals from whom he learned of their inconvenience having to travel to Umzinto to access the range of goods that a shop like Sarika's carried. During one of her sleepovers at Crofton, the subject of a second store was discussed.

"When you consider that Park Rynie has the only proper racecourse on the South Coast which attracts punters from far and wide on a regular basis, the lack of a general store stands out like a sore thumb. So, there's a market to exploit by locating a replica of your Umzinto store in Park Rynie. Another reason is the string of sugar estates – Ellingham, Woodhouse Lea, Preston, Ellangowan and Crofton. They are all closer to Park Rynie than to Umzinto. With exception of Crofton, each one has a family with a variety of needs. A branch of Sarika's in Park Rynie would be very convenient for them," said Hugh.

"Well, Hugh, what you have said has not merely convinced me. It's excited me. When I worked with my late Father in the *dukahwallah* trade, finding new customers was always a thrill because it grew the business. For a while I have felt a lack of challenge. My Umzinto store has a solid customer base. It turns a good profit, but I sense a degree of boredom in Emma. Like me she needs a new challenge. Without hesitation, I would post Emma to manage the Park Rynie store."

Having agreed that Hugh would advise on a suitable location in Park Rynie, the first step was to consult Alex Brander as the Land Commissioner and for him to draw up the plot details which would then be conveyed to the Surveyor General's Office for registration. Later, in bed, before passions became inflamed, Hugh asked her if she had ever thought about buying a sugar estate.

****

Stewart Harrington's social life was non-existent. Two years had passed since his brief liaison with Lucy ended. His consistent work ethic routine on Preston absorbed his energy and preoccupied his interest. His close relationship with Eric on Woodhouse Lea enabled him to learn a great deal in assisting his father to optimise the potential of Preston and thereby produce better sugar, coffee and maize harvests.

While Emily and John admired their son's passion and commitment, at 20 years of age, they worried about his lack of social growth. When the sports fun day was advertised at Park Rynie, they urged him to take a day off and see a different side of life. Almost reluctantly, he agreed. So as not to clash with Priscilla's visit to the fun day, he attended on the day after her (ostensibly) scheduled visit with Geoffrey.

His interest in horses immediately drew him to the gymkhana. Two teams were in contest – one from Richmond and the other from Ifafa – to clear the most fences on the course. Having noticed that one of the riders in the Ifafa team was a girl his interest and attention immediately perked up. Effortlessly she cleared one fence after another with minimal coaxing of her horse and was instrumental in the Ifafa team winning. When she dismounted, he thought about going across to introduce himself, but shied away when he saw a young man talking to her and leading her horse back into the temporary stable.

Although somewhat disappointed, he noted that a polo match was one of the scheduled afternoon events and wondered if she would be participating in it. Drifting away from the paddocks Stewart headed for the parade ground where the Alexandra Mounted Rifles were displaying their marching skills in a military tattoo.

Since it was about lunch time, he went to the food tent and selected a large slice of beef accompanied by beans and sweet potato smothered in gravy. To his surprise, he saw the girl from the Ifafa team seated at a table eating her lunch in the company of the same young man who had been with her after the gymkhana. She was casually dressed, having removed her jodhpurs and riding jacket. Eyeing her discretely, he noted that she had short, dark hair. Her tanned face suggested her preference for outdoor life. Conversation between her and the young man seemed intermittent until suddenly he left the table.

Eager to make her acquaintance yet at the same time hesitant lest he might be intruding on an issue that had caused her lunch partner to leave rather abruptly, nonetheless, Stewart decided to throw caution to the wind. Quietly he got up and crossed over to her table.

"Hello! I hope I am not intruding. My name is Stewart, and I just wanted to compliment you on your riding in the gymkhana. Will you be participating in the polo match this afternoon?"

"Oh! Thank you, Stewart. Please have a seat. No, you're not intruding. That was my brother, Roger. He's gone to check on the stable. My name is Patricia, but everyone calls me Trish. Yes, I'm in the Ifafa team for the polo match. Do you do much riding?"

"Well, my riding is simply local visits to Umzinto or to the nearest store," he replied diffidently as he processed the fact that the young man was her brother. Somewhat relieved that their introductory exchange had been friendly, Stewart felt emboldened to move the conversation onto a more personal level. “So, Trish, what’s life like down in Ifafa?”

“I live with my parents on an estate where we breed horses which is why I am passionate about equestrian events. I’ve been riding since I was seven years’ old and my aim in life is to own a stable of horses for equestrian and racing events – not transport. With its racecourse, Park Rynie is already an established horse racing venue alongside Durban and Pietermaritzburg. So, there is a commercial future here for that. What’s your line of work, Stewart? Are you from this area?”

Impressed if not somewhat intimidated by her direct and confident articulation, he replied that he was an assistant on the nearby Preston estate which he hoped to inherit one day. She smiled in response but said she had to get back to the stable. “We can chat further after the polo match,” she said as she dashed off. Heartened by her response, Stewart wandered over to the refreshment tent bought a beer and waited for the polo teams to take the field.

Trish was the only female rider when the two teams of four riders each took the field. The Ifafa team’s opponents were the current champions who hailed from Mooi River. Within minutes of the first of the scheduled five chukkas the Mooi River team scored twice. At the end of that chukka, as the rules permit, several riders changed mounts, Trish being one of them. From the onset of the second chukka, the pace of her new mount enabled her to intercept a long shot by one of the Mooi River riders and re-direct it towards the goal mouth. Cantering after the ball, some 30 yards from the goal mouth her swinging mallet connected and drove the ball firmly through the uprights.

After four chukkas, each being seven minutes in duration, the scores were level at three goals each. Excitement mounted among the spectators as the riders took to the field for the final chukka. During the regulation three-minute interval between chukkas, the Mooi River riders had huddled together for a quick team talk. Their reputation as the champions was under threat from the relatively inexperienced Ifafa team which, to add to their consternation, included a female rider.

Several unsuccessful shots at goal by both teams ensured that the fifth and final chukka was a nail-biting affair. In the final seconds, Trish managed to intercept and re-direct a wild hit by one of the Mooi River riders. Although more than 70 yards from the goal mouth, she was able to maintain control over the ball for a fair distance. Seeing a challenge looming, she flicked the ball across to one of her teammates. He was able to intercept it and despatch it decisively into the goal mouth. The match was over. Ifafa had defeated Mooi River by four goals to three.

Celebrations marked the rest of the afternoon. Dignified in defeat, the Mooi River riders were gracious in commending Trish on how well she had acquitted herself. Later in the refreshment tent, sipping a goblet of punch, Trish turned her attention to Stewart inviting him to spend a weekend in Ifafa where she would show him around her stables. He beamed with pleasure in accepting her offer.

At dinner that night, Stewart recounted his day at the sports fun day and his meeting with Trish who had won a gymkhana event and scored a goal in the polo match. Emily and John were delighted to hear of his liaison with this talented young lady. Priscilla was particularly interested in obtaining more details about Trish because she recognised the relevance of her equestrian ability for Victoria Snell's reformist movement. Later that evening she penned an article about Trish to Victoria and mailed it on her way to work at Sarika's the next morning. A week later the sports page of the *Mercury* included reference to Trish in an article on Park Rynie's sports day headed "Lady rider excels in equestrian events."

That *Mercury* article served to enliven discussion amongst the regulars at the Royal Hotel bar. Old timer James Ross thought it was unacceptable for a woman to be playing polo in the first place, never mind as a replacement for a man in the team. "Where is this going to lead?" he asked irascibly. Eric Harrison's acquaintance with Victoria Snell's reformist movement enabled him to present a more informed view.

"If we look at the bigger picture, James, we should not ignore the role women are playing and need to play in many parts of the colony to ensure roles are fulfilled. I refer to ferry keepers, post mistresses, pound mistresses, librarians, school principals, highly trained nurses. My wife, Frances, has been Beneva estate's secretary for 15 years handling all the issues involved with indentured labour. She also recently defended our home and children against that axe-wielding intruder by shooting him. We need to accept that the many tasks women undertake are competently and efficiently performed. So the argument that they are weak and need to be socially constrained is untrue and unfair."

"Anyway, James, the young lass who played in the Ifafa polo team was a substitute for one of their regular riders who had injured his arm. So, I don't think it means the fairer sex is going to elbow men out of polo teams. Ifafa would have had to take the field one rider short if the lass had not been available to participate."

"As district surgeon I see many aspects of colonial life in my travels around Alex County and concur with Eric. We are living in a frontier environment where conventional roles Victorian society esteems to be cast in stone simply don't apply given the reality of prevailing circumstances," observed Dr Lancelot Booth.

"My son, Stewart, is an acquaintance of the young lass referred to in that *Mercury* article. He told me she has been riding horses since she was seven years of age and that her goal in life is to run a stable of horses trained for equestrian purposes. I think that is admirable. Before my wife and I left Lancashire, we noted that women were being employed in technical positions in textile factories in Preston," John Harrington pointed out.

“Gentlemen, I think we must acknowledge that change evolves. Here’s a curved ball for you to consider: Would you be objecting if instead of me behind the bar counter I hired a buxom barmaid?” enquired proprietor William Thornton jovially.

****

Sarika was not a person who procrastinated. Before returning to Umzinto following her latest Crofton sleepover, Hugh accompanied her to the small business area of Park Rynie to get an idea of where she could site her new store. They decided on a vacant plot in the vicinity of the tavern. There was a grove of trees on the south side of the plot which would afford shade for customers’ horses and prove something of a barrier to the gusty south westerly winds. Back in Umzinto, she made an appointment with Land Commissioner Brander to mark out the half-acre plot she wanted and to register it. “Since the establishment of the racecourse, economic activity has increased with cottages offering accommodation to racing punters. As a result, there has been an increase in land prices,” remarked Brander as he wrote out a receipt for the £4 Sarika was paying to purchase the plot.

She then posted a letter to William Joyner enquiring if he was available to construct her new store.

****

CHAPTER 12

Opportunities to repeat the erotic romp they had indulged in when they were supposed to have been at the Park Rynie sports day did not materialise in the weeks that followed. Instead, by the end of October Priscilla began to experience bouts of nausea and loss of appetite. Embarrassed to confide in her mother she approached Sarika who confirmed her suspicions. She was pregnant. Sympathetic to her situation, Sarika assured her that she could continue working in the shop for as long as she felt she could manage. Sarika also agreed to accompany her to Preston and be in support when Priscilla broke the news to her parents.

If they were upset, Emily and John did not show it nor did they clamour for Priscilla and Geoffrey to marry in haste. "We don't want to increase your anxiety by placing any demands on you. Whatever you and Geoffrey decide, we will abide by," said John. "What's done is done. Pregnancy can be life threatening. The less anxiety to which you are subjected the better." Tearfully, Priscilla hugged her parents grateful for their understanding and acceptance.

When Geoffrey called at the shop the next day, Sarika summoned him and Priscilla into her office and gently told him the news. Although somewhat shocked, he too was accepting saying he would like to discuss the way forward with Priscilla before making any decision or announcement.

Privately, Emily saw Priscilla's pregnancy as filling the void David's tragic death had left in the family.

****

Stewart received word from Trish inviting him for the weekend she had promised. The Glenmore estate of her parents, Angus and Frida Smith, was about an hour's ride from Preston. She was waiting for him when he arrived and introduced him to her parents and her brother, Roger. "I've just been mucking out the stables, so that accounts for my boots and farm girl attire," she said as he took in her very informal appearance. "Let's go inside and have tea. I need to change out of these smelly, horsey clothes!"

Returning to the sitting room a few minutes later, Stewart was pleasantly surprised by her transformed appearance thinking she looked quite feminine. After indulging in some small talk with her family over tea and muffins, he accompanied Trish to the paddock. "There are fifteen horses here we are training for gymkhana events. They're all appaloosas which are the best breed for gymkhanas."

Stewart was then given a lecture on the various events that can feature at a gymkhana. In detail Trish described what was required for a flag race, a barrel race, a stake race and a pole bending race. "As you can appreciate, that requires an awful lot of training and practice. Just clearing fences as I did at Park Rynie is straightforward."

Suitably impressed, he asked her if she was going to demonstrate any of those challenges. "Tomorrow Roger and I will set up poles on our course to demonstrate a barrel race," said. "Anyway, Stewart, enough about horses for the moment, we need to find out more about each other. We'll go the courtyard where it's cooler and have a chat."

Sipping glasses of fruit cordial, Trish listened to Stewart's brief account of his life from when he was born in Victoria County in 1860 to the family's move to Preston and the tragic death of his young brother. "Actually, David's death was the second one we have suffered. I was about four when dysentery claimed the life of little Mark who was barely a year old," he added sombrely.

"Dysentery is such a dreadful disease," remarked Trish sympathetically. "Fortunately, our family has been spared such a tragedy. We have not been in Natal as long as you have. In fact, both Roger and I were born in England. He's your age and I'm 17. My parents ran a small holding in Devonshire and immigrated in 1871 on the settler scheme offered by the Natal government. They got a good price for their Devonshire small holding and so were able to buy Glenmore outright, invest in the appaloosas and develop the estate."

After lunch, Trish suggested they saddle up and go for a ride. "There's a pleasant spot I know of on the Ifafa River where we can water the horses and paddle our feet." Stewart was impressed by the way she navigated the route to the river which indicated that she had made the ride often. After almost half an hour they reached the spot Trish had mentioned. The river's flow was impeded by several large boulders around which fairly deep pools had formed. They led their horses to where they had easy access to drink before tethering them to a nearby tree. "We don't want them bolting for some reason," she cautioned.

Having removed their boots, they sat side by side on one of the boulders with their toes ruffling the water surface. Reaching for Stewart's hand, she said she was pleased to have met him. "You're the first male acquaintance I have made who is interested in what I do and not just interested because of my gender. I've had to endure some spiteful types who have ridiculed me and resented the fact that someone of the fairer sex can ride a horse competitively. In that regard I really appreciated the graciousness of the Mooi River team in complimenting me after the polo match."

"My social contact with girls was limited to one I met on a Congregational Church camp. But nothing came of it as our interests were incompatible. So, Trish thank you for the compliment you have just paid me," said Stewart as he leaned across and kissed her on the cheek. They passed the next few moments in a silent embrace which was disrupted by a loud splash in the water. They both saw what had caused it. Just yards away a crocodile had plunged into the water and was headed into the pool in which they were dangling their feet.

In the nick of time, they both scrambled away from the edge of the boulder as the crocodile surfaced where their feet had been just seconds earlier. Clearly shaken by what could have been a tragedy, Trish clung to Stewart in shock. "I am horrified by this. I've come here several times alone and never seen a crocodile or noted any signs that one could be present. The realisation of what could have happened to me is too ghastly to think about." In response, Stewart hugged her tightly and said that the brute must have been alerted by the movement their feet were making in the water and decided to investigate.

Mounting their horses they rode back slowly to the estate. "After that shock, I need a big mug of tea," declared Trish as they returned the horses to the stable. At supper that evening their brush with tragedy was discussed. "It is widely believed that with the exception of the Mkomanzi and probably the Mzimkulu, there are no longer crocodiles in the rivers of Alexandra County," said Trish's father, Angus. "However, I do remember John Bazley advising me soon after we arrived here to be wary of crocodiles in the Ifafa River. So, Trish, it upsets me to think that you have been riding to the Ifafa alone in the past. Thank heavens, you were never attacked. Anyway, tomorrow you will show me where this crocodile lurks so I can shoot it."

Straight after breakfast, Sunday morning, with Angus, Roger and Stewart following, Trish led them to the area where the crocodile had been seen. Cautiously they surveyed the riverbanks and the shallows but saw no sign of their quarry. "It's possibly sitting on the bottom of one of these deepish pools which is why it is difficult to detect. Perhaps if we drop in a few heavy rocks, it might be forced to move," Roger suggested. His idea worked. Sure enough, there was a thrashing noise as the crocodile rapidly surfaced and made its way toward the riverbank. Aiming to kill a moving crocodile is particularly difficult as its eyes are the only vulnerable part of its body. On his second attempt, Angus wounded the reptile in the upper part of its right rear leg, slowing it down somewhat as it headed for its secluded lair in the riverbank. That gave Angus time to manoeuvre in front of it. At close range he killed it by despatching a bullet through one of its eyes.

"Well done, Papa!" exclaimed Trish. "Let's hope there are no others around."

"I hope so, as this one looks fairly young judging by its length. There's a law that encourages the eradication of what are called noxious creatures. If you can prove you killed a crocodile or a jackal, you can claim a payment of ten shillings from the government. But having to hack the head off this brute and transport it either to the magistrate or the Field Cornet in Umzinto as proof, is hardly worth the effort," said Angus dismissively.

After lunch, as promised, with Roger's assistance, Trish set up the poles on the training course to demonstrate the barrel race. Having selected her favourite appaloosa and saddled up she gave a cantering demonstration of how the horse threaded its way in and out of the poles. Watching her at close quarters, Stewart noted the rhythm which required rider and horse to fling their weight in unison in order not to upset the poles. It also occurred to him that few men could manage such fluid riding.

When she dismounted at the end of the display, he embraced her saying, "You make it look so easy and natural but I'm sure it took a lot of practice." She smiled, nodded her head and squeezed his hand. Accompanying her to the stables to fetch his horse as it was time to return to Preston, she thanked him for his visit. "When will I see you again, Stewart? I have really enjoyed your company."

"You're welcome to spend time with us on Preston. Just let me know. I'm not much good at writing letters but I'll try and send one soon."

Looking fervently into his eyes, she said she looked forward to staying in contact. Then she hugged and kissed him ardently. He reciprocated her kiss but before emotions grew any more delicate, he mounted his horse and departed swiftly.

With an hour's ride ahead of him before he reached Preston, Stewart had time to reflect on seventeen-year-old Trish Smith. Foremost in his assessment was that she did not bait his attraction. She was an exceptionally down to earth person bereft of shallow airs and graces. That was what appealed to him. She was also very mature for her age. He ascribed that to her love of outdoor life and her special interest in horses. While physically she lacked the voluptuous appeal that had inspired his dalliance with Lucy at the Congregational church, that was more than compensated for by her modesty and sincerity. All in all, he concluded that he would like her to be part of his future.

****

William Joyner had agreed to construct Sarika's store in Park Rynie based on the same plans as the Umzinto one. However, he cautioned her that prices had increased over the past three years. Consequently, he estimated that construction would cost around £60 and asked for a deposit of £20. In her favour, he said, was that the plot she had bought was on flat, even ground, unlike the Umzinto one which had required a great deal of excavation in locating her house.

In 1876, Sarika had had the insurance money from Michael's death to finance the construction of her residence and shop together with its stock. To afford the full £60 Joyner was asking and at least a further £40 to purchase basic stock for the new shop, she needed to obtain a bank loan and duly made an application for £100 to Natal Bank. One of the conditions the Bank specified was the provision of a surety in the event she defaulted on the loan. To fulfil that requirement, she asked Victoria and Gordon Snell if they would agree to provide that cover. They promptly assented and invited her to stay with them when she came to Durban to sign the necessary documentation.

For Victoria it was an honour to assist Sarika in her new business venture. She saw it as exemplifying the reformist policies she espoused - promoting women's rights and welfare. Added to that was Sarika's Asian identity. Victoria was adamant that ethnicity should not be an excuse to erect social barriers. Nor should it impede conformity to accepted standards. As always, Gordon admired his wife's reformist campaign and was happy to append his signature as surety to Sarika's loan application.

****

Sarika was fortunate to return to Umzinto before communication between Alexandra County and Durban was cut off. Exceptionally heavy rain late in November produced floods which transformed the Mkomanzi River into a raging torrent that swept away the pont and all light river craft. The wagon tracks which passed for roads, of course, became impassable.

But Alexandra County's isolation was not complete thanks to the sea link the *Somtseu* provided with Durban. The ship was able to make a series of voyages into the Mzimkulu bringing badly needed supplies which were distributed by carts and wagons northwards to Umzinto and the settler nodes on the coast.

At the Wiltshire, Charles Reynolds remarked that his Father had presented a petition to the council from residents of both Alex and Alfred counties calling for the construction of proper harbour works on the Mzimkulu. "Our reliance on the *Somtseu* as the only means of communication and supply during the floods more than justifies the expense required for wharf construction. Great effort and expense has gone into the erection of sidings and stations along the railway from Durban to Maritzburg, so it is only fair and reasonable that the *Somtseu* should be able to load and unload goods alongside a proper wharf instead of the rickety little jetty that is now is use."

"That's a sensible request, Charles, but I remain a sceptic. For 15 years our appeals for a bridge over the Mkomanzi have been ignored. The council's outlook is focused only on railway development. Construction of the line to Ladysmith is the new priority. Thomas Reynolds has an uphill battle on his hands trying to provide for the South Coast's needs," said Captain Tucker disconsolately.

****

Thanks to a revolution in transport, Christmas 1880 was a special one for many families who wished to spend it visiting relatives in either the environs of Durban or Pietermaritzburg. After almost five years, the railway line from Durban to Pietermaritzburg was officially opened on December 1, 1880. Pulling five carriages, the locomotive managed the inaugural journey to Pietermaritzburg in just under six hours. In 1863 when Bishop Colenso had travelled by ox wagon from Pietermaritzburg to Durban, his journey took nearly three days.

The celebration of Christmas 1880 was a Prescott family reunion. For the families of Simon and Victoria, it was especially memorable because of their train journey to be with Anne at Taunton Manor. Anticipating a great demand for tickets for the trip to Pietermaritzburg station, Victoria made the seat reservations well in advance. Although in 1867 Simon and Cynthia had experienced train travel during their honeymoon in the Cape, for their two boys, George and James, train travel was a novelty. It began at Isipingo where the Prescotts boarded the train on the newly opened line to Durban. Disembarking at Durban station, they met Gordon, Victoria and Lily. The children were fascinated by the sights, sounds and bustle of the station as they waited for a porter to load their suitcases into the coach they had reserved in the first-class section.

The journey from Durban station involved several stops of which the ones at Botha's Hill and Camperdown were quite lengthy allowing passengers time to buy food and refreshments at the canteens. George and James relished the opportunity to stretch their legs along the station platforms. Upon arriving at the rail terminus in Pietermaritzburg, they hired a carriage to ferry them to Martin and Anne Pryce's home in Taunton Manor, a distance of almost four miles.

George, aged almost ten and his cousin Lily, who had just celebrated her 12th birthday, seemed compatible in each other's company playing in the tree house Martin had built. Eleanor entertained James in the playroom. By the sounds of their chatter and laughter, the two four-year-olds got on well together while also keeping baby Elizabeth amused.

While having a few beers on the patio, business matters dominated the conversation amongst the three men. Legal business from the Natal government concerning railway development was keeping Martin's branch of Goodricke's permanently busy. "As the line moves progressively northward, we are inundated with land expropriations, fencing issues and compensations to the point that I am really looking forward to our three weeks break in January which we are going to spend in the Cape."

"We've had a bumper sugar harvest in Alex County, so Dewsbury has enabled us to afford a holiday also in the Cape during the first two weeks of January," said Simon. "It will be George and James' first experience on a ship and of course their first journey outside of Natal. Once again, we are so fortunate to have Emma and Peter living on the estate to take care of the place while we're away."

Gordon noted that progress in transport matters was proving a boon to the liquor trade. "Obviously the rail link has not only speeded up the despatch of orders but made delivery much safer. On many occasions in the past deliveries by wagon would be late or not arrive at all when a wagon toppled over in muddy conditions resulting in crates of smashed liquor bottles. Of course, shipping access to the Mzimkulu is a tremendous development which is going to result in rapid economic progress in Port Shepstone."

In between their food preparation efforts in the kitchen, Anne, Victoria and Cynthia chatted about their children and how they were growing up. Victoria said she had worried about schooling for Lily on account of the absence of a girls' high school in Durban. "She will be a teenager next year. Gordon and I have discussed this and have decided to enrol her at St Anne's here in Pietermaritzburg. We met the Lady Principal, Miss Usherwood, a month ago and she told us that fees for boarding are 50 guineas per annum. Although Lily will be a boarder, at least she will have family here and I am sure, Anne, you and Martin could have her over during weekends. Of course, it occurs to me with the convenience of rail travel, I suppose she would want to come home to us in Durban now and then."

"George is doing well at Umzinto Primary, but we are uncertain about his schooling beyond that level. We have mixed feelings about sending him to Durban High School where he would have to be a boarder. Unlike Edward Harrison who is a born farmer and will be assisting his grandfather on Beneva in a few years' time, George does not show much interest in agricultural matters on Dewsbury," said Cynthia. "I often wonder if he is not destined for a career in law like my father. But I suppose it's too early to tell."

"Now that I am the mother of two little girls, my intention to resume school teaching has faded. Besides, the best grounding one can give one's children as a mother is to be at home with them. It's a once-only opportunity. I remember Mama telling us how difficult life was in England when we were very young and she had to work part time to earn extra shillings to enable the family to survive," said Anne.

"Do you intend having any more children?" asked Cynthia.

"Yes, because Martin is very keen to have a son."

Later during Christmas dinner, toasts were drunk to parents and brothers who had passed on –George and Eleanor Prescott, Martin Pryce's parents, William Prescott and Michael Moodie.

Then glasses were lifted to grandparents – the Snells and the Moodies. Sensing that Cynthia was missing being with her family, Simon said he hoped the railway line was closer to Ladysmith by 1881 to facilitate spending Christmas with Cynthia's parents, James and Margaret Moodie.

****

Christmas 1880 for Trish and Stewart was what they hoped would be the first of many together. Angus and Frida Smith had given their daughter permission to spend it with the Harringtons. Stewart had ridden to Glenmore estate to accompany Trish on the ride to Preston. Their thrill at being together again was mutual. In response to Stewart's apology for having written to her only once, she said she understood his limitations and pacified him with a kiss.

John and Emily were delighted to meet Trish about whom they had heard so much. After lunch, Stewart gave Trish a quick tour of the stables. "Ours are very modest, as you can see. No appaloosas here – only riding and transport horses," said Stewart apologetically. Nuzzling the head of one of the horses, Trish said with the right temperament most horses could be trained to perform as well as her appaloosas.

Returning hand in hand to the main house, Trish asked Emily if she could help in the kitchen preparing food for Christmas lunch the next day. Emily was impressed by Trish's good manners and her willingness to help, especially as Priscilla had begged off on account of the nausea she was experiencing with her pregnancy.

After a light supper that evening, they sang carols and played card games. In bed later, Stewart wondered what gift Trish might have brought for him. He was pleased with what he had had purchased for her. It was a simple sterling silver necklace featuring a small plaque on which the jeweller in Scottburgh had engraved her name.

Before lunch on Christmas day, gifts were exchanged. Trish was thrilled with her necklace which Stewart helped to fasten around her neck. Her gift to him was a riding crop with his name engraved on its shaft. "When you are holding it, just pretend you are holding my hand and when you are using it, it's to spur your horse to bring you to me speedily!" she exclaimed lovingly.

Also present at the lunch was Geoffrey. He had ridden down from Ellangowan not only to be with Priscilla, but to make an announcement. She had spent some time with him in recent weeks on the estate when they had discussed their future. After John Harrington had wished everyone a happy Christmas and good cheer to which a toast was drunk, he said a prayer in memory of their son David who had died tragically earlier in the year. "We all miss him dearly. But we know he is watching over us today and wishes us to fulfil our lives," said John reverently.

Rising immediately to lift spirits, Geoffrey said he had an announcement to make. He and Priscilla had decided to get married as soon as was convenient. "We have discussed our situation and feel it is the right thing to do and also because we feel compatible as a couple. And so, I now want to present Priscilla with an engagement ring." She beamed with pleasure as he slid the ring onto her finger and embraced him. Emily and John were relieved at this development, having quietly speculated what might become of their pregnant daughter's relationship with Geoffrey Southam. Rising to toast the couple, John congratulated them. "Emily and I are delighted that you have found it within yourselves to have made what is a difficult decision, especially when one considers social conventions. Geoffrey, we welcome you to the Harrington family and look forward to a long and prosperous relationship. Seeing as you want to be wedded fairly soon, we'll need to make preparations regarding the church and a reception venue."

For Trish and Stewart just being in each other's company was a sufficient way to spend the rest of her three day stay on Preston. By sharing experiences, they found the extent to which they had much in common and, consequently, how compatible they were. It prompted her to admit that she found it easier to talk to Stewart than to her mother.

After lunch on December 26, Stewart accompanied Trish on her ride back home to Glenmore estate. Their farewells were tender and tearful. Both promised to write to each other.

****

CHAPTER 13

The death of the governor, Sir George Colley, at the hands of the Transvaal

Boers in February 1881 during the battle of Amajuba in the far north of the colony raised little interest in the Royal Hotel bar. Britain's conflict with the Boers was remote from Alexandra County. A more significant issue was the corporate growth of the sugar business in the county.

"The reason I left Victoria County was because I could see little chance of ever owning my own sugar estate. Besides the big sugar men like Binns and Saunders, corporates like Natal Plantations, Natal Central Sugar, Glasgow and Natal Sugar were snapping up small estates in auction sales. It was financially impossible to beat their offers. Now I see a similar trend underway in Alex County," observed John Harrington.

"John's got a point there," said Eric Harrison. "About eight years ago that observation was made here by a Scotsman, Andrew Muir, when he cited what John has just mentioned and how that process was evolving in Isipingo where De Pass, Spence of Cape Town had acquired several sugar estates. Muir labelled the emergence of corporate ownership as a 'sugarocracy' and was very unpopular as a result."

"Has anyone considered that Sam Crookes might be duplicating that trend? Since his first estate, Ellingham, he has bought Renishaw and Maryland from Joseph Landers. Now he has added Restalrig which, I understand, originally belonged to Charles Sinclair who now runs a transport business," noted John.

Continuing to make his case, he then cited T Reynolds & Sons. "Besides extensive estate ownership in Victoria County, Umzinto Sugar at 8,500 acres is the largest sugar estate in Alex County. Now the Reynolds are buying Umzinto Lodge which has gone into receivership. Craigieburn with 2,700 acres is another possibility given its uncertain financial circumstances although with its proximity to Crookes' estates, Sam may consider purchasing it at some future point."

"While your observations can't be disputed, John, how are they relevant to your own estate?" enquired proprietor William Thornton.

"Last year we all had bumper sugar crops. In fact, sugar exports from Natal posted the highest earnings ever - £215,000. That enabled many of us to clear debts. But it takes only a poor harvest or a slump in the sugar prices to place smaller estates on the brink of bankruptcy. In such circumstances selling out to a corporate and becoming a renter or accepting an appointment as a manager would be the Hobson's choice one faced."

"But, John, surely being able to sustain an existence as a renter or a manager is better than poverty and penury?" remarked William.

Frank Reynolds who had been listening to this exchange decided to weigh in with some comment. "John and Eric, I understand your concerns and I agree with what William has just stated. If you look at any enterprise that has commenced in a colony, the pattern is always the same. Enterprising individuals establish a market. As it grows, more individuals are attracted to it. That was very much the case in the 1860s in Natal until the credit crunch wiped out many. Those who survived, like my father and his brother, Lewis, consolidated their holdings. Edward Hawksworth, here in Alex County, was a survivor who used the opportunity to add three estates to his existing Beneva estate. That is the cycle of capitalism. As you just pointed out, John, last year's crop was the best ever. But we don't know what this year's harvest will yield. Agriculture is a risky business because of its dependence on nature, the vagaries of labour and the economics of the market."

"As a final observation, gentlemen, you need to appreciate that enterprise is not a limited exercise. It requires endeavour. The question to ask is: to what extent are you willing to endeavour? The answer depends on the individual. It just so happens that my father does not see limits in endeavours. He sees opportunities as extending endeavours because there are no boundaries in enterprise."

"Well said, Frank. But there is just one spoke in your wheel: that's all well and good if government does not interfere or prescribe boundaries!" quipped William Thornton.

****

Although William Joyner and his sons completed the building of Sarika's new store in Park Rynie in under two months, the construction of shelving and other fixtures took several more weeks since the timber had to be sourced from Durban. The store's official opening took place on Wednesday March 16, 1881.Having been advertised by means of handbills, public response was gratifying which indicated the little settler node's need for a comprehensive one-stop store. Emma was delighted to have earned Sarika's confidence to manage her new investment.

Before the end of January, Priscilla and Geoffrey were married. They exchanged vows in St Patrick's Church before a small number of guests who then gathered at the Royal Hotel for the wedding reception. Geoffrey did not have any family members present as his parents were visiting family in Britain. Priscilla continued to work in Sarika's Umzinto store until the end of March when, at six months pregnant, she found it too tiring.

But just as Priscilla's employment at the store was short lived, so was her marriage. Geoffrey began to lose weight and found coping with the chores on Ellangowan physically exhausting. Copious amounts of Dr Collis Browne's Chlorodyne failed to lessen the debilitating effects of dysentery. His death in May coincided with that of William Arbuthnot of Greenwood estate, also from dysentery. For Priscilla and the Harringtons, Geoffrey's death was a devastating blow. Priscilla was eight months pregnant and had no means of supporting herself, a situation exacerbated by Geoffrey's lack of life insurance cover.

For Priscilla it seemed fate was intent on denying her relationships with the opposite sex. Four years earlier, her teenage affair with Lawrence Paglar ended in tragedy when he drowned in the surf at Park Rynie. The death of her brother David was still fresh in her mind. Now Geoffrey's demise at just 26 years of age had dashed her hopes of having a family and of her baby ever seeing its father. Traumatised and emotionally distraught, her body went into pre-mature labour. The same mid-wife from Park Rynie who had delivered Frances' sons was hastily summoned to Preston. After an exhausting eight hours little Stella was born, approximately a month before her due time. During Priscilla's pregnancy, Geoffrey had indicated his preference for the name 'Stella' if the baby was a girl.

Stella's birth was a bitter-sweet experience for the Harringtons. Priscilla's joy was compromised by her physically exhausted state after eight hours in labour and, of course, by Geoffrey's absence. For John and Emily, their joy in realising they had become grandparents of a healthy little girl was clouded by sadness for their widowed daughter. Privately, Emily had regarded Priscilla's pregnancy as filling the void David's tragic death had left in the family. Little Stella's presence would certainly help in that regard but at the same time it would never fill the void left by her father's death.

In the days and weeks that followed, Sarika visited Preston regularly to comfort and counsel Priscilla. They shared the same tragic experience: death had robbed them of their husbands while they were pregnant. To help with Priscilla's emotional recovery, Sarika insisted that she work in the shop on a part-time basis. "I want you to come whenever you like and to spend however much time you feel you can manage in the store. Your mother is more than willing to take care of Stella in your absence and has told me how much she understands your need to spend time away from Preston."

Geoffrey's death prompted Ellangowan's owner, James Ely, to put the estate up for sale. Named after a field of daisies by its original owner, William Joyner, Ely had lost interest in Ellangowan and had been contemplating terminating Geoffrey's role as assistant. Having once before enquired whether Sarika had considered buying a sugar estate, Hugh Lawson raised the issue with her on one of her frequent sleepovers at Crofton.

"I would need to borrow a great deal of money to afford it. Now I have that £100 loan from Natal Bank which the Park Rynie shop is paying off. What price do you think Ellangowan would fetch?" she asked.

"The mill has been neglected for the past year. I question what Geoffrey Southam was doing on the place. Anyway, Ellangowan is not in great shape which should reduce its resale value. I'd say it's not worth more than £750 at the most," said Hugh.

"If I put both my properties up as collateral, they would amount to about half that sum. I would need a partner to put up the balance. I wonder if Gordon Snell or even E Snell & Co would be interested being either joint-owners or buying Ellangowan outright. I'll write to Gordon and enquire," said Sarika.

Gordon's response was swift. He said it was not company policy for E Snell & Co to buy and manage sugar estates. However, he personally might be interested in partnering Sarika in purchasing Ellangowan. But before committing himself he needed informed opinion about the condition and prospects of the estate and had asked his brother-in-law, Simon Prescott of Dewsbury, to make an assessment.

Simon obliged with alacrity. In his opinion the mill was obsolete and should be scrapped. No more than 200 acres was suitable for cane which was why having a mill was neither necessary nor economical. Overall, he believed Ellangowan was not worth more than £650. In correspondence with Gordon, Sarika felt she could negotiate a loan of £300 from Natal Bank based on the value of her properties and asked if Gordon would be willing to put up the balance of £350. He agreed but had reservations about who would manage their investment. Simon mollified him saying there were prospective estate assistants at the cricket club who would be suitable.

Natal Bank required the title deeds of Sarika's properties as surety before they were prepared to make a loan of £300 available to her. Once that documentation was in hand, the Bank provided a letter confirming Sarika's credit worthiness which she would need to present to the auctioneer as proof that she was a bona fide bidder. Gordon fulfilled his side of their deal accordingly.

The date, time and venue of the auction of Ellangowan to be conducted by Acutt's was duly advertised in the press and by means of handbills in Umzinto, Park Rynie, Scottburgh and Umkomaas. The occasion was the subject of an unusual degree of interest in the district, particularly at the Royal Hotel bar. Eric Harrison and John Harrington had let it be known that Sarika intended to bid for Ellangowan. "It's going to be a unique occasion in Alex County since not only will it be the first time that a former indentured Indian is bidding for a sugar estate, but that the bidder is a female. However, I understand that Sarika's bid is a joint one with Gordon Snell of Durban," remarked William Thornton.

"What I find significant is that Sarika is a resident of Alex County. If she is successful in bidding, it prevents one of those corporates from another county or from the Cape getting a foothold here," opined James Ross.

Frank Reynolds was present in the bar that evening but refrained from involvement in the discussion.

****

Letter-writing for Trish and Stewart became something of a mini-industry which proved cathartic in expressing their growing affection for each other.

Since neither were churchgoers, opportunities to see each other on a regular basis were few and far between. However, an invitation to the Ifafa equestrian team to participate in a gymkhana at Clairmont in Durban provided a hopeful prospect.

Trish explained that although the gymkhana would take place over a weekend, they would need to have a full day in advance to practice with the horses that would be available. "We don't take our own horses as the 60-mile journey would be tiring enough for them besides the risk of incurring an injury on the way," she wrote. "I would love you to accompany me on this five-day excursion. Having you there would also be a big help for Roger, my brother, in preparing and stabling the horses we have to select for the various events."

John Harrington had no reservations in allowing his assistant son to attend the Clairmont gymkhana. "There's nothing much requiring attention on Preston during these autumn months, Stewart. So go along with Trish and the Ifafa team. It will do you good to get away and see a different slice of life."

Clairmont, situated near the Umhlatuzana River south of the town of Durban, was an established horse racing and equestrian venue dating back to 1852. Except for Alfred County, Clairmont's autumn gymkhana attracted teams from the colony's other seven counties. The Ifafa team representing Alexandra County was regarded as joint favourite with the Weenen County team since its champion Mooi River-based riders had been beaten at Park Rynie in September 1880 by the Ifafa team. Trish and one of the team members from Umvoti were the only female participants. Their separate accommodation from the male-dominated teams was provided by the owners of a nearby small holding.

Trish found the practice day very frustrating in trying to find a horse suited to her lightweight and responsive to her riding style. Stewart and Roger spent hours saddling and unsaddling one mount after another until eventually Trish found a grey gelding best suited to her needs. After an exhausting day in the hot sun, Trish said she needed an early night and asked Stewart to accompany her to the small holding where she would be sleeping. Although it was only some 500 yards distant, the opportunity to have some private moments together in the moonlight ensured that walking those 500 yards took more than half an hour. Ardent embraces and kisses were interspersed with expressions of endearment, caressing, and fondling until Trish wisely decided against further incitement of their passions.

The gymkhana events over the two days included flag races, barrel races, stake races, pole bending races, and the most popular and hotly contested event – the steeplechase. Each team entered its top two riders in the various challenges. For Trish, the barrel race and steeplechase were her forte. Her grey gelding proved as good as the appaloosas she was used to riding. As a result, she not only won her events but also won the respect and admiration of the spectators and the other teams. In her quiet, athletic way, Trish unwittingly exposed the fallacy of social convention that women were limited to household chores and raising children.

In terms of the scoreboard, Weenen County was in the lead. Alexandra was lying second with Pietermaritzburg County in third place. The final equestrian event of the two-day meeting was a polo match between the two top teams. Based on her performance in the September Park Rynie match against the Weenen riders, the Alexandra riders were adamant that Trish should be part of their polo team. She did not disappoint them scoring twice and giving a display of riding skills that had the spectators cheering. Although the Weenen team won the match, Trish won the hearts of many while Stewart and Roger beamed with pride.

When news of the performance of the Alexandra team reached the Royal Hotel bar, proprietor William Thornton exclaimed: "Alex County might not have roads, bridges, or the telegraph, but it's got Trish Smith!"

****

The auction of Ellangowan was held at the Umzinto courthouse. The extraordinary number of men present belied their interest in Ellangowan per se. They were there out of curiosity. An ex-indentured female bidding for a sugar estate was an unprecedented event. Promptly at eleven o'clock, the Acutt's official banged his hammer to get everyone's attention. He read out the particulars pertaining to Ellangowan and stated that the seller, James Ely, had stipulated a reserve price of £500.

Eric Harrison, John Harrington, Hugh Lawson and Gordon Snell were clustered around Sarika in support. Quietly Gordon remarked that with their bidding limit of £650, it might be a short-lived event. Opening the bidding at £500, the Acutt's official called for offers. Frank Reynolds offered £550. Gordon raised his hand and offered £575. Reynolds immediately offered £600. Sarika raised her hand and offered £625. Indicating that he was not interested in playing small numbers, Reynolds upped the price to £675. Sarika and Gordon looked at each other and shook their heads. They could not compete with Reynolds. When there was no response to the auctioneer's call for further bids, he banged his hammer and confirmed that Ellangowan was sold to T Reynolds and Sons for £675.

Sarika had prepared a light lunch for her supporters at Michaelhouse to which they all repaired. Asked how she felt, she said she had no regrets. "In one respect, I am relieved that I won't have a bank loan of £300 to bear and the niggling problems that would come with having someone managing Ellangowan. I feel it was not meant for me and I accept that. Nonetheless, as a venture, it was interesting and exciting and I thank Gordon for being willing to be part of it," she said planting a kiss on his cheek. Placing his arm around her shoulder, Gordon expressed admiration for Sarika's willingness to buck social convention and her refusal to be intimidated by it. "My social reformist wife, Victoria, is immensely proud of you. I can almost read her mind of what she will say about today's bidding outcome. She will hail you as the winner for reasons that far transcend a sugar estate." Eric, John, and Hugh politely applauded Gordon's sentiments while Sarika expressed her appreciation by giving him another kiss. Continuing, Gordon made the following observation:

"Beyond the significance of Sarika's challenge though, I think we ought to recognise something else of significance today. Frank Reynolds came to the auction determined to buy Ellangowan. He would have paid £800 if that was bid even though the place is not worth it. The reserve price of £500 tells us that. What I am getting at is T Reynolds & Sons can afford to acquire any estate that's up for sale. Apart from Sam Crookes who, it seems, is assembling his own estate empire, I don't see anyone in Alex County who could seriously challenge Reynolds at an auction. Mark my words, Greenwood, the estate of the late William Arbuthnot, is next on Acutt's auction list. It lies in the heart of the Umzinto/Sezela district where Reynolds and sons have their major sugar interests. In my view, their acquisition of Greenwood is a foregone conclusion."

The declaration Frank Reynolds made at the Royal Hotel bar that enterprise was an exercise which had no boundaries was demonstrated several months later when Greenwood estate was acquired by T Reynolds & Sons.

****

CHAPTER 14

Sarika's historic venture featured prominently in the next issue of Victoria Snell's monthly social reform newsletter. But beyond that, it was a non-event and went unreported by the colonial press. At the Wiltshire Captain Tucker asked Charles Reynolds what he thought of the Ellangowan auction.

"It was just a formality as far as Frank was concerned. That Indian woman's challenge was a publicity stunt. The press obviously recognised that which is why they didn't bother to report it. She and that Snell liquor trader were not serious bidders. That was evident by their unwillingness to match Frank's £675 bid. She needs to stick to coolie stores and stay clear of sugar estates."

Charles Reynolds' view that the auction had been a mere 'formality' left no one in doubt as to the growing influence and ambitions of the Reynolds in Alexandra County.

****

Priscilla's willingness to take up Sarika's offer to perform shop assistant duties whenever she felt inclined gave Emily ample opportunity to look after baby Stella and to relish her role as grandmother. Even though Stella was a month premature, she was putting on weight and feeding well. In looks, Emily thought she was more of a Harrington than a Southam particularly as she appeared to have Priscilla's auburn hair.

****

One night while Hugh and Sarika were having supper in the kitchen at Crofton, there was a knock at the door. Somewhat alarmed since no one was expected and Sarika was the only regular visitor to Crofton, Hugh opened the door cautiously. He was greeted by the sight of an Indian woman, barefoot and dressed in clothes that resembled rags. In between her plaintive cries, she uttered a string of words in a foreign language. Having left the dinner table and joined Hugh at the door, being fluent in Tamil, Sarika understood what the woman was saying and told her to come inside.

After providing her with a mug of tea and some bread and jam, the woman calmed down. Before asking her to explain her presence, Sarika briefly informed Hugh that the woman was an indentured deserter. Speaking in Tamil, the woman said her name was Janki and that she was indentured to Charles Reynolds on the neighbouring node of the Reynolds' sprawling Umzinto Sugar estate.

Janki explained that she could no longer bear Reynolds' treatment of his indentured labour. Elaborating, she claimed they received only 20 minutes for the mid-day meal which invariably comprised of mouldy rice. They were kept out in the cane fields in all weathers until sunset. During that time, they were lashed by *sirdars* if they were deemed to be slacking. The issuing of their food rations was invariably days late. The excuse given was that the suppliers were out of stock. They had little time to forage for firewood and do their cooking outdoors in the dark. If it was raining, they had to cook within their hovels and shanties which leaked in wet weather and were very draughty. There were no ablution facilities. The quality of the water fetched in buckets from a small muddy stream was poor. Janki said they had very little personal time and in any case were exhausted after each day's labours. The condition of her clothes conveyed that fact.

Illness was common but was always dismissed as shamming. Permission to visit the district surgeon was never granted. Too often labourers were afraid to seek permission to lodge a complaint with the magistrate for fear of reprisals. Rations were docked when a labourer missed work through illness. Pregnant women were required to work right up until their time of delivery. It was not uncommon for childbirth to take place in a cane field. Punishments were routine. An entire group of women would be placed on a spare diet (a single bowl of unsalted rice for the entire day) if a task had been poorly carried out or neglected or if the labourer responsible for a misdemeanour failed to own up. Janki said it was not uncommon for *sirdars* to use the lash on women in those circumstances. She said they did not see much of Charles Reynolds because he was mostly busy supervising matters in the mill. But when he was around he was always armed with a whip and used it indiscriminately. She said she had seen him kick and assault male labourers.

Having listened to Janki's outpouring of grief and hardship, Sarika said she was familiar with much of what Janki had said having been indentured herself and heard similar tales of inhumane treatment from others who had been indentured. Nodding his head in dismay, Hugh confirmed that he had seen such treatment on estates in Victoria County when he had worked there. It was the reason he was opposed to indentured labour and was pleased that Crofton employed only native labour.

Sarika reminded Janki that by being off Reynolds' estate without permission, in terms of the law she was liable to a fine and a prison sentence of up to 14 days with hard labour. Janki nodded her head and said she was aware of that, but that if she returned, she would have a nervous breakdown and die under the conditions Reynolds and his *sirdars* imposed.

Discussing the situation that Janki faced, Sarika and Hugh agreed that as a temporary measure the poor woman could stay on Crofton. However, they would have to report her whereabouts as it was against the law to harbour an indentured deserter. After having given Janki more food, some blankets and Holloways ointment to smear on the sores and chafed skin of her body, they placed her in an outbuilding for the rest of the night. Sarika promised to source some new clothing items for her when she returned to Umzinto the next day.

Contemplating Janki's experience while in bed with Hugh, Sarika said it made her feel emotional. "I feel I am reliving what I saw on that Illovo estate where I was indentured which was humane compared to what is going on not just on Reynolds' estate but on other estates." Regarding Janki's predicament, Sarika said she would report it to the acting magistrate, John Hathorn. "Of course, he is going to order Janki's return to Reynolds which will be her death sentence. I think we should offer to buy out the balance of her indentured period. At £3 a year, it should not be more than about £9, depending on how much of her five-year indenture she has still to serve. In the short term, she could be your house assistant on Crofton until a more permanent solution is found."

****

Budget details published in the colonial press stimulated discussion at the Royal Hotel bar. "Well, isn't it nice that for once Alex County is being placed on the same footing as Victoria County by the mandarins in Pietermaritzburg," remarked proprietor William Thornton testily. "They have announced that postal deliveries between Durban and Stanger and between Durban and Umzinto will become a daily service from May. In addition, the postal service between Umzinto and Port Shepstone will be increased to thrice weekly. That just shows how regular shipping on the Mzimkulu is stimulating economic advancement."

"That's true, William, but besides the absence of any items in the budget for roads and bridges for us, what galls me is this article in the *Mercury* concerning the Verulam library. It has just celebrated its 25th year in existence and boasts a collection of 1,600 books. Yet the closest library we have is in Isipingo in Durban County. I think that's an insult to the residents of Alex County and just another example of the neglect this County suffers," bemoaned Robert Anderson.

"On your remark about shipping on the Mzimkulu stimulating economic development, William, I have a bone to pick with the owners of the *Somtseu,*" said Frank Reynolds. "They are charging rates per tonne higher than what overland wagon transport costs. Just because cargo carried by the *Somtseu* reaches Durban in a couple of hours compared to eight days by wagon, I find that unacceptable for the simple reason that the *Somtseu* can move 50 tonnes in a single voyage. So, on sheer bulk TN Price is profiting enormously. To transport that kind of bulk overland requires more than a dozen wagons with overheads of pont fees and wages for the wagon drivers and their native assistants. Mr Price is being greedy. Most of the sugar the *Somtseu* transports to Durban is from Reynolds' estates. If it wasn't for the bulk we are providing, the *Somtseu* would be returning to Durban half empty and thereby making less money," declared Frank Reynolds.

****

Sarika's meeting with acting magistrate Hathorn had a predictable outcome: Janki had to be returned to Reynolds' estate. In motivating his decision, Hathorn accused Sarika of having been taken in by Janki's claims. "Lying is coolie religion," he claimed. "If I had to accede to your offer to take over Janki's indenture, you'd have half the County's indentured clamouring for such a deal."

Sarika was outraged by his remarks, particularly as he implied that she was just another 'coolie liar.' She took exception to his views and demanded an apology failing which she would write to the Attorney-General and report his lack of judicial impartiality. Somewhat taken aback by her tenacity, Hathorn relented and undertook to write to Charles Reynolds concerning the case of Janki and to recommend that he consider Sarika's offer to take over the balance of her indenture contract.

On leaving Hathorn's office, Sarika felt she had achieved a partial victory in dealing with the colonial bureaucracy. Subsequent events, however, proved that her meeting with Hathorn was merely the beginning of a protracted confrontation with the dark side of indenture.

Charles Reynolds, already angered by Janki's desertion, was incandescent with rage upon receiving Hathorn's letter with Sarika's offer to buy out Janki's indenture. "Who does this coolie bitch think she is? First she tries to buy a sugar estate. Now she is interfering in my labour. If she doesn't stay out of my business, I will ruin hers!" he fumed. Replying immediately to Hathorn, he flatly rejected Sarika's offer and demanded Janki's return.

Having been informed of Reynolds' response, Sarika paid a visit to the Harrisons to discuss the situation. While both Eric and Frances were sympathetic, they were unable to offer any firm advice. "We just don't have any experience in a case like this," said Eric ruefully. "Perhaps you should ask Charles Sinclair. He has acted as defence lawyer on occasions in the past."

Sarika met with Sinclair a few days later. He said he was wary of the Reynolds and the way they were throwing their weight around in the County. "I have been informed of Frank Reynolds' remarks he made at the Royal Hotel bar about tariff charges for transport. But what he did not mention was the fact that wagon prices on tonnage are lower simply because he forced me to lower them threatening that he would put me out of business otherwise." Concerning Janki, he asked whether Sarika had any particular angle she felt would be persuasive in securing Janki's discharge. "If I have to go to court to fight for her release from Reynolds, the obvious line of argument to pursue is his inhumane treatment of indentured labour," said Sarika.

"But would you be able to prove that? Regrettably, the prevailing opinion about Indians is that they sham and lie," countered Sinclair. In response, Sarika said she would approach the district surgeon, Dr Lancelot Booth to provide testimony. "He frequently gets calls concerning health issues among the indentured on estates."

After giving the case some thought, Sinclair declined to take it. "Apart from the odd court case I've been involved in, I'm really just a notary and a conveyancer. There won't be a jury because the amount of money remaining on Janki's indenture contract is less than £15. Besides, mistrust of the jury system is widespread. This case would require a close knowledge of the statutes concerning indentured labour. Such expertise would certainly be beyond the average juror. For that reason, Reynolds will probably hire a top lawyer. If you want to beat Reynolds, you need to fight fire with fire."

****

At Charles Reynolds' Esperanza residence, the mood was grim. "This Sarika woman is no longer just a nuisance in this community but an outright opponent of our social conventions. Not only does she own two stores, but she is basically living with that Lawson fellow on Crofton. I think we should approach Crofton's owner to sell his estate then get rid of Lawson once we own the place. That will force him out of the district," said Charles to his brother Frank.

"I hear you have a spot of bother with a deserter who has found her way to Crofton and is being given shelter by Lawson and his coolie lover. What do you intend to do, Charles?"

"The coolie lover, who herself was once indentured, wants to buy out the rest of the deserter's indenture contract. There's no law against that but it would set a bad precedent which is why I have told Hathorn that the deserter must be returned. I'm damned if I'm going to tolerate interference in how we run our labour. If one coolie gets to have his indenture contract bought out or transferred to another employer, it will create havoc. You know how scheming these coolies are. Our labour routine would be disrupted. Troublemakers in the gangs will encourage a mass of applications. The sugar industry could be destabilised. It would also lead to disunity in the ranks of employers if coolies began playing us off against each other."

"I agree, Charles. The whole idea of indentured labour is that employers are guaranteed a labour force for five-year periods. As it is there is enough bother and paperwork involved in keeping registers of their rations, absence from work, wage deductions and discipline records. If buy-outs and transfers were permitted, the clerical aspect would get out of hand completely."

"Of course, there is a way to minimise the chances of that happening. All we must do is keep buying up estates so that coolie troublemakers won't have anywhere to escape or petition for a transfer," said Charles.

"That's true, but in the meantime what's your plan getting that deserter back from Crofton?"

"I have told Hathorn that she must be returned within three days. If that does not happen, I have instructed him to charge Lawson and his lover with harbouring a fugitive. So, there'll be a court case. We need to crush Lawson and his coolie storeowner on this issue because if we don't, the long term consequences will be detrimental for employers of indentured labour. Do you have a suitable litigator in mind, Frank?"

"Yes. I'll contact Tatham and Brown in Maritzburg. Dad found their services worthwhile when he had issues with our Umhlali properties."

****

Without hesitation, Sarika knew whom to contact if she was to beat the Reynolds in court: Martin Pryce of Goodricke's in Pietermaritzburg. In haste, she mailed him the details of her situation regarding Janki and the responses of the acting magistrate and Reynolds.

Having assisted Sarika in the past to obtain compensation for the death of her common-law husband, Michael Moodie, and being opposed to the way social conventions discriminated against Indians, Pryce agreed to provide legal assistance. "Please forward all documentation you received from the magistrate regarding the case so that I can do the necessary research and preparation," he wrote.

Determined to have a legal showdown with Reynolds, Sarika ignored Hathorn's order to return Janki to Reynolds and advised him that she would challenge it in court. In the meanwhile, Janki resided on Crofton and made herself useful as a house help. Wearing new clothes, having decent food and working hours restored her self-esteem.

On the estate from which Janki had absconded, there was an undercurrent of interest among the indentured as to her whereabouts. The fact that she had not been returned, fuelled speculation. The *sirdars* picked up on this and propagated the lie that she had been apprehended and was in prison. To deter others who might attempt to desert, they declared that when Janki returned, she would be publicly flogged – despite the ban of flogging legislated by Law 12 of 1872.

****

An issue which worried all sugar estate owners concerned a fungal disease called 'smut' that was increasingly prevalent in cane plantations. It manifested itself as a mass of black spores on the leaves of the cane, stunting growth, and reducing yield and the quality of cane juice. The China cane varietal, the most grown, was highly susceptible to the smut fungus. After the bumper harvest of 1880, many estate owners realised that a decline in tonnage because of the proliferation of smut was inevitable unless a smut-resistant varietal was planted. Switching to the Green Natal varietal meant that better harvests would occur but only in the second year after planting. That was the reason the 1882 harvest was the poorest since 1868.

For planters having 300 acres or less under cane and who depended on the maximum tonnages their limited acreage could produce, the smut disease was a great threat to their livelihoods. Simon on Dewsbury and Eric on Woodhouse Lea were among those affected. Fortunately, both of them had good coffee crops which helped to offset their loss in sugar earnings. But that was not how others fared. Crofton's sugar crop was less than half its 1880 yield. That news and the prospect of having to replant all its fields with Green Natal persuaded its owner to give Hugh Lawson notice that he intended to sell.

****

CHAPTER 15

Martin Pryce found there were two statutes to consult in preparing his case for Janki and Sarika: Law 2 of 1870 and Law 12 of 1872. Law 2 was a compilation of the existing laws concerning indentured and free Indians. Law 12 expressed the key views of the Commission of inquiry into indentured Indians which took place in 1872. He also wrote to Dr Lancelot Booth, the district surgeon, and advised him that he would be an important witness based on his travels around the county.

The basic charge Reynolds was levelling against Lawson and Sarika was that transferring a labourer to another employer was disruptive of labour routine and therefore not condoned within the planter community. Nonetheless, Pryce found three sections of Law 2 which sanctioned transfers of contract labourers. An additional point he intended to exploit was the obligation of state officials to monitor the conditions of indentured labourers on estates. Primarily, he intended to premise his case on humanitarian grounds by specifically examining causes for desertion such as poor rations, failure to supply adequate clothing, poor accommodation and ill-treatment.

In another building in Pietermaritzburg, Charles Reynolds was deliberating the case with his lawyer, Mr Tatham. "Our central thrust must be that by refusing to return this Janki labourer to my estate, Lawson and his coolie lover are guilty of kidnapping her. This Sarika woman is part of a group of misguided females led by the wife of that Snell liquor trader who aim to promote equal rights for women and their welfare. We also have to argue that Janki has exhibited mental problems which caused her to wander off and desert the estate. Her poor clothing reflects her inability to take care of herself because of her demented state."

"But if that is her condition, Charles, why do you want her back? Surely, she's dead stock and just costing you money?" enquired Mr Tatham.

"We must reject this transfer request as setting a dangerous precedent. Besides, what tasks she performs on the estate is my business because she is contracted to me. If her transfer is condoned, it could prove very disruptive to the industry with labourers clamouring for transfers for any darn reason."

In answer to Mr Tatham's question about visits by the district surgeon, Reynolds said he had made only two cursory visits in the past three years. "As a witness, Dr Booth will be more concerned to deflect attention away from his failure to do his job properly. Officials are supposed to make two visits a year. But none of them does," replied Charles.

****

The *Somtseu's* regular voyages to both the Mzimkulu and the Mkomanzi inspired conversation among the regulars at the Royal Hotel bar. David Aiken, who had twice visited Durban as a passenger on the ship, remarked how the *Somtseu's* routine service was proving a tonic to settlers in the Port Shepstone district. "There's a new spirit amongst the locals which is reflected in the construction of a hotel some three miles up the river." In support of that, Aiken cited a report in the *Mercury* which read: "The redoubtable little steamer's movements are so frequent that a daily issue of a newspaper can scarcely keep pace with her."

The general consensus was that shipping on the Mzimkulu was an established reality with long-term prospects. A report by the colonial engineer, Albert Hime, seemed to confirm that. To improve the scour in the entrance channel, a 370-yard-long training wall was planned. Hime calculated that it would require 2,800 cubic yards of stone and cost about £10,000 over a four-year period. However, he cautioned that whatever improvements were made in navigating the Mzimkulu, there would always be days when high seas outside the river mouth would prevent the *Somtseu* from entering or leaving.

****

Networking among Indian traders and suppliers was one of the ways in which they undercut white-owned stores in terms of prices. It occurred to Sarika that by networking she could get back at the Reynolds' intention to ruin her business. To that end, she contacted Aboobaker Amod. Besides owning several stores in Durban, he had extensive contacts with India. By sourcing rice, coriander, ghee oil, dholl, turmeric, tamarind, garlic and chillies through Amod's connections, her objective was to become the bulk stockist in the county of the food items required by employers of indentured labour. From Port Shepstone she sourced dried fish - another important indentured food item. Charles Sinclair's dislike of the Reynolds made him a willing ally in providing for Sarika's transport needs in return for which he gave her a discount. As a consequence of her adroit business manoeuvring, Sarika's stores had the widest range of indentured food items at the lowest prices. To cope with the increased sales traffic, she hired extra staff and a carpenter to erect an additional storeroom.

As the employer of over 400 indentured Indians, the Reynolds were the biggest purchasers of Indian food requisites in the county. At the Wiltshire, Charles Reynolds fumed at being outmanoeuvred and placed at a disadvantage. "I'll fix this little coolie bitch yet for trying to be smart. I intend to approach Hawksworth and Crookes. They both have quite large numbers of indentured coolies. My idea is to form our own bulk buying business and, in that way, cut out two of her biggest customers."

But Charles' intended manoeuvre failed. Edward Hawksworth, whose three estates were surrounded by Reynolds' property holdings had no desire to become part of a Reynolds' food supply syndicate. Sam Crookes was also wary of the Reynolds influence in the county and did not reply to Charles' letter on the subject. Besides, he found Ellingham's close proximity to Sarika's Park Rynie store very convenient for his purchases of indentured food items.

****

Meanwhile, Thomas Reynolds, Alexandra and Alfred counties' representative in the Legislative Council, had his detractors. One of them was the man he defeated in the 1880 election – William Hawksworth. In a letter published in the *Mercury,* he accused Reynolds of "deception and chicanery" for having ignored the petition he had submitted on behalf of others concerning the omission of their names from the county's voters' roll. One of those omitted was Sam Crookes. In his response, Reynolds claimed that the Council was "not the proper tribunal" to deal with such matters. Calling him "the member for Cloudland," Hawksworth scoffed at his excuse and insisted it was in the public interest.

In Frank Reynolds' absence, speculative opinion surfaced in the Royal Hotel bar regarding his father's apparent indifference to this issue. Eric Harrison said he thought it reflected Reynolds' unstated resentment towards the growing extent of Sam Crookes' sugar enterprise in the county. Dr Lancelot Booth adopted a softer view on the matter. "I think Hawksworth is just out to needle Reynolds using voters' roll omissions to do so. If one's name is omitted from the roll, the simple solution is to inform the magistrate." William Thornton agreed but felt that where Reynolds had erred was in ignoring Hawksworth's petition. "In public life, one has to observe courtesies, regardless of whom they concern or their implications," he counselled.

Another issue involving Thomas Reynolds was his request for a refund of the Customs duty he was charged on the tramway system he had imported for erection on his sugar estates. He argued that to obtain optimum juice extraction from freshly cut cane, it was necessary to get it to the crushing mill as speedily as possible which is what the tram system in the cane fields facilitated. Referring to a press report on the matter, John Harrington noted that the Chief Customs Officer, George Rutherford, had rejected Reynolds' request because the tramway could be used for a variety of purposes and not solely in agriculture. "Colonial Secretary Mitchell says the government is within its rights in claiming payment," the report states.

"The interesting aspect of this dispute with the government is that Reynolds has succeeded in waking up inland farmers like Frederick Moor of Weenen County. Suddenly, he is now asserting that fencing and all agricultural plant machinery should be exempt from Customs duty," observed John Redman. "I can't see that happening. If agricultural equipment was exempted what would be next? After all, almost every manufactured article or item is imported and therefore is liable for Customs duty."

"What strikes me about Thomas Reynolds' request is that he is sharp and perceptive in money matters. In all likelihood, Frederick Moor would not have cottoned on to the wider implications of the matter if Reynolds had not raised his imported tramway system in the first place. I think the conclusion we need to draw is that the Reynolds are ambitious and shrewd operators," ventured proprietor William Thornton as he sipped his beer.

****

Travelling together from Pietermaritzburg, two of the colony's top lawyers hired to handle the Janki deserter case, Tatham and Pryce, arrived in Umzinto over the weekend preceding the start of the case. Tatham was accommodated by Charles Reynolds at his Esperanza mansion while Sarika hosted Martin Pryce at Michaelhouse.

During pre-supper drinks, Martin fielded questions from Sarika about how his family were keeping at Taunton Manor.

"You will be pleased to hear that Anne is pregnant and this time I am hoping for a son," he announced exuberantly. "Eleanor and Elizabeth are respectively five and three years old and keep Anne dotingly occupied! We are going to have to hire a Nanny when the new baby comes along. But not a day passes that I do not remind myself how fortunate I was to find and marry Anne. She is just so naturally maternal with little children. I remember Reverend Barker of St Patrick's saying to me how he regretted Anne leaving his school for Indian children when we married and moved to Taunton because as a teacher Anne had such a warm rapport with them."

`**********

The Reynolds-Janki case opened in the Umzinto courtroom on Tuesday morning, October 18, 1881 – a cold, windy day. The courtroom was packed with interested and curious local residents eyeing the two London-trained lawyers from Pietermaritzburg resplendent in their morning coats - Tatham representing the plaintiff and Pryce on behalf of the defendants. The clerk of the court announced the entry of Acting Magistrate JW Hathorn. The serious business of adjudicating a controversial subject was about to commence.

At issue was the desertion of an indentured labourer; the demand that she be returned; the accusation of harbouring a fugitive and the offer to purchase the balance of her indentured contract. Hathorn then invited the legal representatives to present an outline of their cases.

Speaking first, Mr Tatham's initial statement elicited mutters of surprise from those assembled: "It is our contention that the fugitive indentured labourer known as Janki, who absconded from Umzinto Sugar estate, is being held on Crofton Estate against her will by one Mr Lawson and his Asiatic companion Sarika Singh. They have refused to return the labourer to whom she is contracted."

"We, submit, therefore, that the defendants are guilty of defying the process involved in dealing with an absconding indentured labourer. As such, they should be fined the sum of £10 as the law prescribes in addition to a further eight shillings for every day they have been holding Janki in defiance of the court order to return her to Mr Reynolds' estate."

Smiling as he rose to present the defendants' case, Mr Pryce posed the question of why the failure of an indentured labourer to return to Umzinto Sugar estate from which she had fled, can be ascribed to the contention that she was being held against her will at the place where she had sought and been granted sanctuary. "Therefore, the motive for Janki's fugitive status will form a major part of our case along with an argument to substantiate my clients' offer to purchase the balance owing on her indentured contract."

With a nod of his head, Hathorn indicated that Tatham should motivate his case. "Estate records show that Janki has exhibited mental problems which, from time to time, have caused her to wander off the estate. Her poor clothing reflects her lack of conscientiousness in taking care of herself. Consequently, she is lightly tasked on the estate while she fulfils her labour contract. It is my client's contention that she is actually a beneficiary of sheltered employment and faces destitution once her contract expires given the extreme unlikelihood of her acquiring gainful employment. In that context, we assert that it is in Janki's best interests to return to Umzinto Sugar estate where for the balance of her contract period she is guaranteed food and shelter. At the end of her contract the Indian Immigration Trust Board will be consulted. The Board repatriates labourers whose mental or physical condition renders them unemployable in Natal."

Rising to challenge Tatham's argument, Martin Pryce said he would like to call Mr Hugh Lawson as a witness. After relating his background experience with indentured labour during his time in Victoria County where he had worked on three different estates, Pryce asked him to describe Janki's condition when she arrived at Crofton.

"Her condition resembled the worst of what I saw in Victoria County. Besides her tattered clothing and barefoot state, when we changed her into some new clothes, we saw sores and lesions on her arms, legs and back. From experience I recognise those as a consequence of being beaten and whipped," Lawson testified.

"Mr Tatham has alleged that Janki has mental problems. Based on the time she has been on your estate; would you concur with that?" asked Pryce.

"In the three weeks she has been on Crofton she has shown herself to be alert, capable and conscientious in performing household chores. She has also proved lucid in relating her experiences in Tamil to my companion, Sarika Singh."

"Mr Tatham has stated that Janki was lightly tasked and essentially afforded sheltered employment. From your companion's conversation with her, was that view corroborated?"

"Definitely not! Janki was part of a women's work gang in the cane fields. They were obliged to work in all weathers regardless of conditions. She said that also applied to pregnant women and that there were occasions when childbirth occurred in a cane field. Treatment by *sirdars* was brutal in driving the gang to complete a task. Another form of punishment was the docking of rations for what *sirdars* deemed to be slacking or insubordination. In that respect, it was clear to us when Janki arrived at Crofton that she was in a very under-nourished state. She said that besides the mere 20 minutes they were given to eat their mid-day ration, the mealie meal or rice was often mouldy."

While Hugh Lawson was testifying, Mr Tatham was looking increasingly agitated as a result of remarks Charles Reynolds was whispering to him. Taking advantage of a sudden break in Lawson's testimony, he asked for permission to cross-question him.

"Mr Lawson, what you related about Janki's treatment was what your companion reported to you about her conversation in Tamil with Janki. How do you know what was translated into English was the correct version of what

Janki said? How do you know if your companion's command of Tamil is sufficient to understand what Janki was saying? I ask these questions because it is well known that grave errors in accuracy are common among interpreters of Tamil and other Indian languages. I should also point out that lying is almost a religion amongst Indians," declared Tatham.

Amidst exclamations of protest from some of those in the courtroom, Martin Pryce expressed his indignation at Tatham's remark. "I must absolutely reject your attempt to smear the evidence relayed by Mr Lawson because it questions Miss Singh's language proficiency and the inference that she propagated falsehoods regarding Janki's experiences. I have had dealings with her over the years and can vouch for her integrity along with others in this district."

Sensing that tempers had become inflamed, Hathorn ordered a twenty-minute recess in the proceedings. Outside the courtroom Pryce said he was going to call Dr Booth as his next witness. After that, he intended to present aspects of Law 2 of 1870 which would place Reynolds in a precarious position. Huddled with Tatham, Charles Reynolds urged him to redirect the focus on the illegality of harbouring a fugitive. "That is where this case has to go. But at the same time, keep questioning the veracity of anything based on a coolie's words."

Back in session, Martin Pryce called Dr Lancelot Booth as his witness. "As district surgeon, you no doubt see a diverse range of health issues. In his testimony, Mr Lawson referred to lesions on Janki's body. Could you tell the court how those may have been caused?"

"Based on the description given by Mr Lawson, those lesions are wounds where the flesh below the skin has been ruptured and infection has set in. Without cleaning the wound with something as basic as a saltwater solution and keeping it dressed, the healing process would be stunted – hence what is called a lesion."

"Thank you, Dr Booth. In that Mr Lawson witnessed the widespread existence of lesions on Janki's body, what, in your opinion, caused them?"

"In Janki's case, particularly as they appear on her back, they could not have been the result of self-inflicted mutilation. Therefore, it is reasonable to conclude that they were caused by violent ill-treatment such as assault or whipping."

Indicating that he would like to cross-question Dr Booth, Mr Tatham asked how frequently he visited estates which had indentured labourers. Embarrassed, Dr Booth conceded that he did not visit them as often as he should. Citing section 33 of Law 2 of 1870, Tatham noted that the Coolie Agent or the district surgeon was required to make two visits a year to inspect the condition of indentured labour. "According to Mr Reynolds, in the past three years, Dr Booth, you have visited Umzinto Sugar estate only twice. Each visit was perfunctory. You did not ask to hear complaints, nor did you ask to inspect the medical register. On those grounds, I submit that your remarks about lesions amount to conjecture."

Aware that Tatham had planted doubt in his case, to regain credibility Martin Pryce recalled Hugh Lawson. "From your experience in Victoria County as an assistant estate manager, did you witness brutality in the treatment of indentured labour? Moreover, how frequently were inspections conducted by the Coolie Agent or the district surgeon?"

"Ill-treatment was not uncommon and was mostly carried out by *sirdars.* But not all of them were what I would term lash happy. However, I did witness brutality, and I have no doubt that the lesions on Janki's body are the result of *sirdar* brutality. As far as inspections by officials were concerned, like Mr Tatham mentioned, they were perfunctory and infrequent."

"Did you ever witness the Coolie Agent or district surgeon addressing the labourers and calling for complaints?" asked Pryce. Responding, Lawson said he witnessed such an occasion only once and ascertained that labourers were too afraid to make public criticisms of their treatment for fear of reprisals which could take the form of lashes or the docking of rations.

Addressing the court, Martin Pryce said that based on Mr Lawson's observations, Dr Booth's concessions and Mr Reynolds' statements, it was evident that despite the requirements of Law 2 of 1870 and Law 12 of 1872 which prohibited flogging or whipping, the state was negligent in its defence of the rights and welfare of indentured labour. "What we have established, therefore, is that regulations are flouted and human rights violations do occur. This is a grave travesty and shows that the recommendations of the 1872 Coolie Commission are being ignored. There is a reason for that which I found in a statement by the previous Alexandra County resident magistrate, Mr James Moodie. He admitted that he did not fulfil the requirements of the law by visiting estates twice a year. His reason is very interesting: he said it was awkward to indict the social lions of his district if he found they were violating regulations."

"Further to the issue of conditions on estates, I refer the court's attention to the findings of a government commission of inquiry into the pollution of water sources by sugar mills published in the *Government Gazette* last month. Amongst the estates the commissioners visited was Umzinto Sugar. They found the absence of latrines at the barracks for indentured labourers resulted in them relieving themselves on the banks of streams. As a result, faecal pollution was contributing to ill health. Adding to the polluted state of streams was the discharge of dunder from the mill."

With a frustrated demeanour, Mr Tatham rose and thanked Mr Pryce for his homily on the shortcomings of the government in monitoring indentured labour conditions. "We seem to have strayed from the reason this case was brought: the harbouring of a fugitive and the contract of that fugitive with Mr Reynolds. To that end, I wish to cite the findings of the Shire Commission of 1862. It concerned the absconding of several indentured labourers from Henry

Shire's Umhlanga estate and the request to have their contracts transferred to other employers. The commission rejected that request on the grounds it would set a precedent which would permit labourers to clamour for contract transfers for any number of contrived reasons. To date, the only transfers that have occurred have been in cases where estates have been sold or the employer has passed on."

"The purpose of indentured labour is to give employers five years of uninterrupted service. If contract transfers are freely countenanced, they will play havoc with the stability of labour on estates and destabilise the industry by playing off one employer against another," opined Mr Tatham as Mr Pryce rose to rebut his statements.

"Significantly, Mr Tatham omits to mention the reason some 20 indentured labourers wanted a transfer from Shire's estate. It was for the same reason that Janki fled from Reynolds' estate: ill-treatment. Nonetheless, the precedent of the Shire case on which Mr Tatham hangs his hat ceased to be relevant when Law 2 of 1870 was promulgated. Sections 18, 21, 24 and 42 all refer to conditions of transfer of indentured contracts. Essentially, as section 24 specifies, with the consent of the Immigration Agent, now called the Protector, an employer simply cedes the services of the labourer to a new employer who then completes whatever payments on the labourer's contract are outstanding."

"Based on section 24, Janki's contract could be transferred to Mr Lawson without any further ado. I use the word 'ado' with some trepidation because of information relayed to me by one of Mr Sinclair's transport workers delivering goods to Mr Reynolds' estate. He was told that a *sirdar* has promised to subject Janki to a public flogging when she returned," said Pryce to gasps of dismay.

Ignoring Pryce's reference to the *sirdar's* brutal intentions, Tatham redirected attention to his client's charge against Lawson. "While Mr Pryce attempts to resolve this case to his satisfaction, he blithely ignores what section 36 of Law 2 states: harbouring a coolie not assigned to you and whose services you are not entitled to, carries a fine of £10 in addition to the payment of eight shillings for every day the fugitive is harboured. That is the nub of the issue in this case. Mr Lawson and his companion have violated section 36 and therefore must bear the consequences which have mounted up considerably. Having harboured the fugitive for three weeks at eight shillings per day in penalties, Mr Lawson and his companion are now liable to an additional £8 and 8 shillings."

"To conclude my argument, Mr Lawson's testimony concerning the lesions on Janki's body is not empirically based. Those lesions could have occurred before she was indentured. His claim that she is lucid and competent does not disprove her mental state on Mr Reynolds' estate. If anything, Mr Lawson's contention needs to be weighed against the ability of Indians to sham and to lie. In that context, reservations need to be applied in considering the veracity of translations from Tamil into English. Mr Pryce's attempts to emphasise the shortcomings of officials in monitoring conditions prevailing on estates employing indentured labour are a red herring. They have nothing to do with the charge of harbouring an indentured fugitive."

"Finally, Mr Pryce's second-hand information about Janki being subjected to a public flogging on her return is a ploy intended to evoke emotional distraction and should be ignored," concluded Mr Tatham resuming his seat.

Before commencing his concluding appeal on behalf of his clients, Martin Pryce looked smilingly around the courtroom while he adjusted his bowtie. "I can understand why my esteemed colleague is eager to wrap up this case based purely on section 36 of Law 2 of 1870. It's because on the evidence heard today, there are dark issues which overshadow not only the plight of Janki but of conditions on Mr Reynolds' estate. Those dark issues form an integral part of Janki's motive for escaping from that estate. Significantly, Mr Tatham did not dwell on her motive for deserting. Instead, he was content to ascribe it to what his client alleges is her mental illness which causes her to 'wander off,' as he phrased it."

"For the three weeks that Janki has been in the company of Mr Lawson and Miss Singh, they have not observed any symptoms of cognitive impairment. Thus, the claim that shamming and lying are common characteristics among the indentured is baseless in Janki's case. Miss Singh is very familiar with the Tamil language. So, the suggestion that her understanding of Tamil may be sub-standard must be rejected. Moreover, her proficiency in English rivals that of many colonists. The veracity of her translations of Janki's experiences, therefore, cannot be disputed."

"While the failure of officials tasked with observing and monitoring circumstances on indentured estates is not central to the case, their negligence needs to be reproached because it is a contributing factor in the circumstances which motivated Janki to escape from Mr Reynolds' estate."

"What needs to be questioned is where the guilt lies. Is it merely in terms of section 36 or in the circumstances which resulted in Janki becoming a fugitive? If the court believes in the former it will not only be closing its eyes to underlying issues but facilitating their continuance. If the humanitarian recommendations of the 1872 Coolie Commission are to be upheld, the outcome of this case needs to probe what goes on at Umzinto Sugar estate. Record books, medical registers, food supplies, the condition of accommodation and ablutions need to be examined and kept under observation for a lengthy period – particularly the physical treatment of the labourers. To carry out this task would require men who will not quibble before the social lions of the district."

"This is not a cut-and-dried case. It has manifold implications which must be taken into account in arriving at a verdict," Pryce concluded.

Thanking Tatham and Pryce for their presentations, Acting Magistrate Hathorn said he would consider the evidence and reconvene the court when he had arrived at his verdict.

****

PART THREE

CHAPTER 16

Outside the courtroom, Charles Reynolds expressed outrage at Martin Pryce's concluding remarks. "Obviously Pryce has swallowed the reformist claptrap that Snell woman spouts. Typical ivory tower lawyer! Thinks sugar estates are benevolent societies. But of one thing Pryce can be certain and it is that T Reynolds & Sons will never give any legal business to Goodricke's attorneys."

Some distance away from the Reynolds' group, Eric Harrison, John Harrington, Hugh Lawson and Sarika were clustered around Martin Pryce complimenting him on his concluding remarks. "Reynolds' anger is because the case he brought has boomeranged on him. By putting your finger on where the real guilt lies, Martin, you have turned the tables on him," declared Sarika gleefully. "The last thing Reynolds wants is exposure of what goes on at Umzinto Sugar."

Deliberating in the confines of his office, Hathorn had no illusions about the difficulty of his position. As the most affluent people in the county, he felt intimidated by the Reynolds. The fact they had hired a top lawyer for the case indicated they were prepared to pay to get their way. At the same time, he was aware that Martin Pryce had a proven record in high-profile cases and had adduced a very sound argument which had troubling implications for the Reynolds. Wrestling with his thoughts, he decided that compromise was his best option. He would uphold section 36 and fine Lawson but would disallow Janki's return to Umzinto Sugar on the grounds that he had concerns about her treatment there. She would be transferred to Lawson. Regarding Pryce's humanitarian concerns, he ruled that the recommendations of the Coolie Commission were to be assiduously applied. With those stipulations, he felt he had arrived at a fair and balanced verdict by which he could not be accused of serving the interests of the social lions.

Reconvening the court an hour later, he read out his verdict, declared the case closed and returned to his office.

Gathered back at Michaelhouse for refreshments and a review of the outcome of the case, Sarika expressed her thanks to Martin for broaching the subject of human rights on estates. "I feel you have opened the door on that issue which needs to be probed. I'm also heartened that Reynolds has had to back down on transferring Janki to Hugh. That poor woman would have died had she been returned to Umzinto Sugar."

"Have you any idea about Janki's future?" asked John Harrington "I know Emily would welcome her as a house help on Preston now that she has baby Stella taking up a lot of her time."

"Oh, that's a great solution," said Hugh. "There's actually very little for her to do on Crofton with just me living on the premises. Anyway, once the remainder of her indenture is paid off – it's just £6 – which I will remit shortly to the Indian Immigration Trust Board, Janki will be a free person."

At Charles Reynolds' Esperanza residence several large whiskies had not assuaged his mood. "That damned Hathorn has now set a precedent in this county. I can just see coolies lining up for transfers all over the place. Well, it's not going to happen on our estates. As I said to Frank recently, the more estates we can buy and own, the tighter our control over everything, especially indentured labour. Regarding the requirement that the Coolie Commission's recommendations are applied, I can't see Dr Booth coming anywhere near our estates," declared Charles belligerently.

"Charles, you should be thankful that Hathorn did not go more for what Pryce was advocating. Instead, he spun a very neat compromise between giving some of what you wanted and tilting slightly to the line Pryce hewed," counselled Mr Tatham. "I think you should also be grateful for the absence of the press as they might have decided to explore some of Pryce's statements."

****

Despite Sarika providing a balanced report to the *Mercury* and the *Witness* about the case, not a word of it appeared in print. At the Royal Hotel bar that issue was raised by William Thornton who asked Frank Reynolds his thoughts on the matter.

"It's very simple, Gentlemen. In the first place, a case involving a single indentured fugitive does not warrant a press report because such incidents are quite common. For those of you involved it may be significant, but outside of this immediate community, it's not even a talking point. In the second place, whatever case that lawyer Pryce was trying to make, is not in the interests of the colony. We have had the Coolie Commission which appointed a Protector of Indian Immigrants. It's his job to get on with protecting them, not yours. What we don't need is alarmism, which is what we had ten years ago when, as a result, the India government very nearly banned all further indentured immigration to Natal. The sugar industry, railway construction, the harbour and even inland agriculture need indentured labour. Now that coal has been discovered, that will be another area requiring indentured labour. So we don't need to project this Janki case in a way that renews concerns by the India government of how indentured labour is allegedly treated here," declared Frank Reynolds.

Soon after Frank had finished his beer and left the bar, John Redman posed a question: "If the case was just over a single fugitive, as Frank put it, why did the Reynolds hire a top lawyer to represent them?"

"Besides being able to afford to hire Tatham, I think they wanted to intimidate Lawson and Sarika while at the same time being prepared to shut down a contrary line of evidence," suggested John Harrington.

"Well, they failed there, thanks to Pryce's tenacious efforts. But considering what Frank said earlier, I get the impression economic interests are a priority and that humanitarian concerns are trifling," remarked Robert Anderson.

"Frank's views raise another concern. He basically told us to leave conditions of indentured labour on estates to the Protector. But the Protector is a government official and given the government's commitment to economic development, to what extent would the Protector want to jeopardise that development by harping on humanitarian concerns?" asked Eric Harrison.

"I think you have hit the nail on the head, Eric. The evidence of what goes on at Umzinto Sugar, begs the question: where was the Protector? I don't like to say this, but it would seem there is collusion in high places on this subject," declared William Thornton.

His suspicions were later given some substance by Magistrate Lucas. In a private conversation with Thornton, Lucas disclosed that on 12 February 1879, Thomas Reynolds had written to the colonial secretary requesting that his son, Charles, be exempted from border duties with the Alexandra Mounted Rifles and replaced by his other son, Arthur, of Victoria County. The reason given was that Charles' role overseeing more than 200 indentured labourers on Umzinto Estate was indispensable. The request was granted. Yet a similar request to the colonial secretary by George Clarence, who managed 150 indentured labourers on Delta Estate in Isipingo, was denied.

****

Since the gymkhana at Clairmont in April, Trish and Stewart had not seen each other. Apart from an occasional exchange of letters, their relationship lacked physical contact. What he loved about her was how different she was from other girls, epitomised by her rejection of that quip that while 'horses sweat and gentlemen perspire, women just glow.' So, for Stewart, the looming annual July festival at Park Rynie meant the opportunity to spend that weekend together.

Having hired a furnished tent for the duration of the weekend, intimacy was as much on their agenda as Trish's prospects in the various equestrian events in which she intended to participate. Early on the Friday morning, Stewart rode down to Glenmore estate to accompany her to Park Rynie and assist in carrying her bag of clothing and extras. Despite the almost three-month hiatus in physical contact, the flame of their love had not diminished. That was evident from their exchange of embraces and kisses when Stewart arrived at Glenmore.

After stabling their horses at the Fairgrounds, they went directly to the refreshment tent and had lunch. Eager to be on the programme for the various equestrian events, Trish located the events' organiser and had her name entered for the gymkhana and the open races. She asked to be considered for a polo team if one of the teams was short of a rider. Somewhat fatigued after their ride up from Glenmore estate, they retired to their hired tent for some afternoon intimacy.

Elated at being together again, Stewart asked the question that was on both of their minds: "Where do we go from here?" Cuddling up to him, straight-talking Trish said she wanted them to be married and to move to another county. "I would fancy moving to Weenen County which has a very strong equestrian membership. It's where my goal of a stable of appaloosas can be realised. It's also, of course, a very fertile agricultural area, so Stewart, darling, you would have no difficulty in being employed as a farm assistant. From there we could aim to own our own estate for the family we are going to produce!"

“I like those ideas! I also feel that the never-ending eighteen-month cycle of sugar – plant, burn, cut, harvest, grind - is not something I would want to be dealing with for the rest of my life. Agriculture is more varied in Weenen County. From what you said, it is clear that you see a better equestrian future in Weenen County than here on the South Coast.”

“Unquestionably! Then clearly, we are agreed that life in Alex County for us means stagnation. We need challenges. Let’s walk to the nearby shop and buy a newspaper to see if there are any advertisements concerning opportunities in Weenen County,” urged Trish. “We may get an idea of what’s available and who we could contact.” The copy of the *Natal Witness* they purchased provided substance to their desires.

There amongst the spread of advertisements on the front page was a request for a farm assistant in the Rosetta district and an advertisement concerning equestrian training. Stewart and Trish looked at each other in amazement. “Stewart, darling, here’s our future! I think the first thing we have to do is to write to the two advertisers and get an idea of how urgent or soon they would like those positions filled.”

Suddenly the programme of events at the fair seemed irrelevant. The future in a different part of the colony beckoned the two lovers. That night after dinner in the food hall, they returned to their tent eager to discuss what would be required in detaching themselves from their respective families and livelihoods before relocating to Weenen County. Interrupting Trish’s rapid-fire stream of enthusiasm, Stewart asked: “Aren’t we overlooking something? Shouldn’t we be married before we undertake this relocation challenge?” Squeezing his hand, Trish asked teasingly: “Is that a proposal, Mr Harrington?” Cupping her face in his hands he kissed her and responded: “Definitely! I am just amazed at how this weekend is working out. We don’t see each other for nearly three months and now we are set on marriage and a new life in a distant part of the colony!” exclaimed Stewart. “I think tomorrow morning when you are not down to participate in any events, we should ride to Scottburgh and find a jeweller's shop where we can buy an engagement ring."

With tears of joy streaming down her face, Trish embraced Stewart. "I can't tell you how happy I feel! Meeting you, dear Stewart, has been a turning point in my life. I had begun to despair of having a social life stuck down at Glenmore estate until I met you. I also realised that my equestrian and outdoor interests and lifestyle do not project the feminine image most men expect. So, thank you for coming into my life! I love you dearly, Stewart, and want to be your wife!"

Emotionally overwrought, they made love and passed the rest of the night wrapped in each other's arms. Early Saturday morning they set off to Scottburgh where Trish chose a ring with a garnet stone setting – symbol of truth, constancy and fidelity. Although she did well in her equestrian events, the rest of the weekend was a blur. Being together was all that mattered. "How do you think your parents will react to our engagement and relocation plans?" enquired Stewart. "My parents don't cling to traditions. They never questioned us being together this weekend. Anyway, you've made a good impression on them, so I think they will be pleased for my sake that I want to become Mrs Harrington!"

****

The negative effects of the smut disease on sugar cane crops drove some of the small-scale planters into insolvency. Crofton estate's modest sugar production was decimated by the disease. Its absentee owner, Mr Butler of Pietermaritzburg, gave notice that since he was going to auction the estate, Hugh Lawson had better seek new employment.

Crofton's fate was briefly a topic of speculation at the Royal Hotel bar regarding what reserve price the owner might fix on the estate for its auction. John Harrington said he could not see more than £450. "The fields are going to have to be completely re-planted with Green Natal. The fact there is no mill on Crofton also reduces its value."

The only other aspect concerning Crofton about which there was no speculation was who its new owner would be. Sure enough, at the auction held in January 1882, there was only one bidder – Frank Reynolds, who bought Crofton for just £450.

Following the wedding of Stewart and Trish and their relocation to Weenen County, Preston's loss of its estate assistant was Hugh Lawson's gain. John Harrington was grateful that Hugh was available as Stewart's replacement. Hugh's departure from Crofton also proved favourable for Sarika because it meant her lover became a Michaelhouse resident.

****

Political issues polarised Alex County in 1882 as the prospect of self-rule was the main issue of deliberation for the future of the colony. If self-rule (responsible government as it was called) was chosen, would Natal be able to defend itself in the face of a Zulu uprising or a Boer invasion? For many, the tragedy of Isandlwana was still vivid. Others, however, were critical of what they saw as 'imperial blundering,' citing the Anglo-Zulu War and the attempt to rule the Transvaal as having been completely unnecessary.

A public meeting held in Umzinto in April 1882 demonstrated the extent to which opinions were divided. After speeches made for and against responsible government, the vote taken was split evenly: 15 for and 15 against. The outcome of the meeting also emboldened criticisms of Thomas Reynolds, the South Coast's sole representative in the legislative council. Whereas in 1880 he had endorsed the principle of self-rule, in 1882 he backtracked on it. In so doing he was labelled a 'refusalist' and deprecated for adhering to 'the present, narrow, untenable course.'

With a general election due in May, opposition to Reynolds rapidly materialised. Edward Hawksworth campaigned in Umkomaas and the Port Shepstone area on the slogan 'measures, not men' and disparaged Reynolds for supporting what he called "a mongrel form of government." Despite his late entry into the campaign, Hawksworth put up what was hailed as a 'gallant' fight losing to Reynolds by just ten votes.

However, the election and the issue on which it had turned produced a rift within the community, particularly as the Father of the District, Alexander Brander, was opposed to Reynolds' anti-responsible policy.

At the Wiltshire, Brander regaled his fellow beer drinkers with the altercation he had had with Thomas Reynolds. "On election day, Reynolds accused me, as the polling officer, of colluding with Hawksworth. I demanded an apology from him which he very grudgingly gave but only after the election."

Present that evening in the bar was Charles Reynolds. Having listened to Brander's remarks, he swiftly rallied to his father's defence. "You people have no idea how irresponsible you are for even thinking about self-rule. The recent war with the Zulu should tell you how inadequate we are in simply defending ourselves. If imperial forces had not been summoned, we would have faced a holocaust. So, we were very alert about how the election proceeded because we are aware of the anti-Reynolds undercurrent in this county."

An uneasy tension followed Charles' remarks. Exploiting that silence, he angrily proclaimed he was "done drinking with a bunch of plebians." Then slamming his empty glass down on the counter, he stormed out of the bar.

"Well, I guess we might have seen the last of him here, but we won't have heard the last of the Reynolds clan," observed Bunting Johnstone. "Their arrogance is getting to me. Did you read what the Alexandra Letter published in the *Mercury* called them? It referred to them as 'the Lords of Oaklands.' And that's what they are. I don't think the Reynolds were too popular when they lived on Oaklands estate in Victoria County which may partly explain why Thomas came down here after his brother Lewis died."

Hard on the heels of the election controversy, Thomas Reynolds made himself extremely unpopular through his failure to promote petitions calling for the establishment of telegraphic links between Kokstad and the South Coast settlements. Since the line linking Durban and Pietermaritzburg with Cape Town passed through Kokstad, the petitioners rightly recognised that an extension of it from Kokstad to Harding and the coast would end the South Coast's communication isolation.

Retired General and prominent Alfred County landowner and resident, Sir John Jarvis Bisett, presented a petition on the issue endorsed by 35 residents. Former South Coast MLC, James Aiken, forwarded a petition signed by 72 Alexandra County residents. But Reynolds withdrew both of them claiming he had consulted the general manager of the Telegraph Department, James Sivewright, who had "frightened" him by the costs involved. As a result, he felt the petitions were futile.

Added to an estimated cost of £12,500 to erect the line would be an annual maintenance charge of £950. Sivewright was of the view that usage of the line would not defray the costs involved. "The time has not arrived at which the coastal settlements would warrant such a large expense," he asserted.

In the July issue of the *Mercury's* Alexandra Letter Reynolds was roasted for his lack of courage in failing to justify the petitions. "Is this the manner in which our member redeems his promise to the electors?" In March Reynolds had made the following boast: "My persistent advocacy of all that affects your welfare is the best guarantee that your interests will be my first care and will be in safe hands."

At the Royal Hotel bar, William Thornton raised an interesting question: "How many times have Alex County residents petitioned the government for a bridge over the Mkomanzi, only to be told there was no budget for it or that there were more pressing requirements in the colony? Yet for twenty years we have persisted in forwarding petitions on the issue. To the best of my knowledge, no other county has presented as many petitions as Alex County."

"You're absolutely right, William," said John Redman. "Our persistence has earned us respect. It's the reason we have significant allies in the Council like *Mercury* editor John Robinson of Durban Borough to champion our cause. So, by Thomas Reynolds withdrawing those petitions he has achieved two negatives: he has lost an opportunity within the Council to muster support for the telegraph proposal, while, unwittingly, he has created the impression that we are not really serious about wanting that telegraph extension."

"Somehow, I'm not surprised at Reynolds' posturing," remarked Robert Anderson. "When he first stood for election in 1880, he was probably the only candidate in the colony who did not promote a railway for his constituency."

"Another point to consider is that Reynolds has no vintage as an Alex County resident. He's from Victoria County where he still owns property and was criticised after winning the 1880 election for spending six months on his Oaklands estate. At least our two previous Council representatives were established Alex County residents," commented James Ross.

****

CHAPTER 17

News of developments on the Mzimkulu and at Port Shepstone prompted Simon and Cynthia to take a mid-year break from Dewsbury and spend a few days in Alfred County together with their sons, George, who was eleven and James who was six years old. "We'll book into the new hotel which is situated about three miles up the river. Apparently, it's near where the *Somtseu* moors to load and unload cargo. The experience should be exciting for our boys," said Simon to Cynthia as they washed and dried the dishes after supper one July evening.

The carriage journey to Port Shepstone took an entire day. The most arduous part was negotiating the declivity into the Umtwalume River valley. Both Simon and Cynthia agreed that it was as steep and risky as the route to the fording area of the Mkomanzi. "I'm glad I hired one of Charles Sinclair's carriages and drivers for this trip. I've been only as far south as the Ifafa area previously and then always on horseback," remarked Simon as finally they neared the Mzimkulu and awaited the pont to winch them across the widest river in the colony.

For George and James staying in a hotel was a novelty as they excitedly inspected their bedroom and the ablution facilities. "The first thing you boys are going to do is get into the bathtub and have a good wash. When you're dressed, we'll all go to the dining room and have supper," said Cynthia instructively.

In the dining area, the boys were treated to flavoured soft drinks of their choice while Cynthia sipped a gin and tonic and Simon sampled the local beer. "What are we going to do tomorrow, Dad?" asked George. "Can we go swimming and fishing?" Simon assured him that those activities would feature along with others. “But tomorrow we are going to the river mouth because I am told the *Somtseu* is expected to arrive around noon when the tide is full. It will be interesting to see how the little ship enters the river. Then if all goes well and the ship is moored near the hotel, I’ll ask the captain to let us come aboard and be shown around.”

Calm inshore conditions and a full spring high tide enabled the *Somtseu* to negotiate a safe entry into the river mouth, which it acknowledged by a blast of its horn. A while later when the little ship was moored alongside a rickety wooden wharf, Simon asked the captain if his family could have a quick look inside. They were amazed at how compact it was. There were two cabins for crew and passengers, a tiny kitchen and holds which could accommodate up to 50 tonnes of cargo. The *Somtseu* had a crew of eleven including the captain. Steam-powered, the ship was propelled by twin screws. Coal for the boilers was housed in the bows.

The captain said he was relieved to have made a quick and safe entry to the river. He told Simon that on his previous voyage, three days were spent off the river mouth rolling in heavy seas until it was safe to enter. He also remarked that the arrival of the *Somtseu* in this isolated frontier node of the colony reminded him of a stagecoach entering a remote village in England. “People would rush out of their dwellings anxious to hear the latest news and to receive any parcels due to them.”

After spending two more days swimming, fishing, boating on the river, enjoying the luxury of not having to cope with domestic chores and having food prepared and served to them in the hotel, the Prescotts returned to Dewsbury.

****

Widowed and being the mother of a child at the age of 20, Priscilla’s future prospects did not appear very promising, especially where marriage was concerned. Although with her auburn hair and willowy figure she remained youthful and attractive, her social life was non-existent. When she was not working in Sarika's shop, she was at Preston looking after baby Stella.

To be closer to Preston, Sarika had transferred her to the Park Rynie store. It was there that one morning a customer enquired about tennis apparel. As it was an unusual request, Priscilla asked Emma who acknowledged that the store had no stock but undertook to order the necessary sizes from Durban.

Pleased with the store's readiness to acquire the required items and in no hurry to leave, the lady customer engaged Priscilla in conversation introducing herself as Dulcie Lister. "I'm the secretary of the Park Rynie Tennis Club," she said. After Priscilla had reciprocated the introduction, Dulcie enquired whether she would be interested in joining the club. "You're young and seem athletic, Priscilla. The club needs more lady members. Besides, there's a pleasant social environment which I think you'd enjoy."

Without hesitating, Priscilla expressed interest. "I've never played tennis before, but it is a sport that appeals to me. Would the club be able to coach me?" Delighted to oblige, Dulcie and Priscilla exchanged contact details. "Please come to the club this coming Saturday afternoon. I'll introduce you and put you in touch with Yvonne Clark who can coach you. We do play on Wednesday afternoons as well, but with your work here at the store that would probably preclude you," she said as she smiled at Emma.

That evening at Preston, Emily and John were delighted to hear of Priscilla's intention to join the local tennis club. "This is just the sort of outlet and social dimension you need, darling," said John. "Your Mother and I have been most perturbed by your circumstances since Geoffrey's death and the birth of Stella. I think once you've had a bit of coaching, you'll be great on the court especially with your height and reach opponents will struggle to get a ball past you!" he exclaimed enthusiastically.

Following her time spent at the tennis club that Saturday, Priscilla felt her self-confidence energised. After being courteously introduced to the members, Priscilla was accompanied by the club coach, Yvonne Clark, to learn the basics of racket grip and ball control against the back wall of the clubhouse. After watching Yvonne's forehand, backhand, and overhead returns, Priscilla found she had a natural ability when Yvonne put her to the test. "Like everything in life, practice makes perfect," said Yvonne encouragingly. "When we get you onto the court, I'll show you how to serve. With your height, you should have no difficulty in delivering deep serves which will oblige your opponent to stay close to the baseline. In that way, you can dictate how the game is played!"

After six weeks of practicing both at the club and on a barn wall at Preston, Yvonne was suitably impressed by the progress Priscilla exhibited during a practice game against her. A month later, Priscilla was considered good enough to take part in a friendly set of doubles.

****

At the Wiltshire, the atmosphere was a lot more relaxed since Charles Reynolds' departure. "Good riddance! I say," declared Charles Sinclair. "Ever since I struck up that transport deal with Sarika's stores for indentured Indian food supplies, both Charles and Frank have been trying to kill my business. The smug way in which Charles stormed out of here calling us 'plebians' shows that he considers himself of the gentry class which disparages and seeks to distance itself from us ordinary folk."

"That view certainly ties in with their attempt to patronise us by making benevolent donations. The land on which the new Volunteers Memorial Hall in Umzinto has been built was donated by the Reynolds," observed James McMillan.

“If you remember when Thomas campaigned for the Council seat in 1880, he supplied a free lunch and drinks at the Royal Hotel. That was really nothing more than a brazen effort to buy votes. It was also on that occasion that he boasted of their financial clout saying that his company had ‘a substantial balance on the right side.’ Now I note the Reynolds are building a massive mill on that estate named Umhlanga south of Umzinto. According to a press report, at an estimated £17,000 it’s the biggest investment ever made on the South Coast to date.”

“Well, on the positive side I suppose it certainly shows confidence in the county which may serve to motivate afresh the need for bridges and proper roads,” opined Captain Tucker.

****

At the Royal Hotel bar, issues other than the Reynolds were the topic of conversation. Alarm was expressed following district surgeon Dr Booth’s disclosure that 15 deaths from dysentery had occurred amongst the native population in the area between the Umzumbe and Mzimkulu Rivers. Mindful of the death from dysentery of William Arbuthnot in 1881, Dr Booth was asked if there was any medical cure. “Regrettably, there isn’t. Purgatives are prescribed in the belief that clearing the bowels would remove the disease.

But that is not helping and actually weakens patients. I'm not a researcher but to my mind, dysentery must be caused by some micro-organism that inhabits the bowels and on which standard prescriptions simply have no deleterious effect. Commonly you will note that chlorodyne is advertised for the treatment of dysentery. It was originally manufactured for the treatment of cholera."

"On a more cheerful note, gentlemen, Alfred County has just received the largest single influx of immigrants the colony has seen since the Byrne settlement era – 229 Norwegian settlers. In my view they are very brave people coming to an area that is bereft of even the most basic aspects of civilisation," remarked William Thornton. "I read that the government is housing them in native-like rondavels; also, that many of them had their precious possessions broken when some of the wagons transporting them to Marburg overturned. More recently, they have discovered that the 100 acre plots the government has granted them are mostly unsuitable to support even a subsistence existence."

"Shocking though their situation is I suppose we should not be surprised. Remember how those of us who immigrated under the Byrne scheme were treated and how we were expected to make a living out of 20 acres of bush and trees. My bet is that those Norwegians will very quickly learn that to survive and prosper in Natal requires initiative and enterprise – two attributes governments don't have!" declared John Redman.

****

Charles Reynolds had already expressed his intention of ruining Sarika's business because of her near monopoly on food requirements for indentured labour. Frank Reynolds had forced Charles Sinclair to lower his wagon transport prices. As the Reynolds bought up estates, their grip on the county's economy became increasingly powerful. Spitefully, Charles proposed that another avenue to get back at their detractors was in the rum trade.

"Alexandra County is producing a steady 25,000-28,000 gallons of rum annually. Most of it is the result of our cane fields. Yet we are allowing a monopoly in the form of Snell Wine and Spirit merchants to buy up all the rum that is not locally consumed. That representative of theirs, Gordon Snell, is married to that reformist Prescott woman, Victoria, who is an admirer and supporter of the coolie bitch, Sarika. I think it's time we clipped their wings." And so the Reynolds began to ship all their rum directly to a Cape merchant thereby significantly reducing Alexandra County's rum contribution to E Snell & Co.

At the Wiltshire news of that development was greeted warily. David Aiken, who was in the area and had popped in for a chat, regaled the regulars about the pressure the Reynolds were putting on the owners of the *Somtseu.*

"Just because the bulk of the sugar the ship carries to Durban comes from Reynolds' estates, they have demanded discounted charges per tonne. They claim that without their sugar, the ship's return voyage to Durban would scarcely be economical. What they don't take into account is that at least one in three of the *Somtseu's* voyages either has to be aborted because of sea and river conditions or is delayed for days in the river as a result. Those setbacks cost money. Of necessity, therefore, TN Price's tariffs include that risk factor. They are running a business not a benevolent service and they certainly are not subjected to that kind of pressure when they trade at Port St Johns."

"It looks as though we have an economic leviathan in the county and there seems no way to counter it," observed Captain Tucker ruefully.

****

Four months after joining the Park Rynie Tennis Club, Priscilla's ability on the court had progressed to the point where she was a sought-after doubles partner. Just as Sarika had given her a life beyond her isolation and low esteem on Preston by employing her as a shop assistant, so participation both on and off the court at the tennis club had done wonders for her well-being and confidence.

As the youngest member of the club, she was also noticed by the male members resulting in individual requests to participate in mixed doubles friendlies. Besides her athleticism, youth, and advantage in height, Priscilla was also left-handed. Partnered with a right-handed player, their combination was awesome regardless of an opponent's placement of the ball.

A tournament invitation from the Scottburgh Tennis Club resulted in her being selected to play in Park Rynie's doubles and mixed doubles teams. On the day she excelled herself, never losing her service and frustrating her opponents with her powerful left-handed returns. Enjoying refreshments after the tournament, Priscilla found herself getting close attention from one of the male members of the Scottburgh club.

His name was Tony Hassall, the local hotelkeeper. At 30 years of age he was slightly taller than Priscilla, clean-shaven and stoutly built. Extrovert in character, he was popular at the club and attentive to the needs and comfort of visiting players. Introducing himself he complimented her on the way she had acquitted herself on the court and enquired about her life in Park Rynie.

Having given an account of her situation, she enquired about his occupation and background. "My parents moved to Scottburgh from Durban in 1862 when I was ten years old and started Hassall's Inn. About ten years ago they upgraded it and it became Hassall's Hotel. I manage it now since the death of my Father last year."

After engaging in further everyday conversation topics, it was time for Priscilla to join the Park Rynie team's homeward journey. Hastily, Tony enquired if she would care to have lunch with him at the hotel on the following Saturday. Delighted at her acceptance, he promised to send a spider carriage to fetch her from Preston.

On the journey homeward, Dulcie, the Club secretary, who was aware of Priscilla's personal circumstances, said she was pleased to note Tony's apparent interest. "He's a very decent gentlemen and a great asset not only to the Scottburgh tennis club but to the community at large. I don't know if he told you, but he was once married. Tragically, about three years ago, his wife suffered a terrible miscarriage and died as a result."

Back at Preston, John and Emily were thrilled at Priscilla's account of her day at Scottburgh. "We thank the Lord that you are thriving in tennis and hope that something good will come of your forthcoming lunch date with Mr Hassall," said John as he embraced and fondly kissed his daughter.

****

An issue which rocked the County concerned voters' roll irregularities. Queries about the seemingly arbitrary way in which voters were struck off the roll or whose names simply did not appear on the roll resulted in the Alexandra County Association undertaking an investigation.

Its findings pointed fingers at Field Cornet Alex Brander. For 16 years he had been entrusted with maintaining the roll, yet the committee found that of 31 names struck off the roll, only two were justified. Those removed included all local clergy members, prominent sugar planter Sam Crookes, and residents of 20 years standing in the County. The committee found "a loose, irregular, and unsystematic manner in which revision was conducted."

The matter was escalated to the attention of the colonial secretary and the acting attorney-general who expressed serious concern that Brander had "for years been allowed to publish a false voters' roll," particularly as those who objected to exclusion or removal had not appeared in court to challenge his decisions as was their right.

Despite glaring evidence of laxity and irregularity in the compilation and maintenance of the voters' roll, Brander denied any wrongdoing. Nonetheless, in December 1883 he resigned as Field Cornet having held the position since 1865.

In the wake of the voters' roll controversy speculation abounded as to the outcomes of closely contested elections since 1877. "William Hawksworth's single vote victory in 1877 against Arbuthnot could have been far different if the roll had been fairly compiled," averred James McMillan in the Wiltshire.

At the Royal Hotel bar, William Thornton questioned whether Reynolds was the county's legitimate representative. "He defeated Edward Hawksworth by just 10 votes. How do we know those votes were legitimate? We can only speculate how many more votes Edward might have received but may have been denied thanks to Brander's irregular compilation of the roll."

"Well, there's an election coming up in 1883. We need to scrutinise the roll and the procedure instead of just presuming all is well," said James Ross.

Sure enough, in April 1883 requisitions for candidates were published in the press. Edward Hawksworth and Reynolds each received requests to stand for election. Prospects for Reynolds were initially very bleak. At a public meeting in Harding, he was accused of "lukewarmness" for not promoting residents' petition for a branch telegraph line. A motion of confidence in him attracted only a single vote in support while votes in favour of Hawksworth were almost unanimous.

But opinions were quite different in Umzinto where Hawksworth was persuaded to withdraw from the contest on the somewhat specious basis that Reynolds should "be permitted to complete his work." As a result, Reynolds was unopposed and the state of the voters' roll was not subjected to election scrutiny.

Hawksworth claimed at the time that a further election was likely as he anticipated Alfred County being granted its own seat in the legislature. But that did not transpire until 1889. Speculation in the Royal Hotel bar suggested that Charles and Frank Reynolds had been active in promoting the view that their father should not be bothered by an election campaign. In raising that opinion, Robert Anderson asserted that it showed the extent of the Reynolds influence in the county. "Have we reached a point where the Reynolds can exert pressure on wagon transporters, shipping in the Mzimkulu, rum sales, and now political representation?" he asked.

****

At about an hour before noon on Saturday, the spider carriage arrived at Preston to transport Priscilla to Hassall's Hotel for her lunch date with Tony. Wearing a short-sleeved dress as the weather was warm and windless, Priscilla had rolled her auburn hair into an attractive chignon.

Tony was waiting at the hotel entrance to receive her. Having previously seen her only in her tennis apparel, he was visibly awed by her appearance and how her deep green eyes contrasted with the shimmering white of her dress. Kissing her lightly on the cheek he gently guided her to the lounge in his private quarters.

Having established what refreshment she would like, they made small talk until their drinks arrived. Enquiring whether she had any aspirations beyond working in Sarika's shop, Priscilla impressed him with her unambiguous response. "I certainly have no desire to become a governess!" she smilingly exclaimed. "I find working as a shop assistant rewarding from both a business and a social point of view. I wouldn't be here now if I had not met Dulcie Lister in the shop because until that moment, I had never given a single thought to playing tennis."

"That's fascinating," said Tony. "Fate so often provides a virtuous dimension. I am very pleased for your sake that Dulcie's visit to Sarika's store appears to be having positive consequences."

Before continuing their chat, Tony asked her to peruse the menu to decide what she would like to order for lunch. Noting her choice of seafood as both an entrée and the main course, Tony ordered a chilled white wine and invited her to accompany him to his private dining room.

Over lunch, their conversation broached the personal tragedies in their respective lives. From his remarks about his father, Priscilla noted that Tony had been very close to him and was still grieving his sudden death as a result of a heart attack. Commiserating with him, she said she also enjoyed a very close relationship with her father. "Daddy is so supportive and understanding. Unlike most heads of family, he never raged at me about my illegitimate pregnancy. I owe him and Mum so much for their understanding and support."

"You are indeed very fortunate, Priscilla. You have both your parents and little Stella. I can't claim that. I lost my wife and what would have been our child three years ago." Pausing, he asked her to excuse his emotions as he dabbed his eyes with his handkerchief. Reaching across the table, Priscilla clasped his hand in sympathy.

Thanking her he suggested they have coffee on the veranda. Seeking to engage in a more neutral topic, Priscilla asked him about Scottburgh's economy since Sarika was toying with the possibility of establishing a store there. Eagerly warming to the question, he said he thought Scottburgh had better potential than Park Rynie. "I can understand Sarika's logic in having a store in Park Rynie because of the racecourse, the July festival and the string of sugar estates from Ellingham down to Ellangowan. But long term, I can't see prospects in Park Rynie getting any better. In contrast, Scottburgh as a settlement is growing faster than Park Rynie. It is also growing popular as a tourist destination. The fact that there are three hotels here as opposed to one in Park Rynie proves that."

Having thoughtfully absorbed his remarks, Priscilla asked if he could arrange the spider to return her to Preston. Thanking Tony for the occasion, she bade him farewell kissing him on the cheek before boarding the carriage. The hour or so of the homeward journey afforded her time to reflect on Tony Hassall. In that they were both widowed, emotionally they had much in common. The family was another mutual area of value. Her interest in commerce, which Sarika had nurtured, was aligned with Tony's. Then, of course, on a lighter note, tennis was what had led to their acquaintance.

Having mapped out what they had in common, she asked herself what the prospects were of a relationship and decided there was plenty of time. She also noted that he had not expressed a follow-up liaison. "Unlike my overheated indulgence with Geoffrey, I am now older and wiser. I think I like Tony but let's just see what develops," she told herself.

Watching her carriage draw away from his hotel, Tony cursed himself for not suggesting a future meeting. "I'll write to her and propose another outing," he murmured. "I'd be a fool to neglect such a beautiful, charming and sensible lady."

****

CHAPTER 18

Remote though the County of Alexandra may be from the chief centres of population, it nevertheless sets an example that might well be followed by other larger communities. In no part of the colony is there more persistent and healthy discussion of public questions than obtains in Umzinto - editorial comment in *the Natal Mercury.*

The neglect of Alexandra County's infrastructure riled the patrons of the Wiltshire having read Governor Henry Bulwer's remarks in the press introducing the 1883 session of the Legislative Council. Bulwer spoke glowingly of the construction of bridges over the Little Sterkspruit near Greytown, the Ingagane near Newcastle, the Sundays River and Incandu in Klip River County and the Tongaat River in Victoria County.

"I can see why we are being neglected," said David Aiken. "The government is relying on the initiative of private enterprise regarding shipping on the Mzimkulu and the Mkomanzi to ignore our appeals for bridges on the South Coast. The fact that 4,000 tonnes of produce and merchandise were winched across the Mkomanzi by pont last year surely underlines the dire need for a bridge. But with the news of significant coal deposits in Klip River County, it's a case of full steam ahead to build railways and bridges to expedite the transport of coal."

"If coal had been discovered on the South Coast, roads, rails and bridges would be the government's priority. Even if Alexandra County produced more sugar than Victoria County, I think we might have had a bridge over the Mkomanzi. But we don't, which is why the North Coast has bridges over the Mhloti and Tongaat Rivers. Of the eight counties in the colony, Alex and

Alfred are the only ones without bridges. Unofficially, it would seem, we are the 'Cinderella' counties," observed Charles Sinclair morosely.

Scrutiny of the speeches of Thomas Reynolds in the Legislative Council proved a regular topic of conversation at the Royal Hotel bar during the winter months of 1883 when the Council was in session.

Having read a verbatim account of the debate on the sale of alcohol to natives and Indians published in the *Mercury,* proprietor William Thornton laughed out aloud. "Our Mr Reynolds says that selling alcohol to our darker brethren is having a 'demoralising' effect on them. I find that a bit rich considering that in Victoria County the sale of Reynolds' rum to all and sundry was known as 'Umhlali water.' They made lots of money from that 'water,' so Thomas's paternalistic plea that it should be illegal to sell liquor to natives and Indians is really rather disingenuous."

"You're quite right, William! Reynolds also shows little appreciation of the vast disparity in numbers between the white and non-white population. In that whites makeup no more than eight percent of the colony, Reynolds is not going to find favour with sugar planters who own distilleries if they are denied the right to sell rum to natives and Indians. It's a quick cash income on which they depend. Alex County alone is producing over 30,000 gallons of rum per annum. To limit sales to whites only, planters are going to sit with thousands of surplus gallons of rum," remarked Robert Anderson deprecatingly. "Anyway, now that the Reynolds are selling their rum produced in Alex County to the Cape, they have no idea whose lives they may be 'demoralising'!"

"From this speech of his, it would seem Reynolds is canvassing the Temperance Society vote for the next election!" jested John Redman.

The issue of flogging or whipping was the subject of the next contentious debate in the Council. Reynolds presented a petition on behalf of his son,

Charles, and 52 others from Alex County requesting revision of the 1850 Master and Servants Ordinance so that magistrates did not require the Governor's assent to order flogging. In Thomas Reynolds' view, corporal punishment of natives was necessary to demonstrate the hegemony of white colonial rule. "The prisoners in our gaols are nothing but a lot of porridge eaters who get no punishment," he stated.

Eric Harrison and John Harrington both expressed their opposition to whipping as 'barbaric.' "I've employed native labour on Woodhouse Lea since 1867 and never even carried a whip. What's more, I've seldom been short of native labour," said Eric.

"I have the same approach on Preston," said John. "There are other ways of upholding discipline and encouraging compliance and cooperation such as withholding wages and reducing food rations. From the native's point of view, given their in-fighting and combative existence with other native groups, a white man brandishing a whip at an unarmed native may compel cooperation but in the long term, does such an act of supremacy engender respect or does it plant a seed of vengeance and resentment?"

Sadly, as in the case of social reforms regarding women, humane reform of the system of punishment was resisted. Flogging of natives and Indians persisted into the early years of the twentieth century.

****

An article titled 'A month in Alexandra County' published in the *Natal Mercury* expressed admiration for the extent of social activity in the county: "*Balls, parties, picnics, cricket matches, tennis matches, fishing excursions follow each other with amazing rapidity down here.*" Membership of the tennis clubs was said to exceed 70. The most recent annual ball had attracted more than 60 couples.

Since her first lunch date with him, their relationship had grown steadily thanks to further luncheons, tennis matches, a day at the Park Rynie fair and the endearing notes attached to occasional bouquets of flowers Tony delivered to Priscilla at the Park Rynie store. Having experienced tragedy himself, he was mindful not to pressure her into commitment but to give her time to heal and to grow in their relationship.

A direction of her personal growth concerned her business ambition. In that regard she had related Tony's remarks about business prospects in Scottburgh to Sarika who had warmed to the idea of establishing another store. The economic downturn in the colony in the wake of the withdrawal of British troops after the Anglo-Zulu war provided opportunities for bargain purchases. Buoyed by that prospect, Sarika met Tony in Scottburgh for a business discussion.

He recommended that she establish her store on the village's main thoroughfare – Scott Street. With the help of a property agent, vacant premises were purchased for just £35. Tony's builder undertook to modify and extend them for £40. Two months later the modifications and additions were complete. Charles Sinclair was tasked with delivering stock from Durban which was then arranged on shelves and counters by Priscilla in her role as manager of Sarika's Scottburgh branch.

To mark the occasion of the official opening of the store, a *soirée* was held on the premises catered for by Hassall's Hotel. Among those present were Priscilla's father John Harrington, Emma and Peter from Dewsbury, Eric and Frances Harrison from Woodhouse Lea, Charles Sinclair and, of course, Tony and Sarika's partner – Hugh Lawson. Several local residents also attended taking advantage of the free snacks and drinks.

Sarika spoke sincerely about Priscilla's diligent work ethic and enthusiasm and that it thrilled her to appoint her as manager of her third shop. Referring to Victoria Snell's women's reform movement, Sarika said she was proud to be able to promote it and to add impetus to awareness of the roles of which women were capable. "It's a blot on society that women are overlooked because social convention stereotypes them as unsuitable for most occupations beyond domesticity and childbearing."

Tony Hassall beamed with delight at the praise Sarika lavished on Priscilla. He hoped to be able to persuade her to sleepover at the hotel instead of returning to Preston with her father. But although she coquettishly declined his suggestion, she kissed and hugged him while accepting his invitation to be his partner at the upcoming ball in Umzinto.

****

News of Sarika's new shop in Scottburgh had Charles Reynolds fuming. "That's the ninth coolie-owned store in the county and the second one managed on the coolie bitch's behalf by white females," he raged. His attempt to marginalise Sarika commercially by forming a bulk food supply syndicate for indentured labour had failed when Sam Crookes and Edward Hawksworth declined to participate. Instead, his efforts unwittingly strengthened Charles Sinclair's transport business by consolidating its relationship with Sarika's store business. As a result, the Reynolds decided to investigate the possibilities of beach-wise shipping to compete aggressively with wagon transport of sugar to Durban.

In the 1862 the colonial engineer, Peter Paterson, had made a study of suitable spots along the coast whereby cargo could be transferred from a steamer offshore onto lighters and brought ashore and vice versa. Scottburgh and the mouth of the Umzinto River, called Mzinto Bay, were considered suitable places. In September 1883 Thomas Reynolds informed the Legislative Council that he and his sons had formed the Victoria Wharfage Company to develop shipment facilities at Mzinto Bay. As the biggest producers of sugar in the county, (2,300 tonnes in 1883), the Reynolds could afford to be independent. Accordingly, a warehouse was erected and a hawser installed with a 250-yard cable that could reach a steamer waiting offshore. A diminutive vessel called the *Carnarvon* moved the first load of 60 tonnes of sugar at a cost of £2. 6 pence per tonne – 15 shillings cheaper than wagon transport and in a fraction of the time wagons took to reach Durban. But like shipping on the Mzimkulu, sea conditions frequently ruled out cargo shipments from Mzinto Bay.

Another attempt by the Reynolds to marginalise Sarika's stores was to generate complaints about 'coolie stores' being open for trade in violation of Sunday Observance while white-owned stores remained closed. The monthly 'Alexandra Letter' in the *Mercury* complained of the desecration of Sunday Observance by Indian traders and the lack of enforcement by justices of the peace. Having repeatedly argued in favour of standards, Sarika ensured that, except for her Umzinto store, her Scottburgh and Park Rynie ones were closed on Sundays. She felt the large Indian population in the Umzinto area warranted that exception. It also amused her to note that notwithstanding the convention of Sunday Observance, some white colonists availed themselves of the convenience of shopping at her Umzinto store on Sundays.

****

Education for white children was a challenge in frontier areas like Alfred and Alexandra counties. In 1883 the only government school for white children was in Umkomaas and was limited to primary education. Significantly, thanks to the private initiative of the American Mission Board there were several mission schools for natives. A state-aided school for Indians was established in Umzinto in 1882. There was also one at Equeefa in the Sezela district by 1884. Prior to that, the Reverend Barker had run a small private school for Indians in Umzinto where Simon Prescott's sister, Anne, had taught before marrying and moving to Taunton Manor above Pietermaritzburg.

Education for young George Prescott had been limited to what his mother Cynthia could manage from her teaching experience when she had been employed at the state-aided school in Umzinto before George's birth in 1871. But at the age of 12 in 1883, she and Simon realised that he needed some high school tuition. The problem was they could not afford to send him to Durban as a boarder at Durban High School on the Berea. Their predicament was pretty much what other parents faced. As such, a comment in the annual *Natal Almanac* that "Alexandra County is the most neglected and backward as far as education is concerned" was no exaggeration.

Fortunately, establishment of a private school in the county headed by Reverend JC Manners-Coyte resolved their dilemma. All they wanted was for George to have two years in formal senior education until the age of 14 when it was usual for boys to quit school and pursue a trade. In George's case however, from his lack of interest in farming and outdoor work it looked as though he would be suited to a clerical or technical type occupation.

Edward Harrison, son of Frances and Eric, was 16 in 1883 and had received a fair education from Frances who had been a governess before marrying. Since an early age, Edward had been clear on wanting to follow in his father's and his Grandfather's footsteps in agriculture. Grandfather Hawksworth on Beneva had long since earmarked him as his next estate assistant.

****

Managing Sarika's Scottburgh store placed Priscilla in close proximity to Tony since his hotel was in the same street. When the store was closed during lunch hour, she invariably had lunch with him. On Saturday afternoons he was a frequent visitor at Park Rynie Tennis Club and occasionally managed to be slotted in for a set of mixed doubles with her. Ever courteous and hospitable, once a month he hosted the Harringtons for Sunday lunch. They reciprocated by having him to lunches at Preston.

As the months past, Priscilla's parents speculated on when their daughter would tie the knot with Tony. At almost 22 years of age, Priscilla was mature and sensible. Her judicious inventory of the volumes of items sold in the store impressed Sarika since, in that way, she was able to ensure constant re-stocking so that customers could never complain of items being out of stock.

Speculation about the couple ended on Valentine's Day 1884 when Tony asked Priscilla for her hand in marriage. He did so in his private dining room in Hassall's Hotel while having dinner with her. She had anticipated that something was afoot when he had made an excuse about not being available for lunch that day and instead asked her to stay after the close of business and to dine with him. Ever the caring lover, he had sent a messenger to Preston informing the Harringtons that Priscilla would be late in returning as she would be having an early dinner with him. Knowing her food preference, he had asked his chef to prepare a seafood platter. Instead of the usual bottle of white wine, a bottle of *Veuve Clicquot* champagne nestled in an ice bucket next to his place setting at the table indicating that the occasion was exceptional.

At an appropriate moment during their dinner, Tony left his place at the table and went around to where Priscilla was seated. He bent down on one knee and proposed to her as he held out an ornate little box cradling an exquisite white diamond ring. She immediately stood up, embraced and kissed him. In a voice hushed by emotion, she indicated her acceptance. "Yes, dear Tony, I love you and want to be Mrs Hassall!" In the moments which followed Tony placing the ring on her finger, joyous emotion overwhelmed them. Their chance liaison through tennis and their respective tragic life experiences which preceded their meeting echoed the prescience of the observation Tony had made at their first meeting – 'fate often provides a virtuous dimension.'

In their daze of happiness, the champagne was almost forgotten. But after sharing a toast and embracing passionately, Tony said he would accompany her to Preston to inform her parents. Emily and John were elated at the news. "We are so pleased for you, Priscilla, darling! We wish you all the happiness you deserve after the sadness you have endured! And to Tony: our heartiest welcome into our family! We are thrilled and honoured to have you as our son-in-law, and we know you will treasure our dear daughter and little Stella."

After hugs, kisses and handshakes, glasses were clinked, and toasts were drunk. Since it was quite late, Tony said he would need to return to Scottburgh. Kissing his fiancée tenderly, he boarded his carriage and spurred the horse on its way.

Two months later Priscilla and Tony were married at the Scottburgh Anglican Church where three-year-old Stella was Priscilla's flower girl. In attendance were most of the members of the Park Rynie and Scottburgh tennis clubs, the Harrisons, Emma and Peter from Dewsbury, Charles Sinclair, several Royal Hotel bar patrons and, of course, Sarika and Hugh Lawson. Ill health prevented Trish and Stewart traveling from Weenen County to be present. The day after the wedding reception at Hassall's Hotel, Tony and Priscilla left for Durban from where they boarded a train bound for the Midlands and their honeymoon retreat.

****

Evidence of the dark issues to which Martin Pryce had referred in the Janki case emerged during a series of court cases presided over by acting magistrate William Rose Gordon in Umzinto in July 1884. Of 28 cases, nine concerned brutal assaults by white colonists on indentured and free Indians. Routinely the accused claimed they had been provoked by the Indian. In several cases employers were found guilty of failing to pay wages or for refusing passes to indentured labourers to leave the estate in order to see the magistrate or district surgeon. In every case the white colonist was subjected to a small fine ranging from ten shillings to just £1.

Punishment for Indians charged for being absent without leave, disobedience, misconduct or not having a pass from an estate, ranged from imprisonment for 14 days to loss of wages and severe curtailment of rations. But these cases were what was visible to the public. Unseen was the routine thrashing of labour on estates for any number of contrived reasons. One of Charles Reynolds' overseers by the name of Edgar was twice convicted of violent assault yet Reynolds refused to dismiss him.

Having been present at the court during several of the recent cases, David Aiken related his observations during a visit to the Royal Hotel bar. Apart from Frank Reynolds who was only occasionally present, the regulars were all supportive of the critical remarks Martin Pryce had made in the Janki case. "Are we going to accept what Frank said when he was last here that treatment of Indians is purely the concern of the Protector and none of our business?" enquired Robert Anderson angrily.

"I know when Sarika hears of this spate of cases and how acting magistrate Gordon has handled them, she is going to be incensed," said Eric Harrison. "It is obvious that the application of humanitarian principles, which acting magistrate Hathorn endorsed in his ruling on the Janki case, is being ignored. The Protector is not doing his job and needs to be held accountable."

"I have a suggestion. Why don't we see if we can rally the Alexandra County Association to take a stand against this blatant injustice?" ventured proprietor William Thornton. "We should ask ourselves if we would sit back and do nothing if Sarika was charged with some misdemeanour and subjected to an excessive fine or imprisonment just because she is an Indian."

"Well, let's not forget how the County Association positioned itself when Sarika applied to buy a plot of land. The majority of those who attended the meeting ignored the right of a settler to own land, regardless of race. Instead, the prospect of what was termed "another coolie store," allowed emotions to determine their opinion," cautioned John Harrington.

"I think we ought to realise by taking a stand on human rights abuse, we are going up against the Reynolds empire in this county. Where will it get us? Just look at the influence they already wield in terms of sugar production, rum sales, political representation in the Council, buying support and compliance with donations?" asked James Ross disconsolately.

"While all of what has been said is valid, I think we need to stand up for what is right. There may be all sorts of risks in doing so, but the alternative is submission, compliance and acceptance. And somehow, that doesn't wash with me. Just look how Sarika stood up to Brander and then she stood up to Reynolds in the Janki case. She put many in the county to shame by challenging Reynolds. We need to take a stand on the principles which Her Majesty Queen Victoria has exhorted. In so doing we may encourage others in the colony to do likewise," argued John Redman.

"I don't know whether it's the liquor that is emboldening us, but you're right, John. The principles at stake need to be upheld. So, with your permission I am going to draft a letter to the County Association calling for a meeting to take a firm stand on implementing the humanitarian recommendations of the Coolie Commission of 1872. And whatever the outcome of that effort is, Attorney-General Gallwey should be informed and requested to act in the spirit of the Queen's intentions," declared William Thornton.

As there were no dissenting voices, out of a sense of camaraderie William announced a round of drinks at half price.

****

Soon after proprietor William Thornton's letter reached the County Association, on July 29, 1884, the Legislative Council in Pietermaritzburg voted to establish a Commission of Inquiry into Indian Immigration. Public agitation against on-going Indian immigration and what was termed the "excrescent growth of the many offshoots" of Indian settlement, served to muster sufficient political will to deal comprehensively with what had come to be called the 'Indian Question.'

Although Thomas Reynolds voted in favour of the Commission of Inquiry, he dismissed it as "a rotten egg which will produce no benefit whatsoever." In his address to the council, he made his attitude to indenture very clear: Indians should all serve a second five-year indenture term and then be sent back to India. But his view did not address the rapidly growing Indian settler population which was the real reason white colonists were becoming anxious. In 1884 the Indian settler population of Natal stood at 29,589 while the total white population was 35,453. In Alex County the Indian settler population had already exceeded that of whites: 793 to 567 and showed every sign of increasing its majority.

****

CHAPTER 19

The initial response of the County Association to William Thornton's letter requesting a firm humanitarian stand on the treatment of Indians was that there was no point getting involved since an official inquiry had been launched to probe all aspects of indentured labour and Indian immigration.

Discussion of the County Association's attitude at the Royal Hotel bar saw Frank Reynolds clashing with William Thornton on the matter. "You people are just soapbox orators. The Association's job has nothing to do with the welfare of the indentured. I've already told you, that is the Protector's concern."

Agitatedly, William Thornton interrupted Reynolds reminding him that the Association's mandate could only be determined by a representative meeting of its members. "Until a public meeting on this issue has been held and the sentiments of those present have been voted on, the Association cannot claim to have a particular standpoint."

"Some of us in this County, Frank, believe in open, democratic expression which is why we are going to demand a public meeting of the Alex County Association as is our right," exclaimed Robert Anderson defiantly.

Sensing that the mood of the bar patrons was decidedly against him, Frank Reynolds finished his beer and headed for the door. "Suit yourselves. But I can tell you not only are you wasting your time, but you may regret your actions," he said as he departed.

"Well, if that is not a threat, then I'm confused," commented John Redman. "I say to hell with Reynolds' attitude! It's just another example of how they throw their weight around. We must insist on a public meeting of the ACA. This fancy, official inquiry is unlikely to start before next January. In the meantime, humanitarian abuses continue. In any event, I'll wager in advance that whoever the commissioners are, their findings will favour employers like the Reynolds."

If anything, Frank Reynolds' attempt at intimidation reinforced the opinion of the bar regulars to proceed in demanding a public meeting of the County Association.

****

Reluctantly the secretary of the ACA advertised the meeting as requested. On the appointed day, about 30 men gathered at the Umzinto Memorial Hall. In advance Sarika had decided she would attend since together with Hugh Lawson they had instigated the Janki case. In support of her were most of the Royal Hotel bar room regulars.

"I strongly expect your presence to provoke emotion and to deflect focus from what we want to achieve," remarked Eric Harrison to her. "I also expect the Reynolds will be present to stir things up and basically shut down the meeting," he warned.

"Thank you, Eric, for your concern, but I refuse to be intimidated. If I can bring a case to court, I can take a stand at a public meeting," said Sarika defiantly.

The substance of the motion before the ACA was an appeal to the Protector to be proactive in monitoring human rights on estates as the 1872 Coolie Commission advocated; also, that magistrates punish violations of those rights far more severely. First to speak in support of the motion was Sarika.

Before she had even stood up to address the meeting barracking commenced from a group of men Eric identified as assistant managers on Reynolds' estates. "Go back to your shop and mind your own business!" yelled one of them. "Go back to India!" yelled another. Nervously the ACA chairman, John Kirkman, attempted to call the meeting to order. "Gentlemen, I appeal to you to exercise restraint. Sarika is a stakeholder in the county and as such deserves the right to be heard!"

"Thank you, Mr Kirkman," said Sarika loudly and with determination. "There are some of us in this community who do not accept the price of economic benefit and profit without concern for the human suffering on which it is achieved. Twelve years have passed since the publication of the report of the Coolie Commission, yet its humanitarian recommendations continue to be flouted and neglected on some sugar estates."

"The indenture contract does not give employers the right to act as judge, jury and executioner in the treatment of their labour. The basis of my appeal today is that indenture contracts are applied humanely. Britain abolished slavery 50 years ago, yet the worst aspects of slavery are evident on some estates employing indentured labour."

A fresh round of heckling and derisive comments erupted as Sarika paused in her address. "Most of the indentured are the scum of India," declared one of the Reynolds' managers. "The only thing they understand is forceful treatment. It's the only way to counter their lying and shamming," he said to loud cheers and applause.

Realising that her presence was provoking the unruly state of the meeting and that she could not hope to regain a degree of attention, Sarika asked Hugh Lawson to try and conclude what she had intended to say. Unperturbed by shouts of "coolie lover" as he stood up to speak, Hugh, banged on the table and riposted: "You call the indentured 'scum' but your conduct is hardly civilised!"

After chairman Kirkman had intervened again, the meeting quietened down somewhat which enabled Lawson to make the points Sarika had intended. "All we are asking the ACA to endorse is that treatment of the indentured is tempered with reasonableness and in the spirit the Coolie Commission intended. It is insensitive to force women in advanced stages of pregnancy to work in the fields. It is unreasonable to compel work to be done in the pouring rain. It is wrong and unhealthy to issue maize or rice which is mouldy. It breeds resentment when rations are not timeously issued or when passes are vindictively denied for visits to the village, the magistrate or district surgeon. By providing proper ablutions, better health will result and a better worker/employer relationship. By adhering to such standards compliance and co-operation prospers. Surely, as the representatives of the enlightened civilisation the British Empire claims to be, such considerations should determine how to treat our labour?"

Uproar erupted once again. "Where have you been hiding, Lawson?" yelled one of the Reynolds managers. "Indentured labour is not a holiday camp. Without pressure on them nothing gets done because of their damn shamming and laziness."

"Why don't you take a look at John Bazley's Nil Desperandum estate?" countered Lawson. "His indentured have responded positively to his provision of proper housing, proper ablutions and fair treatment. Their health is good. He has no desertions and never uses the lash – unlike what occurs on certain Reynolds' estates!" he thundered.

Hugh Lawson's last statement proved too much for the Reynolds' crowd. "Get back to Victoria County!" screamed one of them, "and take your coolie lover with you!" Sensing that the mood had turned ugly and even threatening, chairman Kirkman declared the meeting abandoned.

****

The mood at the Royal Hotel bar was somewhat subdued in the wake of the failed ACA meeting. "The influence of the Reynolds was on full display at that meeting," said John Harrington ruefully. "It means we can add another notch to the extent to which they control this county. From the comments their assistant managers made at the meeting, we get an idea of how they are going to pull the wool over the eyes of the commissioners when they arrive to conduct their inquiry in Alex County."

"Yes, I was hoping that our motion might have been endorsed, but with hindsight, that was naïve thinking. At least, it could have served to alert the commissioners to the fact that circumstances prevail here which bear serious probing," remarked proprietor William Thornton.

"Let's take heart, gentlemen. By ignoring Frank Reynolds' dismissive remark not to waste our time, we showed initiative and courage. We stood up to the Reynolds – well, Sarika and Hugh Lawson did, and in commendable fashion. Anyway, that's to our overall credit. Our motion didn't fail. It simply was not put to the vote because the meeting was abandoned. So, our case remains intact. When the commissioners arrive here next year, as a group, we can demand to make submissions to them," declared John Redman.

As had been the case with the Janki trial, the 'Country Notes' columns in the press were silent about the Alexandra County Association meeting. Only Victoria Snell's monthly newsletter to her reformist ladies group carried the story. In praising the role Sarika played, Victoria urged her ladies to exploit county associations whenever issues called for reform measures to be promoted.

****

In the last months of 1884 Thomas Reynolds experienced fresh bouts of unpopularity. Since the white population of Alfred County exceeded that of Alex County (665 to 567), Alfred County residents were demanding a representative of their own on the Legislative Council. Their frustration was aptly expressed in Resident Magistrate James Giles' annual report. "The County hopes for a whole, visible Member of the Council instead of a share in one whose face it never sees."

Besides that issue, Reynolds' unpopularity stemmed from the fact that he had failed to promote Alfred County's demand for a telegraph link. Then when 44 family heads of the Marburg Norwegian community petitioned him for the relocation of the magistracy from Harding, 50 miles inland, to the coast, Reynolds found himself damned if he did and damned if he didn't. At a public meeting in Harding in December Reynolds was subjected to a vote of no confidence for his failure on the telegraph issue and for wanting to relocate the magistracy to the coast. In both cases Reynolds' plight was the consequence of "financial circumstances" in Natal, which uncomfortably endorsed the perception that Alfred and Alex were the "Cinderella counties," of the colony.

****

While Alfred County residents were seething about the magistracy issue and the non-extension of the telegraph to Harding, Alexandra County residents had new reasons to complain about the Mkomanzi River.

At the Royal Hotel bar, anger was expressed over the failure of the government to take timeous action in replacing the pont. "It's an utter disgrace that after just four years since the previous pont had rotted away, the current one has also had to be withdrawn from service because of wood rot," fumed proprietor William Thornton.

"What's worse is that the wagons now have to risk fording the river at the drift. In the crushing season 120 wagons cross the river each week. And cashing in on our plight is a private ferry charging exorbitant fees for its services," bemoaned James Ross.

At the Wiltshire discussion centred on the latest reasons the government had given to subordinate the county's infrastructure needs to the priority of railway construction to the northern coalfields. "Besides that, colonial engineer Albert Hime says that even though £2,500 features on the Estimates for the coming financial year for the Mkomanzi, he claims the amount is totally inadequate to even start the foundations of a bridge. According to Hime, borings to a depth of up to 41 feet have indicated the soil is too soft to pile foundations, so the £2,500 would get us nowhere," remarked Charles Sinclair.

"Officials love to talk about priorities, but what are we to make of the £17,518 the government is spending on a new lunatic asylum? How can a couple of nutcases enjoy greater priority than the need for a bridge over the Mkomanzi on which an entire county depends? Absolute double standards!" declared James McMillan indignantly.

****

The festive season of 1884 saw family gatherings taking place far and wide. The Harringtons enjoyed a family reunion with the arrival of Trish and Stewart from Weenen County. They had great news: Trish was pregnant. Understandably Emily and John were delighted at the prospect of a second grandchild with John hoping for a boy to continue the Harrington line.

More cheering news followed at lunch on Christmas Day. Priscilla and Tony Hassall announced that they hoped to be parents by June 1885 which would mean the prospect of a third Harrington grandchild. For Tony, Priscilla's pregnancy promised to diminish the tragedy he had experienced when his first wife died in miscarriage several years earlier. Also present at the lunch were Sarika and Hugh. When asked when they intended to be married, they coyly evaded the question insisting they were content with their present relationship.

At Taunton Manor, Victoria and Gordon Snell were hosted by Anne and Martin Pryce. In order for Cynthia to have a rare visit to her parents, James and Margaret Moodie in Ladysmith, Simon Prescott ceded the opportunity to be with his sisters. In so doing the Prescotts missed out on seeing the new addition to the Pryce family: Lyndon, the son Martin had hoped for and named after his deceased father, was born in July 1882. His two sisters, Eleanor aged eight and Elizabeth aged six, doted on their little brother fulfilling the togetherness of family Martin had not experienced as an only child.

Victoria and Gordon's only child, Lily was already 16 years of age. She had inherited her father's business interests and was clearly a Snell in that regard. But she had also inherited her mother's golden hair, blue eyes and physical attractiveness. "She's going to be joining the Durban office of E Snell & Co doing clerical work. She has shown an interest in product sourcing, costing and sales. Once she's covered the basics, I will have her trained by a firm of accountants," announced Gordon.

"How do you feel about that, Lily?" asked Martin.

"I am so grateful Daddy is giving me the opportunity to have a career in a field that interests me. When I consider the prospects of almost all the girls in my final year at St Anne's, I am indeed very fortunate. Many were resigned to becoming governesses; some saw no prospects beyond helping out on their parents' estates hoping that someday they would meet the right man and marry. I know Mum was a governess until she met Dad. But she was fortunate to have been hired by an exemplary couple, the Greenacres, who, in turn, provided her with a window on life beyond educating their children, Alice and Isabel!" said Lily as she blew a kiss to her mother and hugged her father.

"I am so proud of Lily. She exemplifies my reformist passion of innovation in advancing opportunities for women. And, of course, I am so grateful in having a husband who shares my passion! Thank you, darling Gordon!" declared Victoria as she embraced him.

An item of interest in the conversation amongst the adults concerned Simon and Cynthia's travel to Ladysmith to be with her parents. "When the Prescotts were last here, just after the railway had reached Pietermaritzburg, I remember Simon expressing the hope that before long they would be able to travel by rail all the way to Ladysmith. But that hope has not materialised," remarked Gordon. "From your perspective, Martin, how is rail construction proceeding?"

"At an absolute snail's pace! The cost of the war put a spoke in the wheel, of course. Then the contractors put in claims amounting to more than £228,000 for extra work done. So, at Goodricke's I have been kept busy trying to pare down those costs. Added to that has been the discovery of structural faults in some of the bridges on the main and North Coastlines. Then, incredibly, by providing cheap wagon transport, wagon owners have severely undercut the railway's tariffs thereby reducing rail revenues. In addition to the considerable engineering challenges involved in extending the line from Pietermaritzburg to Howick, a distance of about 17 miles, it was only this year in July that the line reached Howick. So, sadly for the Prescotts a major part of their journey to Ladysmith, the remaining 75 miles, has to be undertaken by wagon. I can't see the railway reaching Ladysmith until probably sometime in 1886."

At the Klip River magistrate's residence in Ladysmith, Cynthia, Simon and their two boys, George aged 13 and James aged 8, arrived on Christmas Eve after a torrid wagon journey from Howick. They were welcomed by James and Margaret Moodie who were delighted to see their two grandchildren. After refreshments and ablutions, they had a light supper. "We'll eat in grand style tomorrow," said Margaret to George and James as she had the rare opportunity of tucking her grandchildren into their beds.

Seated in the drawing room, James and his son-in-law, Simon, engaged in animated conversation while quaffing beers. In updating his father-in-law on life in the Umzinto district, Simon carefully avoided mention of Sarika and her successful stores. He knew that was a taboo subject with the senior

Moodies because of the social embarrassment their son Michael had caused by his relationship with Sarika which had led to his elopement with her to Isipingo and his tragic death at the Reunion mill. Instead, he raised the issue of George possibly having a career in the civil service. "Cynthia and I are aware that George is not interested in agricultural matters on Dewsbury. He reads a lot and unlike us is not the outdoor type which is a bit unusual living in a frontier environment as we do."

Relishing the opportunity to provide guidance and advice, James Moodie pointed out that George would need to complete his high school years. "I understand that he is currently in a private high school in Alex County. I would hope that his curriculum includes classical subjects like Latin as he would need such exposure not merely in the interests of a sound education but also if he wants to pursue a legal vocation. You might want to take him to the Umzinto courthouse during his holidays to get an idea of what is involved. As you are aware from the number of acting magistrates you have had in Alex County since I left, there is a dire shortage of properly trained magistrates in the colony. Your current resident magistrate, Gould Arthur Lucas, is actually a military man with the rank of Captain who was drafted into the civil service very reluctantly by the General Officer commanding Her Majesty's forces in Southern Africa."

"Of course, Simon, there are many other avenues for George to have a career in the civil service, but they would require him to live in Pietermaritzburg where the heart of the administration is based. George could also consider the Post Office and the railways. With the sure prospect of Alex County eventually being connected by rail to Durban, railway administration in Alex County is going to require suitable clerks and personnel."

While the men were talking in the drawing room Cynthia and her mother were busy in the kitchen preparing food for Christmas Day lunch. Cynthia learned that her younger sister, Ruth, was pregnant. She was married to a cattle rancher in the Colenso district. Enquiring how her mother was coping with life in Klip River County after 16 years in Alex County, Margaret conceded that she preferred the colonial society of Klip River to Alex County. “I noticed how there was a distinct division in Alex between the sugar planters and everyone else. Here we don’t have that. Farming here is very mixed – cattle, sheep, maize. We also don’t have that drunkenness problem which Alex has with those rum distilleries and the large number of indentured Indians. There are some Indian stores here in Ladysmith but nothing like the growing number in Alex County. So European life here is a lot more consolidated and integrated which suits me.”

****

CHAPTER 20

The Indian Immigrants Commission was constituted in January 1885 and came to be called the Wragg Commission after its chairman Supreme Court judge Walter Wragg. He had been a district judge in Ceylon and was conversant with the Tamil language and Eastern ways. The commissioners spent 18 months collecting evidence and visited 21 estates between Stanger and Umzinto.

In anticipation of the arrival of the commissioners, the Royal Hotel bar group, whose attempt to get the Alexandra County Association to consider the application of humanitarian rights on estates had been unsuccessful, decided to meet with Magistrate Gould Arthur Lucas.

Since his return from overseas Lucas had expressed great criticism of the poor condition of the tributary which joined the Umzinto River. "He has regularly complained about what he calls the 'filth' from the Reynolds' distillery in Equeefa. In a recent report he described it as 'prejudicial to health.' I feel that his willingness to condemn Reynolds' pollution of the environment shows that he is unafraid of the social lions of the district," observed Sarika. "For that reason, I think we should approach him to organise a meeting with the commissioners where we can render our submissions first hand."

As a result, on behalf of the Royal Hotel bar group Sarika and Hugh Lawson had a private meeting with Magistrate Lucas. After accepting their written submissions in which incidents and observations of inhumane treatment were detailed, they were greatly impressed by an account he gave of an intervention he had attempted on behalf of an indentured woman.

"During one of my intermittent spells here as magistrate when I was not on military duty, I visited the Central Hospital in the county and was appalled by the injuries suffered by an indentured woman. Her chest and back bore the marks of the brutal assault when she was assailed by a *sirdar* wielding a weapon with rows of nails on a hook. I reported this to Attorney-General Gallwey enquiring how it was that the Protector, Louis Mason, had not been apprised of her case."

"Mason's response, which was copied to the colonial secretary, was that supervision of the indentured-on estates was 'quite inadequate.' But it was the final sentence of his response that bothers me. He wrote: *It is not possible for me to discover every matter especially if there is a conspiracy to keep me in the dark."*

"So, Sarika, there is much dark truth in your submission that employers of indentured labour are acting as judge, jury and executioner in the treatment of the indentured. Although I have no doubt that some of this is going to be exposed by the commissioners, I am not confident that positive improvements will come about," declared Magistrate Lucas.

****

In June 1885, the Wragg Commission visited Alexandra County. Although Magistrate Lucas assured Sarika and Hugh Lawson that he had handed their submissions over to the commissioners, they were disappointed not to be accorded an opportunity to meet with them. "I suppose they want first hand evidence," said Sarika resignedly.

Accompanying the commissioners to the various estates for security reasons was the head of the Alexandra County constabulary, Constable JC Whitwell. He was to prove very useful in relaying what he witnessed in the course of the commissioners' visitations. The Reynolds' Equeefa estate was their first destination. Managed by Charles Reynolds his first submission to the commissioners was that there was too much absenteeism and that the law did not provide sufficient punishment. “Coolies are masters at shamming,” he grumbled. When the commissioners confronted him with Magistrate Lucas’s assertion that dunder (residue) from Reynolds’ mill was poisoning fish in the stream and thereby polluting the Umzinto River, Reynolds denied all knowledge thereof.

Yet that issue actually went back to March 1884 when the District Surgeon, Dr Bonnar, had requested urgent remedial measures to improve the quality of the water supply by addressing sanitary conditions. But Reynolds had declined to comply. As a result, the Governor wished to forbid any further allotment of Indian labour to Equeefa estate. But the failure of the Legislative Council to pass appropriate legislation preventing defilement of streams negated the Governor’s intentions.

Arising from this issue, in reporting his findings to the Royal Hotel bar patrons, Constable Whitwell claimed he overheard one of the commissioners, James Saunders of Tongaat, insisting that complaints about the quality of water were “very exaggerated” and that, in any event, the general health of the indentured was good.

But one incident that stood out in Constable Whitwell’s observations of how the commissioners went about their investigation concerned the general assembly of the indentured. The commissioners had requested that the entire labour force on Equeefa estate be assembled so that they could be addressed through an interpreter and encouraged to express opinions or grievances. When the commissioners requested Reynolds, his overseers and *sirdars* to withdraw from the gathering, they refused.

Reynolds claimed that withdrawing would enable elements within the indentured to stir up emotions which encouraged exaggeration of issues and stoked defiance. That mindset, he maintained, fostered a breakdown of discipline. In the wake of such exercises, he found it necessary to punish large numbers before "he could get things right."

Having heard Constable Whitwell's account, Sarika referred to Law 2 of 1870, a copy of which Martin Pryce had left after representing her in the October 1881 Janki case. "It astounds me that the commissioners did not deal firmly with Charles Reynolds' refusal to withdraw from that assembly of his labour. After all, section 34 of Law 2 states that obstruction of an official or agent or non-compliance with an instruction is liable to a fine of £10- or 30-days imprisonment."

Asked whether he had heard any reaction from the commissioners to Reynolds' refusal to comply with their request, Constable Whitwell said their general opinion was that they saw no harm in Reynolds and his *sirdars* remaining at the meeting and accepted that he knew best how to manage his labour.

"Well, if that is not collusion in high places, then I'm not William Thornton!" exclaimed the Royal Hotel proprietor. "The investigation into Reynolds' estates is not even two days old and already we are seeing justice compromised."

"Yes, and let's not forget that Thomas Reynolds is on record in the Legislative Council saying that this commission is a waste of time," observed John Redman. "I have a feeling that we are in for more shocks as the process unwinds!"

****

Since the expansion of the structure of the Indian Immigration Trust Board (IITB) in 1880 to include two non-government members, on behalf of Alexandra County, William Hawksworth had petitioned the colonial secretary to include a representative from the South Coast. Although unsuccessful in his first request, in 1884 when a vacancy occurred St George Arbuthnot of Sezela was appointed on Hawksworth's recommendation.

At a gathering at Michaelhouse, Sarika expressed positive acceptance of this development. "Apart from the occasional announcement in the *Government Gazette,* we are kept in the dark about the deliberations of the IITB. But in terms of the legislation governing the Board, it advises on control and management of Indians – free, like myself, and indentured. So, I'm hoping St George can provide us with an inside track about the Board's working and also that he can promote enlightened thinking regarding the treatment of Indians."

****

In May 1885 colonial engineer Albert Hime became Alexandra County's *bête noire* as a result of his response to the largest and latest petition (signed by 99 residents) demanding a bridge over the Mkomanzi. Hime tactlessly rejected the six pertinent reasons the petitioners had submitted in justification of a bridge. "I cannot think that the want of a bridge over the Lower Mkomanzi is a great, or indeed any drawback on the progress of the county."

Uproar reigned at both the Wiltshire and the Royal Hotel bar. Charles Sinclair was incandescent with rage. "How dare Hime claim that the drift is fordable? Six of my wagons have to ford the river each week. It means they have to wait for low tide. When it is neap tide the depth and the current pose great risk to a wagon toppling over. Then when fording is not possible, we have to use the pont which is not only in poor condition but is an added expense."

"By claiming that the width of the river and its soft soil bed makes bridge construction too expensive, is Hime effectively telling us that we just have to accept that until some great turn of financial fortune, the Mkomanzi will not have a bridge?" fumed an exasperated Captain Tucker.

“It amuses me at the same time as it annoys me that Hime rejects our idea of a toll because, in his view, it would not even cover the interest on the cost of bridge construction,” remarked Royal Hotel proprietor William Thornton. “Since when did Hime become an actuary? If he did a bit of research, he would note that the first toll in the colony was established on the Berea in Durban in 1867. That tollgate recouped the total cost of hardening Berea Rd – the gateway to Durban.”

“The fact that we are stuck with Hime as the colonial engineer illustrates the extent to which we are held captive by unelected, appointed officials. If we had a responsible government dispensation, our parliament could sack Hime and replace him with someone sympathetic to Alex County’s transport plight,” declared Robert Anderson.

“I think it is arrogant of Hime to claim that what we as T Reynolds &Sons have initiated at Mzinto Bay is alleviating the county’s transport dilemma. The occasional portage we manage from there is entirely a cargo of sugar. It’s not two-way traffic. So Hime’s claim that shipping from Mzinto Bay should be regarded as a substitute for a bridge over the Mkomanzi is utter nonsense,” said Frank Reynolds dismissively.

“Now that shipping at Port Shepstone is a reality, I get the impression that we are being treated like children: we can’t have a bridge *and* a port. We must be satisfied with what we have. Yet if it was not for the private initiative of James Aiken and the work of William Bazley, there would be no shipping on the Mzimkulu,” opined an angry James Ross.

****

As the local representative on the Indian Immigration Trust Board St George Arbuthnot often accompanied the Wragg commissioners to estates they were investigating. In turn, he served as a conduit in informing Sarika and her group of the daily findings and statements the commissioners were recording.

As Hugh Lawson remarked, "What we are learning from St George and occasionally from Constable Whitwell is very illuminating because much of it is unlikely to feature in the final report of the Commission. And in any case, when will that report be published?" he asked.

At what became a regular gathering at Michaelhouse, lubricated `by fruit cordial and accompanied by vegetable samoosas, St George divulged the latest news of the commissioners' findings. "Does it surprise you that today Charles Reynolds said that all Indians should be kept in agricultural pursuits and not allowed to own stores? That's why he loathes you, Sarika. He also feels that Indians are 'too much protected' and that the protection system, as he calls it, is overdone."

"It's difficult to avoid the conclusion that he is still bitter over having had to allow Janki's indenture contract to be taken over by you, Hugh," remarked John Harrington.

"Yes, John, and we should not underestimate Charles' brother, Frank. He says he supports everything his brother has stated. When asked how treacle from their mill had found its way into the stream, he blamed the indentured," noted St George.

"In contrast, the commissioners' visit to Bazley's Nil Desperandum estate was a heartening eye-opener. There are 126 indentured labourers on the estate and their lodgings are properly constructed with decent ablutions. The register, medical book and wage book were all in perfect order. Contentment amongst the labour was obvious. I just hope the commissioners marked that contrast not only with the Reynolds estates but also with Andrew Sinclair's small Cowick estate," stated St George.

"Sinclair employs only 25 Indians, but the commissioners found that his wage book was a mess and that wages were not up to date. Equally shocking was that Sinclair refused to allow the sick to be hospitalised in Umzinto and made up his own medical concoctions to treat them. He substituted olive oil for ghee oil. When one of his labourers, Sewpersadh, reported this to the magistrate, the poor fellow was fined five shillings for being absent because Sinclair refused to give him a pass. Apparently, Sinclair had once before physically beaten Sewpersadh."

"It's apparent that what you are witnessing, St George, is the proverbial tip of the iceberg. I have no doubt that brutality and inhuman treatment is a daily occurrence on many estates. When I was on that estate in Illovo, such treatment did not occur. But subsequently, when I mixed with *dukahwallah* traders in Umzinto, I became aware that many of them bore the scars of brutality they had suffered during their indenture contracts," said Sarika wistfully.

"How should we be responding to these revelations? Just because there's an investigation taking place why should a blanket of silence be cast over what is being exposed?" asked Eric Harrison.

"One thing is certain: expecting Thomas Reynolds to lift the lid on what we are finding out is never going to happen," sneered Robert Anderson.

"If the Alexandra County Association was not beholden to the Reynolds, it could serve as a vocal mouthpiece in exposing what's going on. But that avenue is closed, as we know from recent experience. Of course, we could hold our own public meeting in the Umzinto Memorial Hall," suggested William Thornton.

"Good idea, William. It grates me that we live in a community which frequents the same stores and churches, yet we remain silent about terrible human rights abuses that are going on around us," observed Sarika.

****

In reporting Thomas Reynolds' death on 10 June 1885 from a ruptured liver, the *Mercury* referred to his name as a 'household word on the South Coast.' He was buried in St Patrick's church yard yet strangely no details were published about his funeral. Such occasions were usually comprehensively reported – from the salient aspects of the eulogies delivered to the names of prominent residents in attendance.

At both the Wiltshire and the Royal Hotel bar his passing was the subject of discussion. "The absence of any comments or letters in the *Mercury* concerning Reynolds somehow does not surprise me," commented Charles Sinclair. "Thomas certainly was not popular among Alfred County residents for wanting to move the magistracy from Harding and for failing to promote their petitions calling for a telegraphic connection."

"I think opinion of him has soured in recent years because of the arrogance of his sons and the way they throw their weight around in Alex County. His political backtracking on responsible government also did not endear him to at least half the residents," suggested James McMillan.

"Any ideas as to who is going to succeed Reynolds as our sole public representative?" enquired William Thornton as he polished some beer glasses in the Royal Hotel bar. Dr Jones, who had replaced Dr Booth as District Surgeon, said he had heard that it might be someone from Alfred County. "I suppose the Alfred folk feel that if they can't have their own representative and have to share one with Alex County, then the next best thing is to ensure that the new representative is one of their own."

Dr Jones' thinking proved correct. Since the late 1860s, Sir John Jarvis Bisset had owned property on the Alfred County coast. Promoted to the rank of Major General in 1867, Bisset was a distinguished soldier having fought in the Eastern Cape frontier wars.

"It will be interesting to see what opinion he holds on to the Indian Question. Apparently, he employs about 30 indentured Indians on his Barrow Green estate," said Robert Anderson.

Bisset's election manifesto provided the answer. He favoured the return to India of all Indian labourers upon completion of ten years of indenture. Subsequently, he even went as far as saying that 'no more coolies should be brought from India.'

At one of the regular gatherings at Michaelhouse, Sarika expressed dismay at Bisset's anti-Indian views. "What I find distressing is that an educated, experienced man like Bisset does not distinguish between Indians as settlers and Indians as labourers. What his opinion says to me is that I should be back in India. Across the colony there are Indians like me who as settlers are contributing not only to the economy but serving as mechanics, tailors and clerks while many are providing fruit, fish and vegetables in abundance to white colonists."

"It distresses me," said Sarika, "that our new public representative on the Council is unaware of the very pertinent remark which Sir Garnet Wolseley made in 1875 when he was briefly administrator of the colony. He said that without Indians, commerce in Natal would languish and its revenue would be seriously reduced. He made that observation ten years ago. How much more relevant is it now?"

****

In pursuing the idea of having a public meeting in the Memorial Hall on the topic of humanitarian concern for indentured labour, Sarika and her fellow organisers encountered an early setback. It had been their intention to have the Protector of Indian immigrants, Louis Mason, as the guest speaker. But as a government official he had expressed reservations. In response, however, Sarika reminded him that speaking at a public meeting was no different from speaking in committee at Council meetings where his every word was recorded in Hansard and published.

A few days after Sarika's attempts to persuade Mason to address her intended public meeting, she received a letter from him politely stating that he was not available.

"I have no doubt that somebody we know got to Mason. The situation stinks of intimidation and collusion in high places," said Eric Harrison. "Let's recall what magistrate Lucas told Sarika about the fear Mason expressed in a letter to Attorney-General Gallwey. He spoke about a 'conspiracy to keep him in the dark.' Well, it seems that keeping all of us in the dark is the agenda regarding what goes on at indentured estates."

The next setback Sarika received was that the Memorial Hall was booked up until the end of the year, so, therefore, it was not available.

"Considering that the Reynolds donated the land on which the hall was built and made a donation to its construction, it is obvious that they are behind denying us the hall as a venue to discuss a topic they have a vested interest in keeping quiet," declared William Thornton with disgust.

The next possible venue to consider was the private Indian school run by Reverend Joseph Barker. But shortly after enquiring whether it could be used for a public meeting, Sarika received a letter from Reverend Barker begging her to withdraw her request.

"This is really revealing about who controls just about everything in this county. Reverend Barker receives financial support from the Reynolds to run that private school. Of course, it's very generous of them. But they are now leaning on him because our agenda is not to their liking," said James Ross.

The final negative against Sarika wanting to hold a public meeting arrived in the form of an anonymous letter. It warned her to desist from trying to stir up trouble or face malicious damage to her property.

At a special meeting called at Michaelhouse attended by all the Royal Hotel bar regulars, the situation confronting them was discussed. "We clearly have touched a sensitive nerve in attempting to create awareness about what the Wragg Commission is supposed to be exposing," said Sarika. "Just consider this statement from the commissioners about the condition of the indentured which St George Arbuthnot recorded at the conclusion of their visit to one of the Reynolds' estates: 'We are pleased with the sympathy which appeared to guide Reynolds arrangements for their comfort and welfare.' With that kind of shut-eyed outlook, I despair of the Commission making any difference in how indenture is managed."

"Equally disturbing is the silence of the press on treatment we know is occurring on estates. Evidence of the web of collusion is just so obvious: it's the sugarocracy, the press and the government," declared John Harrington.

"So, what are we to do? I can think of only one option and that is to write to the Colonial Secretary for Colonies in London. I think it is currently Earl Granville. But in advance, I can almost read his response: we have to await the outcome of the Wragg Commission,"ventured Sarika dejectedly.

"What about the churches?" enquired John Redman. "The men of the cloth are good at delivering sermons exhorting Christ-like behaviour and attitudes. Yet they are silent on exploitation of human lives right under their noses."

"In that the Anglican Church is effectively the church of the Empire, I can't see it waving a big stick on this issue because, wittingly or unwittingly, it is part of the whole colonisation process. The Catholics are a minority denomination in the colony along with the Congregationalists. Moreover, their mission schools get small state grants which they might be loath to jeopardise through some form of confrontation," advised William Thornton.

"If Bishop Colenso were alive, I feel his great humanitarian outlook would have been moved to intercede on behalf of the plight of the indentured," said Dr Jones reflectively.

****

CHAPTER 21

The Reynolds acquisition of estates continued with Andrew Sinclair's Cowick estate being absorbed along with Ifafa sugar and the small Dunragil estate near Umzinto. Pondering these developments one evening with Cynthia, Simon said the coastal area of Alex County seemed to be squeezed between two sugar empires: Crookes in the northern sector and Reynolds in southern part.

"What does that mean for us here on Dewsbury?" asked Cynthia.

"At the moment we are fine. Dewsbury provides us with a good living. We get our cane milled on Hawksworth's Beneva estate. Our coffee crop is substantial and the distillery sales to E Snell & Co are satisfactory. I think what really helps our cash flow situation is that we do not have indentured labour or a mill. Those elements have proved the undoing of smaller estates. Eric on Woodhouse Lea has remarked to me how much time Frances spends maintaining her father's wage book and register for his indentured labour on Beneva," said Simon.

"But our circumstances do not exempt us from suffering consecutive bad seasons and becoming insolvent. That's when the likes of Crookes or Reynolds come along and buy out estates at bargain prices. That has been the trend throughout the sugar growing coastal areas."

****

Before writing to the Secretary of State for Colonies, Sarika consulted Magistrate Lucas on her proposed action. He informed her that mail going out of the colony to the Imperial government had to be routed through the

Governor's office otherwise it would not reach its destination. "There are regulations to be complied with in forwarding documentation to London," he advised.

Three months after she had complied with the regulations and forwarded a list of human rights violations of the letter and spirit of the 1872 Coolie Commission's stipulations to Earl Granville, Sarika received a brief acknowledgement. As she had anticipated, Earl Granville evaded the issues she had raised. Instead, he advised that he did not wish to pre-empt the findings of the Wragg Commission.

Discussing the outcome of her effort with her support group at Michaelhouse, Dr Jones pointed out that Sarika's documentation had likely been accompanied by a letter from Governor Havelock highly critical of her. "We can be sure that since the Janki case in 1881, the mandarins of Government House in Pietermaritzburg have been kept abreast of your efforts to expose the human rights abuses on the sugar estates. I have no doubt that through Thomas Reynolds your name in government circles has been disparaged. Corridor talk in the Legislative Council amongst the colluders is undoubtedly part of the process which is why the press plays along in giving your exposures the silent treatment."

****

That night Sarika's stores in Scottburgh and Park Rynie were vandalised. The doors to the shops were forced open; bags of rice were cut open and spilled onto the floors; bottles of condiments and preserves were smashed; haberdashery items such as cotton reels and needles were found on the floor mixed up with the rice and the broken jam jars. On the counters of both shops a message was scrawled on a piece of paper that read: 'Suffer coolie agitator.'

The incidents were reported to Constable Whitwell who also filed them in his regular crime report to the press. When his report was published it excluded reference to Sarika's shops. As William Thornton remarked in the Royal Hotel bar, if such vandalism had occurred at Knox's or Archibald's shops in Umzinto, there would have been a hue and cry in the press with fingers pointed at Indians and natives.

For two days Sarika's stores were closed for business as Priscilla, Emma and their helpers cleaned up the mess and inventoried the losses which could be claimed on insurance. Not surprisingly Constable Whitwell was unable to find who had perpetrated the vandalism.

****

Picking up her mail at the Umzinto post office, Sarika was intrigued by the contents of an envelope. Although the letter was from an anonymous source, it praised Sarika for her efforts to expose the ill treatment occurring on estates and promised to send her regular accounts of abusive incidents. Sure enough, a few days later a litany of ill treatment incidents arrived in her post box. Without stating the name of the estate or estates on which the abuses occurred, the envelope referenced the following:

During crushing season, no time is allowed for meals; sick men have to work until they cannot not stand; miscarriage or confinement is not accepted as a reason for a woman to be off work; human excrement often fouls water sources; increasing numbers of suicides are being ascribed to overwork; treatments dispensed by overseers are often callous: for example castor oil being used to treat a foot ulcer and for diarrhoea.

At a meeting of Sarika's concerned group, the question asked was: what can we do about these disclosures? As Eric Harrison pointed out, they could not be pinned on any particular estate, nor could they be verified. Nonetheless, in the context of what was already known such abuses were undeniably occurring.

"My suggestion is that we ask Magistrate Lucas to put them on file. At least they may assist a future historian in filling in the silent gaps of the historical record," advocated Robert Anderson. Although Sarika nodded in agreement, she said she wanted the situation addressed in the present, not as the subject of historical inquiry.

The anonymous correspondent did not let up. A fortnight later another envelope arrived in Sarika's post box. It disclosed the following:

High rates of desertions; the sick in the hospital being denied food; all-white juries acquitting overseers of brutalities claiming lack of evidence; severely beaten men left unconscious in the field during a winter night; no treatment for jigger flea infestation which made walking and hand use very painful; diarrhoea common as a result of poor diet and infected water; callous brutality on Reynolds estate institutionalised by Mr WT Pemberton; venereal disease rife.

In correspondence with Simon Prescott's reform-minded sister, Victoria Snell, Sarika was pleased to receive a new suggestion for her campaign to create awareness of the human rights abuses on sugar estates. Victoria pointed out that the late Bishop Colenso had cultivated contact with the Aborigines Protection Society in London as part of his mission to expose and to remedy injustices inflicted on the natives of the colony. Eager to access the Aborigines Protection Society and to see how it could promote awareness of her campaign, Sarika prepared and mailed a dossier on the plight of the indentured to the Society's London address.

Before ending her letter, Victoria had asked whether Sarika could address a meeting of her reformist ladies in Pietermaritzburg.

****

Victoria Snell's reformist ladies movement had gained quiet momentum in recent years. The fact that it had a small following in the capital of the colony was heartening. As her husband, Gordon, pointed out, "to be influential on any subject, Pietermaritzburg is the platform you need. Amongst the politicians' wives and the wives of the heads of the various government departments, there is fertile ground to cultivate awareness of the need for reform of women's rights and roles in society."

Delighted that Sarika was available to address her Pietermaritzburg meeting, Victoria arranged for her to stay over with her sister Anne and her husband Martin Pryce in their home at Taunton Manor. Not only was it Sarika's first visit to the Pryces' home but it was also her first formal meeting with Anne who was thrilled to host Sarika and to catch up with news from Umzinto. Particularly intrigued by Sarika's presence was three-year-old Lyndon, the Pryces' son. "I think he finds the bright colours of your sari unusual and attractive," said Anne, while Lyndon's two sisters, Eleanor and Elizabeth wanted to know if Sarika would make them some samoosas. Eager to please them, Anne led Sarika to the kitchen and showed her the location of the necessary ingredients. "You and Martin have such a delightful domestic atmosphere. I envy you. It is what I had once hoped for," said Sarika wistfully.

At dinner that evening, Martin enquired about the topic of Sarika's address. "It's titled 'A society immersed in convention' and echoes much of what I stated in an address in Durban some years ago. But tomorrow's speech will adduce fresh challenges and venture into waters that are deliberately kept dark."

"Well, I'm sure my sister will be very pleased. She and Gordon would have been here tonight but are staying with E Snell & Co's Pietermaritzburg branch manager. They'll be with us tomorrow night when your address will undoubtedly be the topic of conversation!" remarked Anne confidently.

****

Founded in 1859, the Victoria Club in Longmarket St Pietermaritzburg was a sedate gentlemen's retreat for dining, business and political discussions. The only time women were allowed on the premises was for the occasional special dinner in honour of some dignitary or event. Martin Pryce, as a senior member of the legal fraternity, was a Club member. Thanks to his influence, Victoria was granted permission to host her reformist ladies meeting in the dining room of the Club on condition their proceedings were over before noon.

By 10 o'clock the last of the invited ladies had taken her seat when Victoria accompanied Sarika to the lectern. Dressed to dazzle in a bright, violet-coloured sari with her lustrous ebony hair loosely tied back, golden bangles on her wrists, Sarika was the focus of 25 pairs of eyes. With her usual cordial aplomb, Victoria welcomed everyone and gave a biographical resume of her guest speaker.

Already impressed by Sarika's appearance and genteel disposition, her unaccented erudition ensured the audience's rapt attention.

Thank you, Victoria, for your warm welcome and for the honour and privilege to address your growing following of reform-minded ladies!

This morning, I want us to consider the extent to which as a society, we are immersed in conventions. There's a saying that an emigrant joins someone else's society but a settler replicates the society from which he came. Have you thought of the ways in which lives here in the Colony of Natal are different from how they are lived in England? I will give you three examples. Ownership of land is the basis of fundamental class distinction in England. When we talk about the landed gentry, we refer to a small, elitist minority of people who are the landowners of Britain.

But here in Natal, because land is cheap and as many of you were beneficiaries of the Byrne immigration scheme, you automatically became landowners. So, the convention that applies rigidly in Britain which distinguishes land owners from those who are renters or tenants, scarcely applies here.

A second instance of where convention has been laid aside in Natal concerns the military. In Britain civilian fraternisation with the military is frowned upon. Those in the military lead socially exclusive lives. But the small size of the population and the interdependence of those at Fort Napier with the surrounding civilian population ensures social reciprocity.

A third very distinct abandonment of convention applies to the lives women lead in Natal. Again, the small size of the population has necessitated that women perform roles which would not occur in Britain because convention dictates otherwise. So here we have women post mistresses, women ferry keepers, pound mistresses, librarians, teachers and school principals, hotel managers, newspaper correspondents and shop keepers – which is how I make a living!

On estates, women not only carry out a range of household chores – from butter churning to bottling of preserves, vegetable garden maintenance, undergoing firearm training, engaging in horse riding and carriage transport.

During the Anglo-Zulu war, women kept district economies going while their menfolk were at the frontier. That meant marshalling labour to harvest crops and transporting produce to local markets. Thanks to firearm training, a great friend of mine was able to defend herself and her two children from an axe-wielding intruder on her sugar estate.

So, ladies, as Victoria has undoubtedly questioned on several occasions: why are we denied the right to vote? What more do we need to prove that we are responsible and eligible to exercise the right to choose not only our political representatives but to be candidates ourselves for election?

The usual reasons trotted out by officialdom that women are the weaker sex and would not survive in the political hurly burly, are really tired, empty words. I remember one newspaper editor's response to that very question

Victoria posed. He said that because they are the weaker sex, women already enjoy statutory protection. If they participated in politics, he claimed they would lose that protection!

The conclusion to draw from his response is that he lacked the ability to think for himself. Instead, he sheltered behind convention which ignores the fact that circumstances evolve. He preferred to justify his stance with an argument that exists simply because convention discourages challenges to its legitimacy.

This brings me to a very relevant aspect of life in colonial Natal: political convention. Convention on issues regarding race is strongly adhered to, despite instances that challenge it. I stand before you as an example. According to convention, I should not be a shop owner, particularly as a female. Two weeks ago, two of my three shops were vandalised following a warning that I should desist from questioning the violations of human rights on sugar estates. Nearly seven years ago, my first shop was burnt to the ground because of the unseemly convergence of racial and social convention.

As you are aware, there is a commission of inquiry into what is called the Indian Question. Through contacts I have in Alexandra County, my group of concerned settlers is aware of institutionalised violence, ill treatment and degradation that occurs on sugar estates employing indentured labour. We have caused the local magistrate to file that information for posterity because after three attempts we were prevented from holding a public meeting on it. Even our effort to apprise the Secretary of State for Colonies in London of these human rights abuses has been met with a limp response. He said he did not wish to pre-empt the findings of the Wragg Commission.

Arising from our experiences in Alexandra County we have been confronted with something more than convention. We call it collusion. We have noted collusion between what we call the sugarocracy, government officials and the press in ensuring that a prescribed narrative on indentured labour is adhered to – in other words, a convention. And that convention projects the image that, with minor exceptions, the health and welfare of indentured Indians is satisfactory. Yet mounting evidence challenges that projected image. Sadly, as I have indicated, efforts to expose it have taken the form of intimidation, outright denial and even vandalism.

From that perspective, my appeal to you this morning is to recognise that ***adherence to convention should not mean adherence to what is hypocritical.*** *All societies evolve and from what I have pointed out, it should be clear that much social evolution has unwittingly taken place in Natal amongst the white community.*

Therefore, our plea is to recognise that. To challenge it and not to rest until obsolete and unjust conventions have been consigned to the bin of history. As women, for how much longer are we going to accept being immersed in conventions that have been overtaken by new realities?

Although applause greeted Sarika's address it was not unanimous. Opening the floor to questions, a lady whose husband was a senior officer at Fort Napier said she believed the passage of time and experience justified adherence to social conventions. "From the narrow purview of Alexandra County, I do not agree that circumstances require conventions to be challenged."

Graciously accepting the lady's viewpoint, Sarika premised her response on the need to recognise and adhere to standards. "All Victoria and I are advocating is conformity to standards. Women are proving that they can uphold standards. In so doing they are exposing the unfairness that convention prescribes towards us in certain roles."

Another lady whose husband was a Member of the Legislative Council, took exception to Sarika's claim of collusion between the sugar barons, politicians and the press. "On what grounds do you make such a reproach?" she asked indignantly.

Undaunted by the question, Sarika's response was simply: "Follow the money. Without indentured labour the sugar industry would collapse. If the India government was aware of the ill treatment that takes place, it would stop indentured immigration as it almost did in 1872. So, between the sugar barons, the press and the revenue sugar generates for the government, there is mutual benefit in projecting an image of indentured labour that is not controversial."

****

As Anne had anticipated, Sarika's address was the topic of conversation around the dinner table at Taunton Manor that evening. "I very much doubt whether there will be a press report on your meeting today," said Gordon to his wife. "Although a ladies meeting at the Victoria Club should prompt a report because the venue challenged convention! But then Sarika's topic was just too unconventional for those whose job it is to uphold conventions!" chuckled Gordon.

'Yes, I must agree with you, darling," said Victoria. "But from a contact in London I have received a direction which is very encouraging. It concerns the newspaper known as the *Pall Mall Gazette.* Its editor, William Thomas Stead, is shaking up the London press with his new approach to reporting which he calls 'investigative journalism.' Already he has ruffled the feathers of the establishment with probing articles on child welfare, the penal codes and social legislation. Apparently, his critics are accusing him of 'government by journalism.' So, I think Mr Stead would be very interested in Sarika's address because it reflects the trend he is pursuing."

Accompanied by a covering letter detailing her reformist group's involvement, Victoria despatched a copy of Sarika's Pietermaritzburg address to Mr WT Stead of the *Pall Mall Gazette.* His response almost a month later was most encouraging.

Dear Mrs Snell

I am most grateful to you for alerting me of circumstances in the far-off colony of Natal. It made me realise that our news focus on colonies tends to concern itself only with broad imperial issues. As a result, the commission of inquiry regarding Asians in Natal and the circumstances that brought it about is news to me.

Since reform is very much the lens through which my paper views social issues, I am most interested not only in the address she delivered but also in obtaining biographical details about Sarika. I would be grateful if you could forward those at your convenience so that they can accompany the publication of her speech in the Gazette.

I remain your obedient servant

WT Stead, Editor

London

****

CHAPTER 22

1885 saw John and Emily Harrington become grandparents twice: Francis was born to Trish and Stewart and Robert to Priscilla and Tony Hassall. Tony was delighted by Robert's birth since it filled the tragic loss he had suffered four years earlier. Both young mothers were eager to recover their athleticism after childbirth. Trish was adamant that within a month or so she would be fit enough to compete in gymkhanas. Priscilla was keen to get back on the tennis court after her pregnancy-enforced absence. Both looked forward to 1886 as the year they would resume active competition.

In contrast, thoughts at the Wiltshire and Royal Hotel bar were sober and contemplative as patrons pondered the challenges of 1886.

"This reef of gold that has been discovered in the Boer Republic is having a negative effect on life here in Alex County," said Charles Sinclair gloomily. "It's attracting young men and native labour. I've lost two of my top transport riders. They told me they could earn three times as much on the gold fields because there is an ever-growing demand for transport. Native labour, which is also crucial to my transport operation, is migrating northwards, either to the coal fields on the gold fields."

A similar downcast outlook prevailed at the Royal Hotel bar. "Has anyone noted the latest reason to deny us a bridge over the Mkomanzi, never mind proper roads?" asked proprietor William Thornton. "The £3 million invested in the colony's rail system is costing £130,000 per annum in interest charges. But a shortfall in rail revenue of about £37,000 means that budgets like the one for Alex County have to be trimmed in order to meet the interest costs."

"Another consequence of our depressed economy is that any thoughts of the railway being extended southwards from Isipingo have become even more remote," said Robert Anderson ruefully.

"Cheer up, gentlemen. At least we are not suffering from the stock theft that is occurring in Alfred County. Colonists whose farms are in the vicinity of the Pondo border are in a real pickle. Organised plunder is resulting in sheep being stolen in twos and threes and sometimes in batches of 20 to 50," remarked Dr Jones.

Despite the pinched state of the economy an event which brightened life was the Alexandra County Show, which took place in February. The first such exhibition south of Durban, it boasted over 300 exhibits which were on display at the Umzinto Memorial Hall. They included local art, sewing and embroidery, furnishings, samples of agricultural produce and a range of culinary items. At Frances Harrison's prompting, Sarika had a stand at which she sold samoosas and tubs of biryani that proved wildly popular. Remembering how successful rum punch was at the Park Rynie July festivals, Simon Prescott set up a stall next to Sarika's from which he sold Dewsbury rum punch at tuppence a pint.

Highlight of the exhibition for William Thornton was the dinner hosted by his Royal Hotel. Among the 50 place settings, besides General Bisset, the South Coast's new MLC, were three dignitaries whose presence in the County was novel: Tongaat sugar planter James Saunders who was also a member of the Wragg Commission, retired Secretary of Native Affairs, Sir Theophilus Shepstone and James Liege Hulett, prominent Victoria County MLC and owner of the thriving Kearsney tea estate.

****

In April 1886, Sarika's Pietermaritzburg speech was published in the *Pall Mall Gazette* along with a short biographical reference. In a sub-section of the paper's editorial column William Stead also referred to her and Victoria.

The promotion of social reform and the need to challenge social conventions, as readers are aware, is very much aim of this newspaper. So, it is with respect and appreciation that we acknowledge the progressive efforts of Victoria Snell and Sarika Singh of the Colony of Natal as *published on page seven of today's edition. Indeed, their initiative and enterprise shames many here in England who are better equipped to propagate social reform.*

The publication of Sarika's remarks resulted in her being invited to England by the Aborigines Protection Society to address its branches in London and Manchester. Thanks to the *Pall Mall Gazette,* interest in her accounts of the ill treatment of indentured labour in Natal gained traction in political circles. She met two Indians who subsequently won seats in the House of Commons – Dadabhai Naoroji and Sir Mancherjee Bhownaggree.

Sarika's speeches also triggered critical discussion about indentured labour in other British colonies such as Mauritius, British Guiana and in the Caribbean. Questions were asked in the House of Commons. Officials in the Colonial Office became wary of the scrutiny the subject was attracting and resorted to a standard response: instances of ill treatment were 'exceptional.' The imperial establishment became alarmed when the reformist-minded *Times of India,* which had a wide circulation in India, began to probe the issue.

In London's Lombard Street, the home of banking and high finance, investors in the sugar industry showed signs of nervousness. The prospect of disruption of the supply of indentured labour by the India government on account of ill treatment would prove disastrous for sugar production in the colonies. Shares in colonial sugar production on the London bourse began to reflect a bearish tendency with shares in Europe's sugar beet production benefiting as a result.

Sarika's return to Natal after two months in England went unnoticed by the Natal press which had assiduously avoided publication of her overseas visit and the interest it had provoked. Only Victoria's latest newsletter reported her successful mission to England and the interest it had sparked. To regale her reformist group about her visit, she held a *soiree* at Michaelhouse.

"Sarika, the silence of the Natal press on your visit to England and the interest it caused, I believe, was the result of racial prejudice and politics," asserted Eric Harrison. "If Robert Archibald and his wife had taken a trip to England, the Alexandra County report in the *Mercury* would have provided every detail of their travels. After all, like you, he is also a store owner with a shop in Umzinto and another in Highflats. But the difference is your Asian identity. The other reason is that your standpoint on the treatment of indentured labour does not sit well with the politics of the colony. Until the Wragg Commission presents its report, the subject of Indian indenture is taboo."

"I agree with you, Eric. There seems to be an unwritten rule which dictates that reporting on Indians and their activities can only be pejorative. So, we find that crime cases, complaints about Indian commerce, housing and cultural idiosyncrasies are the staple of press coverage. Anything that contrasts positively with that narrative is ignored," said Sarika.

"It's just what we have already encountered: collusion between the sugar barons, the government and the press," said James Ross reflectively.

"Oh! Most certainly! And we need to be aware of how influential sugar companies like the Reynolds Bros have become. A reliable source has informed me that in the near future CG Smith will acquire ownership of the *Somtseu* as part of his company's intention to manage the bulk of sugar transport and distribution. So, from that we should recognise the extent to which control is being extended over the industry. Economic interests are paramount. There's just too much invested in the sugar market to be distracted by humanitarian concerns," declared William Thornton.

Within three months of her return from England, Sarika received a letter from the Aborigines Protection Society. It informed her that pressure from high places had shut down political and press discussion about indentured labour. The biggest sugar refiner and distributor, Tate and Lyle, had informed the *Pall Mall Gazette* that it would cut its advertising space in the paper if it did not cease publishing articles critical of indentured labour. Similar threats to reduce the *Times of India's* advertising income had also been applied.

****

A communication revolution occurred in January 1887 when finally, Umzinto was linked by telegraph to Durban. Celebrating this milestone at the Royal Hotel bar, William Thornton referred to the comment the *Mercury* made which congratulated 'our friends down south at being brought in rapid touch with the civilised world.'

"It just shows that we are thought of down here as an uncivilised backwater," declared Thornton indignantly. "Yet the smug residents to the north of us have flocked every July to the Park Rynie fair because they don't have an equivalent in their civilised world," he added sneeringly.

"A new reason for them to flock down here is news of a gold discovery on one of the Reynolds estates. Have you seen the ambitious adverts in the press? We are now being referred to as the 'Umzinto gold fields!' One of the adverts placed by a firm in Durban called the Exchange Mart offers tents, portable wood and canvas shelters and waterproof sheets for hire especially for those headed for the Umzinto gold fields! I wonder how long this latest fantasy is going to last. The last one in 1869 when traces of gold were found in the Amahlongwa River proved a damp squib," chuckled Robert Anderson.

At the Wiltshire, Charles Sinclair bemoaned the effect the new CG Smith transport giant was having on his business. "Besides Alex County, I've been doing quite a bit of transport business in Durban County. But CG Smith has bigger wagons and provides a cheaper and more frequent service to Durban. I can't compete with that. It seems that just as Reynolds, Crookes and others are dominating the sugar industry, so the transport business is going the same way thanks to CG Smith. When we eventually get a railway, I can see my transport business being reduced to minor local deliveries."

****

Magistrate Lucas's doubt that the findings of the Wragg Commission would impose strong humanitarian measures to deter ill treatment of the indentured was confirmed by the publication of its report in September 1887. Although instances of poor treatment were scattered throughout the report, overall, the commissioners contented themselves with the view that treatment was generally satisfactory.

Having been invited by Victoria to spend a few days at the Snells' Berea home, Sarika expressed her disappointment with the Report. "It seems the commissioners were concerned mainly with farmers' respective labour preferences – native or indentured. The fingerprint of the sugar barons in the compilation of the report is obvious. Their investment in the sugar industry requires guaranteed labour which is what indenture supplies. Anything that interrupts or disrupts that has to be pushed aside. That is why our attempts to expose the ill treatment of the indentured are silenced," noted Sarika disconsolately.

"Yes, indeed! And a new development that is going to enjoy press attention because it is in the interests of white colonists is the formation of the Natal Working Men's Association. Its manifesto plainly states that it is pledged to safeguard the interests of white workers whose traditional areas of employment are being encroached upon by Indians," noted Victoria.

"The political implications of this organisation guarantee it a great deal of press coverage because it has announced that its members will not vote for candidates who promote indentured labour and Indian employment. So, the plight of the white worker because of Indian competition is the new priority. I can just picture the press condemning us for our indentured concerns instead of rallying to support white workers!" remarked Victoria bitterly.

"While I have no intention of abandoning concern for the welfare of the indentured, I think we should adopt a more practical approach in our reformist movement where Indians are concerned. Of course, our main thrust of promoting women's rights and enfranchisement must continue as before," said Sarika.

"What practical aspect do you have in mind?"

"I was thinking of craft work and literacy education. I would not be known to you, Victoria, if it was not for the literacy education I received from my very compassionate mistress on that Illovo estate during the 1860s.She insisted on employing me for my second term of indenture as her secretary which, with the lessons she provided during my first five years of indenture, enabled me to develop into what I have become."

"To pursue your idea, we are going to need premises. I'm sure Gordon can assist us in both the Durban and Pietermaritzburg areas. E Snell &Co has premises part of which possibly could serve our needs. Do you any ideas for Alex County?"

"Yes, I do. My Park Rynie shop is not really doing that well, despite Emma's management. Two new stores have reduced the already limited commercial appeal of the area. What Tony Hassall pointed out a few years ago about the limited commercial potential of Park Rynie is proving correct whereas my Scottburgh store is booming. So, yes, the premises of my Park Rynie store can be converted into a craft and literacy education centre."

****

Conclusion

At a meeting at Michaelhouse attended by her reformist group members, Tony and Priscilla Hassall, Eric and Frances Harrison and Emma Johnson, Sarika announced her plans regarding the promotion of craft and literacy. Although she had expected Emma to be upset about the closure of the Park Rynie store, that was not the case. Instead, Emma informed the gathering that she and Peter intended to immigrate to Australia.

Justifying her decision to diversify her movement into craft and literacy skills, Sarika cited her own experience as having been crucial in developing her potential. "We need to appreciate that every year in Alex County alone, there are several hundred Indians completing their indenture. Unlike my indentured experience, they are unlikely to have been given any literacy training. Without a passable competence in English, their chances of employment as free Indians are negligible."

"We also need to realise that laws discriminating against Indians are going to increase in number now that there is a white working men's organisation clamping down on certain types of employment for Indians. So, the ability to read the laws that are passed is going to be of great assistance to them. Even though we are all supposed to be settlers with the same rights, contesting discriminatory legislation is a further reason to promote literacy proficiency among Indians."

"I feel excited at where we are steering our reformist movement because it is about direct empowerment. While pleading for women's rights and enfranchisement is well and good, to date our efforts have not born any fruit. But by promoting craft training and literacy we can see immediate benefits and make a positive difference in the lives of those who have ended their indenture contracts without any personal benefit."

By early 1888, premises for the craft and literacy classes Sarika and Victoria had planned were equipped with tables and chairs, pencils, paper and chalk boards. Volunteers had been sourced to provide tuition and guidance. The Aborigines Protection Society in London had donated a crate of dictionaries and booklets on beginners' English. Through Sarika's contact with Indian merchants in Durban, sewing materials, haberdashery and sewing machines had been purchased at greatly discounted prices.

At all three centres, the interest of Indians in learning skills in sewing, tailoring and in literacy was overwhelming. As a result, classes had to be divided into separate schedules in order to cope with the numbers of applicants. Finding suitable tutors posed another headache for Victoria and Sarika. Fortunately, Victoria's sister, Anne Pryce, offered to take classes twice a week in Pietermaritzburg. Having taught at Reverend Barker's private school for Indians when she had lived in Umzinto, Anne was suited to the task at hand.

****

A farewell function was held at the Royal Hotel for Peter Richardson, Dewsbury's departing estate assistant and his long-time companion, Emma Johnson. They intended to settle in Queensland where sugar production was a major industry. Emma said she hoped to be able to gain employment in a shop based on her experience managing Sarika's Park Rynie store. To that end Sarika provided her with a glowing testimonial of her seven years as Park Rynie store manager. Simon handed Peter a well-earned reference noting his skills both as an estate assistant and in managing a rum distillery. "Before you go, Peter, I would like you to train Nicholas Harrison in distillery management. Eric has agreed to allow him to take your place on Dewsbury," said Simon.

At the Wiltshire, discussing the departure of Peter Richardson from Dewsbury, old timer Bunting Johnstone remarked that getting assistant estate managers on small estates like Dewsbury was becoming almost impossible. “Owners like Simon Prescott cannot afford to pay what assistant estate managers are being offered by the Reynolds and Crookes in this county. And it’s easy to understand why. With over 10,000 acres and employing 800 indentured labourers, the challenges on Reynolds’ estates command higher wages.”

“I think Simon is very fortunate that young Nicholas Harrison is going to help out as assistant estate manager on Dewsbury. Hopefully for Simon’s sake he serves long enough until the younger Prescott, James, is old enough to take over – that is, if he is interested. His brother George from a young age showed no interest in farming. I believe he is now being trained by the Department of Works in telegraph signals and maintenance. With a bit of luck he’ll be stationed in Umzinto,” commented Captain Tucker.

“Talking about telegraphs, I see the Port Shepstone folk are having a fight with the General Manager of Telegraphs, Mr Chadwick. He promised that work on connecting Umzinto with Port Shepstone would start on August 1. But here we are, almost Christmas and not a single telegraph pole has been erected. As usual the bureaucrats are blaming one another. Chadwick says it’s Colonial Engineer Hime’s fault for being unable to provide the necessary workmen. Hime says there is insufficient money in his budget to construct the link in the current financial year!” observed Charles Sinclair sardonically.

****

A much larger farewell gathering was held in the Umzinto Memorial Hall in November 1888 for the departure of Resident Magistrate Gould Arthur Lucas. Appointed in 1876 his duties in the County had been frequently interrupted by military call-ups. Nonetheless, he was respected for his decisiveness and his experience having served as a magistrate since his first posting in 1858. He announced that James McLaurin would take up his appointment as Alexandra County resident magistrate in February 1889.

The political climate into which the new magistrate was migrating was well illustrated by one of the last incidents with which Magistrate Lucas had to deal. On his recommendation the Umzinto post office was moved from Archibald's store to the new telegraph office. Not only was it a sensible and logical relocation but it was closer to the hub of the village and the hotels. But that did not suit Charles Reynolds who sent a petition to the colonial secretary signed by his brother and 17 residents objecting to the relocation and expressing outrage because the new location was two miles further from Charles' Esperanza residence.

As William Thornton remarked in the Royal Hotel bar, the issue served as yet another indication of the arrogance of the Reynolds. "With their coaches, carriages and stable of horses, for them accessing any part of the county is child's play. Their objection to the relocation of the post office is just sheer selfishness. I'm glad Magistrate Lucas ignored their attempt to intimidate him. I wonder if the new magistrate, James McLaurin, is going to be able to stand up to them?"

****

Christmas 1888 saw a series of family gatherings. The Harrison grandparents, Ralph and Mary, travelled from Howick to Beneva estate to be with Frances, Eric, Grandfather Edward Hawksworth and the two grandsons, Edward and Nicholas. Edward had been assistant estate manager to his grandfather for the past four years.

Simon, Cynthia and their two boys, George and James, were able to travel the entire distance from Isipingo to Ladysmith by train where they spent Christmas with Cynthia's parents, James and Margaret Moodie. The Moodies were delighted to host the Prescotts and to catch up with news of Alexandra County. Adding to the family gathering was Cynthia's sister, Ruth, who arrived on Christmas Day from Colenso with her husband and their toddler Margaret.

The two Prescott sisters, Victoria and Anne, and their families, Gordon Snell and Lily, Martin Pryce and the three Pryce children, Eleanor, Elizabeth and Lyndon, enjoyed Christmas cheer and family togetherness at Taunton Manor. Victoria and Gordon were very proud of Lily. She had passed her diploma in accounting and was set to occupy a permanent post in E Snell & Co. Teasingly Martin asked if she was "Daddy's Girl" or if she had met a handsome suitor? "Maybe I have," responded Lily challengingly. "That's why I want Daddy to transfer me to the Stellenbosch office! That's my New Year's wish!" she declared, smiling endearingly at her father.

A Harrington reunion took place at Preston estate. Stewart, Trish and their toddler, Francis, travelled down from Rosetta in Weenen County. Priscilla and Tony Hassall were present from nearby Scottburgh with three-year-old Robert. Completing the placings at the lunch table were Sarika and Hugh Lawson. Enjoying drinks before lunch while gifts were exchanged, attention was suddenly drawn to Hugh as he went down on one knee in front of Sarika. Opening a small jewellery box, he asked for her hand in marriage. She promptly accepted and embraced him.

After hugs and congratulations had been expressed, John Harrington said he was curious to find out why Sarika and Hugh had decided on marriage after they had been together for about nine years. "I know, John, it seems odd, but I think we both had our reasons for not wanting to tie the knot earlier. Hugh can give you his, but I felt I needed a long period to dignify and recover from my loss of Michael. Then there was the convention regarding race. I think by just remaining companions we were quietly able to gain some social acceptance over time as a couple."

"But to answer your question directly, John, about the timing of our decision, my involvement in Victoria's reformist movement and the new direction we are pursuing has proved a watershed in my life. Also, I'm getting older! I'll be 40 in 1889! Time with Hugh has proved our compatibility and our love for each other has grown as a result of the circumstances to which we have been exposed."

"Sarika has said much of what I feel about why we have finally taken this decision. Like her, I too was wary of plunging into marriage. I was also aware that she was deeply scarred by the loss of Michael and needed time and space to live through that tragedy. We have much in common: age, no family, experience of relationships across the colour line, a common humanitarian outlook. Time has also proved our compatibility."

"Thank you, Sarika and Hugh, for affording us a glimpse of those private feelings," said John. "We admire you and are thrilled for you. I know Eric and Frances are going to be delighted by your news. I don't know if you have made any plans for celebrating your wedding, but I want to make a request: Sarika, if possible, as a father figure, may I be allowed the honour of giving the bride away to Hugh?"

****

The *Somtseu* having an easy exit from the mouth of the Mzimkulu River

www.ingramcontent.com/pod-product-compliance
Ingram Content Group UK Ltd.
Pitfield, Milton Keynes, MK11 3LW, UK
UKHW062310290726
14090UKWH00018B/988